POLITICAL PARTIES, GROWTH AND EQUALITY

Given the increased openness of countries to international trade and financial flows, the general public and the scholarly literature have grown skeptical about the capacity of policymakers to affect economic performance. Challenging this view, *Political Parties, Growth and Equality* shows that an increasingly interdependent world economy and recent technological shocks have actually exacerbated the dilemmas faced by governments in choosing among various policy objectives, such as generating jobs and reducing income inequality, thereby granting political parties and electoral politics a fundamental and growing role in the economy. To make growth and equality compatible, social democrats employ the public sector to raise the productivity of capital and labor. By contrast, conservatives rely on the private provision of investment. Based on analysis of the economic policies of all OECD countries since the 1960s and in-depth examination of Britain and Spain in the 1980s, this book offers a new understanding of how contemporary democracies work and reinvigorates the claim that they matter.

D1262440

CAMBRIDGE STUDIES IN COMPARATIVE POLITICS

General Editor
PETER LANGE   Duke University

Associate Editors
ROBERT H. BATES   Harvard University
ELLEN COMISSO   University of California, San Diego
PETER HALL   Harvard University
JOEL MIGDAL   University of Washington
HELEN MILNER   Columbia University
RONALD ROGOWSKI   University of California, Los Angeles
SIDNEY TARROW   Cornell University

OTHER BOOKS IN THE SERIES

Catherine Boone, *Merchant Capital and the Roots of State Power in Senegal, 1930–1985*
Michael Bratton and Nicolas van de Walle, *Democratic Experiments in Africa: Regime Transitions in Comparative Perspective*
Donatella della Porta, *Social Movements, Political Violence, and the State*
Roberto Franzosi, *The Puzzle of Strikes: Class and State Strategies in Postwar Italy*
Geoffrey Garrett, *Partisan Politics in the Global Economy*
Miriam Golden, *Heroic Defeats: The Politics of Job Loss*
Frances Hagopian, *Traditional Politics and Regime Change in Brazil*
J. Rogers Hollingsworth and Robert Boyer, *Contemporary Capitalism: The Embeddedness of Institutions*
Ellen Immergut, *Health Politics: Interests and Institutions in Western Europe*
Thomas Janoski and Alexander M. Hicks, eds., *The Comparative Political Economy of the Welfare State*
Robert O. Keohane and Helen B. Milner, eds., *Internationalization and Domestic Politics*
David Knoke, Franz Urban Pappi, Jeffrey Broadbent, and Yutaka Tsujinaka, eds., *Comparing Policy Networks*
Allan Kornberg and Harold D. Clarke, *Citizens and Community: Political Support in a Representative Democracy*
David D. Latin, *Language Repertories and State Construction in Africa*
Mark Irving Lichbach and Alan S. Zuckerman, eds., *Comparative Politics: Rationality, Culture, and Structure*
Doug McAdam, John McCarthy, and Mayer Zald, eds., *Comparative Perspectives on Social Movements*
Scott Mainwaring and Matthew Soberg Shugart, *Presidentialism and Democracy in Latin America*

(Continued on page 281)

POLITICAL PARTIES, GROWTH AND EQUALITY

Conservative and Social Democratic Economic Strategies in the World Economy

CARLES BOIX

The Ohio State University

PUBLISHED BY THE PRESS SYNDICATE OF THE UNIVERSITY OF CAMBRIDGE
The Pitt Building, Trumpington Street, Cambridge CB2 1RP, United Kingdom

CAMBRIDGE UNIVERSITY PRESS
The Edinburgh Building, Cambridge CB2 2RU, United Kingdom
40 West 20th Street, New York, NY 10011-4211, USA
10 Stamford Road, Oakleigh, Melbourne 3166, Australia

First published 1998

Printed in the United States of America

Typeset in Garamond #3

Library of Congress Cataloging-in-Publication Data
Boix, Carles.
Political parties, growth and equality : conservative and social
democratic economic strategies in the world economy / Carles Boix.
p.   cm. — (Cambridge studies in comparative politics)
Includes bibliographical references and index.
ISBN 0-521-58446-9 (hb)   0-521-58595-3 (pb)
1. Political parties.   2. Economic policy.   I. Title.
II. Series.
JF2011.b65   1998
324.2 – dc21   97-27896

A *catalog record for this book is available from*
the British Library

ISBN 0 521 58446 9 hardback
ISBN 0 521 58595 3 paperback

A l'Alícia

CONTENTS

TABLES AND FIGURES

TABLES

FIGURES

PREFACE

Claiming that there is only one possible economic policy to solve the problems of growth, employment, and inequality that all advanced democracies face today has become a normal practice among both our policymakers and the public. This book, which I actually started as an inquiry into the causes of a much-vaunted process of policy convergence in the industrialized world in the last two decades, turns out to contend the opposite. Even in a world of open and interdependent economies, it is still possible to detect widely divergent economic strategies, all of them linked to different political projects, spawning opposed outcomes. As a matter of fact, the accelerated technological change and the process of growing economic integration we are experiencing today are only sharpening the economic and political dilemmas confronted by all advanced nations. Perhaps paradoxically for some, they are intensifying the extent of divergence among the different economic strategies embraced by governments to respond to those dilemmas. And, as this book intends to show, they are probably increasing the autonomy of politics over the economy.

This book derives partly from the doctoral dissertation that I completed at Harvard University in 1994. I would like to express my gratitude to my three thesis advisers, Alberto Alesina, James E. Alt, and Peter A. Hall. Without their support, their comments, and their suggestions, which were informed by rather different intellectual traditions, this study would not have been possible. I also benefited from the questions and extremely stimulating comments by José María Maravall and discussions with Paul A. Beck. Parts of this book have been presented at Harvard University's Center for European Studies, the Juan March Institute's Center for Advanced Study in the Social Sciences, the Wissenschaftszentrum für Sozialforschung in Berlin, the University of Michigan's Department of Political Science, and panels at the American Political Science Association and the Midwest Political Science Association. I wish to thank the participants at these colloquia and particularly José Alvarez-Junco, Geoffrey Garrett, Mauro Guillén and David Soskice. My thanks also go to Alex Hicks, Peter Lange, and Peter Swenson, whose review of the manuscript has proven invaluable. The Department of Political Science of Ohio State University provided the ideal setting to complete this project. I want to thank my colleagues here, in particular the participants of the Junior Faculty Research Meeting. Among them Dean Lacy made very valuable comments to portions of the manuscript draft. Mark Payne was extremely helpful in polishing my English and compiling the index and, all along in these tasks, asking very penetrating questions. Finally, I wish to acknowledge the editorial assistance of Alex Holzman.

I also wish to thank the following institutions, which provided generous financial support during my stay at Harvard: Instituto de Estudios Fiscales, Ministerio de Economía y Hacienda, Spain, 1990–94; Mellon Dissertation Completion Fellowship, 1994; Comissió Interdepartamental per a la Recerca i Investigació Tecnològica de la Generalitat de Catalunya, 1994–95; and Royal College Complutense at Harvard (for research in Spain).

Parts of Chapter 3 have been published in the *American Journal of Political Science* under the title "Political Parties and the Supply Side of the Economy: The Provision of Physical and Human Capital in Advanced Economies, 1960–1990," and are here reprinted by permission of The University of Wisconsin Press. Parts of Chapter 4 have been published in the *British Journal of Political Science* under the title "Privatizing the Public Business Sector in the Eighties: Economic Performance, Partisanship and Divided Governments" and are here reprinted by permission of Cambridge University Press.

This book would not have been possible without the strength derived from my family: my parents, with their unquestioning love; and my sons, who went from none to two – Carles and Enric – during the elaboration of this project. But, naturally, my deepest gratitude is reserved for my wife, Alícia. Without her comments, time, patience, and encouragement, this project would never have been completed. I dedicate this book to her.

1

INTRODUCTION

In the last two decades, under the impact of increasing international integration and two oil shocks, the developed world has suffered broad structural changes in its economy. Since 1973, the average Organization for Economic Cooperation and Development (OECD) annual growth rate, which had fluctuated around 5 percent in the 1960s, has dropped to 2.6 percent. Such a sluggish economic performance has been accompanied by different – and to some extent opposite – phenomena in each advanced nation. In continental Europe, which has a relatively regulated labor market and extensive social policies, the private sector has created few jobs in the last twenty years and the unemployment rate has jumped from less than 3 percent before 1973 to over 10 percent in the mid-1990s. By contrast, in the United States and, to some extent, in the United Kingdom, which have substantially lower levels of labor and welfare protection, employment creation has soared. Yet, unfortunately, they have had to pay a high price for their economic dynamism: median wages have declined and the income distribution has widened – in fact reversing a secular trend that started at the end of World War II.

The economic changes of the last two decades have, in turn, stirred up public life and galvanized the political debate within industrial democracies, hastening the alternation in power of different parties and encouraging experimentation with opposing economic policies in many advanced countries. Inaugurating what has become a growing movement to break away from the postwar consensus, the British Conservative Party came into office in 1979, as Thatcher put it, "with one deliberate intent. To change Britain from a dependent to a self-reliant society – from a give-it-to-me to a do-it-yourself nation; to a get-up-and-go instead of a sit-back-and-wait-for-it Britain."[1] But, on the other hand, in the early 1980s several socialist parties were elected in Southern Europe under a programmatic commitment to employ the state to modernize their countries, boost their economic competitiveness, and equalize social conditions. Social cohesion, rather than deregulation, took precedence there.

What is striking, however, is that, for all the political reverberation of the last twenty years, most scholars – as well as many voters – question whether electoral politics and political parties have any significant impact on the conduct of public affairs and doubt that politicians, and policymakers in general, can design policies to deliver growth and full employment. Focusing on the government's manipulation of the business cycle – to solve the well-known trade-off between unemployment and inflation – political economists have concluded that, due to towering institutional and economic constraints, parties fail to affect economic policies and aggregates permanently. Using even bolder terms, part of the literature is now claiming that a process of growing economic interdependence at the world level is forcing the convergence of national macroeconomic policies in a way that makes partisan forces and electoral politics altogether irrelevant.

Such conclusions seem warranted in the light of many policy decisions made in the last decade and a half. After all, did not ideologically very different governments, such as those headed by Thatcher in the United Kingdom and González in Spain, adopt similar policies, based on macroeconomic discipline and price stability? Did not Mitterrand, after briefly flirting with an expansionary strategy, end up embracing in 1983 the same objectives of low inflation and fiscal austerity? Neglecting the role of politicians and political parties, researchers who wish to theorize about the interaction between the economy and politics emphasize instead the powerful effects that specific sets of institutional structures, that is, stable sets of norms, rules, and organizational systems – such as the internal structure of labor markets or the constitutional arrangements of the state – have on the formulation of policies and on the broad contest for power. Parties are trapped, the academic literature points out, in so-called institutional equilibria, that is, equilibria induced by particular configurations of institutions. Political agency may count – but only embedded within such powerful constraints. Naturally, institutions and norms may be altered by political agents – yet change is only possible in extraordinary historical conjunctures or generated by very large social coalitions. In conclusion, most of the specialized literature explains political–economic outcomes as the result of the set of specific institutions that characterize each polity for long periods of time and within which partisan actors play a rather marginal role.

This book takes a different view. It argues that political parties, as organizers of broad coalitions of interests and ideas, have played a key role in the economic policy-making process. There is no doubt that even though partisan governments may wish to manage the business cycle, they are stringently constrained by the set of institutional structures within which they operate. The scholarly literature is likely to be right. Managing demand has become a rather inane issue in the political arena. But confining our research to the analysis of the determinants of the economic cycle yields a too narrow understanding of the impact of politics on the economy. The problems of stagnation and joblessness that beset Europe today are not rooted in the short-term evolution of the economic cycle. Similarly, the decline of incomes among unskilled American workers is a function of far-reaching structural changes that no expansionary measures will cure.

The growing economic dilemmas of the advanced world reveal, in rather stark terms, what is the staple of basic economics: that although growth partially depends on pursuing the appropriate policies to manage demand, overall economic performance is eventually a function of the level and the quality of the production factors – fixed capital and human capital – that is, the supply side of the economy. Yet, what structural reforms will work to maximize growth and reduce unemployment are a matter of heavy political contention. In other words, supply-side economic policies remain the object of intense, even growing, ideological conflict and party competition. After curbing an accelerating inflation, Thatcher launched a massive privatization program, deregulated the labor market, and overhauled the British tax system. It did not take long for other conservative governments to follow suit across the advanced world. Meanwhile, a Socialist government increased Spanish taxes by a third and employed the public sector to develop the most extensive capital formation plans in Europe in the 1980s. Similar massive investment plans, mostly focused on human capital formation, have been advanced by several social democratic cabinets in Scandinavia, embraced by Mitterrand in France, and advocated, more recently, by the American Democratic Party.

This book shows that there are two main alternative supply-side economic strategies available to policymakers to maximize growth and ensure the international competitiveness of domestic firms. The first strategy consists in reducing taxes to encourage private savings, boost private investment, and accelerate the rate of growth. Lower taxes, however, may imply, at least in the short run, less social spending and more inequality. Accordingly, policymakers who do not want to reduce social spending will have to turn to the second strategy. In this case, the state increases public spending in human and fixed capital to raise the productivity rate of labor and capital: this should encourage private agents to keep investing even in the face of high taxation (needed to pay for social transfers and public investment programs). As systematically tested in this book, which "competitive strategy" countries embrace to affect the supply conditions of the economy is mostly determined by the ideological preferences of the party in power. Left-wing governments, concerned about achieving economic growth and improving the welfare of the least advantaged sectors, seek to raise the productivity of capital and labor through the public sector. Conservative cabinets, relatively less concerned about equality, try to establish the adequate incentive structure to foster private investment rather than intervening more directly. Political parties in office affect the supply side of the economy relatively unconstrained by the domestic institutional variables that limit their autonomy in managing domestic demand. As a matter of fact, the increasing globalization of the economy, which has forced the convergence of national macroeconomic policies, has, on the contrary, magnified the role of (competing) supply-side economic strategies and intensified the importance of parties and partisan agency in the selection of those policies.

To make sense of the impact of parties on the economy while they are in office, I proceed as follows. In the first section of this chapter I present a rather stylized (yet widely accepted) description of the sets of interests and ideological traditions represented by conservative and social democratic parties in advanced democracies. The two following sections briefly review the current state of the political economy literature. In the second section I discuss how their rather divergent preferences push different parties to develop different strategies to manage the business cycle – the question that has focused the attention of most political economists to date. This discussion naturally leads to the presentation, in the following section, of the institutional constraints that beset any partisan manipulation of the business cycle. By the end of that section, the reader should be familiar with the state of the debate and the main findings of the literature and should understand why institutional or structural models are gaining the upper hand in the field of contemporary political economy. Relying on the initial assumptions of the partisan model presented in the next section, the rest of the book can then be devoted to examining the strong impact that, contrary to the central claims of the dominant theoretical literature, political candidates and parties still have on the evolution of economic policies and the economy.

THE POINT OF DEPARTURE: UNDERLYING PARTISAN GOALS

There is wide agreement in the literature that governments controlled by conservative or social democratic parties have distinct partisan economic objectives that they would prefer to pursue in the absence of any external constraints. Socialist governments are expected to intervene extensively in the economy to modify market outcomes and redistribute wealth to favor the least advantaged sectors and advance equality in general. Conservative parties are generally assumed to develop less interventionist policies and to rely on market mechanisms to maximize economic growth and protect individual liberties.[2]

These differences in the parties' positions toward the management of the economy and the role of governmental policies in sustaining and redistributing economic growth derive from a blend of interests (i.e., the redistributive consequences of economic policies) and ideas (here mostly in the sense of instrumental economic models) in the following way.

In the first place, all political parties prefer to develop policies that maximize growth. Since economic growth will increase the real disposable income of the core constituencies of the incumbent party, and of all social strata in general, and will thus boost the electoral strength of the party in office, it is an unavoidable requirement to be met even by those parties with a strong penchant for straightforward redistributive policies.

In the second place, although always attempting to maximize growth, parties adopt distinctive economic strategies depending on their redistributive consequences. Partisan preferences vary with respect to the specific strategies that should be followed to foster economic growth *precisely because* the strategies affect differently the welfare of all social and economic strata and, more generally, have distinct consequences on the level of economic equality in a given country. On the one hand, left-wing or social democratic parties, while still concerned about maximizing growth, especially care about the welfare of workers and the less advantaged social sectors and about equality in general. On the other hand, right-wing or conservative parties care about economic growth per se regardless of its distributive effects.[3] It must be emphasized at this point that although conservative governments are (relatively) indifferent about the redistributive effects of their growth strategy, this does not imply that they oppose the equalization of incomes per se. They only reject any equalization process insofar as they suspect that it either damages growth, upsets deeply held principles of merit or desert, or deteriorates the position of their electoral constituencies. If incomes become more equal across sectors over time as a result of a "natural" process (namely, a progressive convergence of wages taking place through market mechanisms and with no government intervention), conservatives, although relatively indifferent about equality, should not be expected to stop this process. On the contrary, they would certainly welcome that outcome as a sign of the "good" behavior of markets (in rewarding, say, efforts and skills over time).[4] Conservative parties are convinced that the economic strategy they favor (and which I discuss in more detail below) will increase the welfare of the lower socioeconomic strata, and that it will probably increase the latter's welfare more than any socialist economic policy, at least in the long run.[5]

Finally, even though these distinctive partisan positions about growth and equality derive from different preferences toward the distribution of income and wealth in society, they depend as well on the set of existing instrumental models or theories that parties have about how the economy works and about what policies governments can use to improve economic performance. Instrumental theories or economic models convincingly positing certain causal relationships between the goals to be achieved and the instruments to be employed are indispensable to convince policymakers about the feasibility of the goals they would ideally like to pursue. Unless such models exist, politicians may choose not to pursue certain objectives, no matter how deeply they feel about them. Thus, for example, demand-management techniques were adopted by (several) postwar social democratic parties because they represented (or were thought to represent) *feasible* solutions to the problem of unemployment (and to its connected problems, low disposable incomes and poverty). Although social democratic parties had always considered unemployment as a relatively costly condition, they only embraced expansionary policies to reduce it once Keynesian ideas persuaded them that actively fighting unemployment would have only marginal effects on inflation and public deficits and would actually boost long-term economic growth. Similarly, some conservative governments – such as the British cabinets of the 1950s – adopted demand-management policies when they were considered beneficial, in overall terms, because they were held to reduce unemployment with extremely marginal inflationary costs. These governments' underlying preferences – against inflation – probably remained the same. But Keynesian theory altered the *expected* costs of the programs being implemented. When Keynesian techniques seemed to fail in the 1970s, conservative parties willingly dropped them. Socialist governments followed suit once they understood expansionary policies were not, for various reasons, the best means to achieve growth and equality. As shown in detail in Chapter 2, a similar argument – regarding the relationship between partisan goals and instrumental models – is key to understanding the way in which partisan governments choose their supply-side economic strategies.

POLITICAL PARTIES AND THE BUSINESS CYCLE

If the economic position or disposable income of the least-advantaged sectors and the level of economic equality in general were the only concerns of left-wing politicians, they could attempt, once in office, to equalize social conditions simply through massive transfers of income. To compensate for the unbalanced results of a market system, they would direct transfers (in the form of universal pensions, health-care benefits, and so on) from the better-off to the worse-off socioeconomic sectors.

Public transfers of income can only be sustained, however, if they do not threaten growth, or if they reduce growth rates only marginally. If, on the contrary, they deplete a society's pool of savings and investment, public or welfare transfers impoverish the domestic economy in the medium run. In this case, left-wing parties will (have to) scale back any equalization schemes.[6] It was this fundamental trade-off, between the need to grow and the goal of equality, that socialist parties faced as they started gaining access to power in the interwar period and during the Great Depression of the 1930s. According to neoclassical economic ideas, hegemonic among scholars and, more generally, among policymakers at that time, socialist plans to transfer income from capital to the working class would only squeeze the supply of capital indispensable for the economy to grow in the medium run and hence cause permanent economic decline and massive unemployment (Przeworski and Wallerstein 1986). With this diagnosis in hand, socialist governments seemed forced either to nationalize the sources of investment – radically overturning the market economy – or to drop altogether most of the redistributive schemes favoring their constituencies. Convinced about the correctness of the neoclassical economic diagnosis, for example, Baldwin's Labour government in Britain in the early 1930s rejected, in the middle of a widening crisis, any resort to expansionary and interventionist policies. It abided instead by the standard orthodox recipes of spending cuts and a strong pound.[7]

Keynesianism offered, however, the first way out of this zero-sum dilemma. According to Keynesian theory, aggregate demand, rather than supply conditions, determines the level of economic activity. Policymakers can therefore easily manipulate the overall levels of domestic demand through monetary and fiscal stimuli to smooth the business cycle, maximize the sustainable rate of growth, and achieve full employment.[8]

Demand-management policies to achieve full employment made sense to social democratic policymakers as the best means to combat inequality without damaging the economy, even if it meant incurring some inflation. On the one hand, the use of expansionary policies could be cast as a solution that served the economy as a whole (a policy of full employment meant maximizing the use of the total resources of the economy); and that enhanced the welfare of all social groups, since it reduced the likelihood that anyone would lose his job. On the other hand, Keynesianism offered a way to benefit the social democratic electorate and to accomplish the ultimate social democratic goal of more equality. Full employment policies implied stable jobs for everybody, a stronger bargaining position for workers, and steady and higher incomes for the least well-off.[9] In short, Keynesian demand-management policies provided a theoretical framework and a set of policies that apparently reconciled the desirable goals of growth and equality in the eyes of social democratic policymakers.[10]

The strong appeal of Keynesian policies to social democratic parties was promptly noticed, and modeled, by the specialized literature. Echoing a rather widespread interpretation of postwar politics, Przeworski and Wallerstein (1986) claimed that Keynesianism constituted the key basis of social democratic economic policies, which, in turn, played a fundamental role in securing the broad social consensus of Europe after the war.[11]

More specifically, Hibbs was the first to relate, in a systematic manner, distinctive partisan preferences to the management of the business cycle and the determination of different inflation and unemployment equilibria (Hibbs 1977, 1987). In Hibbs's model, whereas most social democratic parties favored pursuing expansionary policies to achieve full employment, conservative governments fought inflation – by supplying the right amount of money and running a balanced budget – even if that pushed unemployment up.[12] In other words, in the framework of a (stable) Phillips curve, conservative parties would choose a low inflation–high unemployment outcome – the opposite of what social democrats preferred.[13] Mainly looking at macroeconomic data for the postwar period until the oil shock of the mid-1970s, Hibbs successfully pointed out how unemployment rates were relatively lower and inflation rates higher under left-wing governments. Exactly opposite results were obtained under right-wing governments.[14]

THE LIMITS TO THE PARTISAN MANAGEMENT OF THE BUSINESS CYCLE: THE CONCEPT OF INSTITUTIONAL EQUILIBRIA

Such an elegant and straightforward model of partisan politics promptly failed to be adequate, however. Its theoretical foundations, that is, the existence of a relatively stable, long-run Phillips curve, were attacked as early as 1968 by Milton Friedman (Friedman 1968). The unemployment–inflation trade-off was shown to be unstable. Expansionary policies were proved to reduce unemployment only for a short period of time. Any governmental countercyclical policies would in-crease prices and induce firms to raise nominal wages and hire more workers. As soon as workers would strive to match higher prices with higher real wages, the economy would return to its natural rate of unemployment. Inflation would be, however, higher. Friedman's arguments were then pushed even further by the "rational expectations" school (Lucas 1972; Sargent and Wallace 1975). Assum-ing that economic agents form their expectations rationally – that is, in the first place, they use all the information that is available about how the economy works and about policymakers' goals and instruments and, in the second place, they do not repeat past mistakes – and that prices and wages adjust freely, the rational expectations school predicted demand-management policies to have no real effects on the economy, even in the short run.

These theoretical critiques coincided with the historical breakdown of a long-term Phillips curve in the 1970s. By the end of that decade, ever-growing infla-tion was joined by increasing unemployment. A previously relatively benign unemployment–inflation trade-off dramatically deteriorated in most advanced nations.

With the initial model of permanent, stable partisan differences along an unemployment–inflation trade-off badly damaged, parties and partisan strategies became increasingly tangential in the academic literature. There was now a grow-ing consensus among scholars that partisan governments and political coalitions developed policies and chose strategies *in* the context of particular institutional frameworks and constrained by international variables. In terms borrowed from the game theory literature, scholars now stressed that political–economic equi-libria were induced by different institutions and norms rather than by ever-changing governing coalitions. Parties only mattered (i.e., policies only responded to the ideological preferences of governing politicians) under rather specific sets of institutions, if at all. Accordingly, political economists turned now to specify which and how distinctive sets, or constellations, of domestic institu-tions and international conditions, rather than domestic political coalitions and partisan governments, could explain particular policy outcomes. This required carefully mapping the institutional organization of, on the one hand, the domestic economy (basically, the structure of labor and capital) and of, on the other hand, the state or political system.

A more exacting exploration of the underlying workings of the labor market, in line with the most contemporary economic modeling, has shown partisan effects on the unemployment–inflation trade-off to be temporary. According to the "rational partisan model," mainly developed by Alesina, governing parties continue to conduct economic policy according to their underlying preferences (Alesina 1987, 1989; Alesina and Rosenthal 1995). Socialist parties attempt to boost the economy to reduce unemployment and improve workers' disposable income. Conservatives care relatively more about price stability than about unemployment. But the model of the economy is substantially different from the one posited in the classical partisan model. On the one hand, following the critiques made by the rational expectations school, economic agents are fully rational in forming their expectations. On the other hand, here following neo-Keynesian theorists, prices and wages do not adjust freely in the short run. Wages do not adjust immediately to exogenous shocks or policy changes, because wage contracts are signed in nominal terms and remain unchanged for a substantial period of time – say one to three years, the standard period in advanced economies.[15] Accordingly, any policy changes taking place after wage contracts have been signed will have real effects in the economy. An unexpected expansionary policy will create growth and employment, although only in the short run. Its effects will last only until wage contracts are renegotiated to adjust for the inflation produced by the government-led expansion. At that point, the level of employment returns to its "natural" rate, that is, the rate the economy sustains without policy interventions.[16] In short, parties can still affect growth rates, unemployment and inflation according to their preferences – but only for a short period of time after being elected to office. Recent empirical work shows, confirming this rational partisan model, that growth rates and unemployment vary along partisan lines for about eighteen to twenty-four months after a change in government. These differences wane completely, however, after two years lapse since the last election (Alesina and Roubini 1992).[17]

The unionization and institutional organization of the labor force affect equally deeply the management of the business cycle. Governments can only pursue noninflationary expansionary policies if economic agents, and in particular the labor movement, agree to pursue moderate wage raises. This requires, in turn, a highly encompassing and centrally organized union movement for two reasons. The larger its membership and the more cohesive its internal structure, the more likely the union movement will be, in the first place, to internalize the output and unemployment costs of excessive wage aggressiveness and the greater incentive it will have to make stable income pacts with business organizations and the government; and, in the second place, the more leverage and strategic capacity it will enjoy to enforce wage restraint on all workers (Olson 1982; Goldthorpe 1984; Calmfors and Driffill 1988). In other words, an encompassing labor movement gives a left-wing government the opportunity to implement its partisan preferences with success: social democratic parties can pursue expansionary policies; in response, unions moderate wage raises, which prevents inflation from creeping up again and undermining the public-sector-led expansion. Under such a "social democratic corporatist" regime, low unemployment rates will go hand in hand with low inflation (Cameron 1984; Lange and Garrett 1985, 1987; Alvarez, Garrett, and Lange 1991). But in the absence of encompassing union movements, socialist parties will eventually introduce stabilizing policies to prevent high inflation, a net loss of competitiveness, and, eventually, electoral defeat (Scharpf 1987, 1991).[18]

An expanding literature has as well started to unearth the impact that different constitutional structures of the state may have on macroeconomic management. The position of ministries and bureaucratic actors ease or constrict, in different ways, the action of politicians (Hall 1986). Highly independent central banks prevent partisan governments from picking inflationary policies (Grilli, Masciandaro, and Tabellini 1991; Alesina and Summers 1993). Excessively fragmented cabinets, a likely result under pure proportional electoral systems, make harder the coordination of governmental policies and may produce loose fiscal policies (Alesina and Perotti 1994).

In summary, although parties may have distinctive preferences toward the governance of the economic cycle, attaching different values to price stability and employment creation, they operate embedded in rather specific institutional environments. How economic agents adjust to governmental policies, how well coordinated firms and employees are, and how the political system within which politicians design policies is structured ultimately affect the success of partisan strategies. Parties are heavily constrained by a large set of structural and institutional variables. Governments may attempt to reform domestic institutions. This is, in fact, where politics matters. To put it differently, politics is restricted in the neoinstitutionalist literature to reforming (or inventing) institutions. Yet that is an extremely costly and uncertain process. And, for part of the literature, even different domestic institutional arrangements have become increasingly irrelevant as a result of growing international economic interdependence.[19] In short, looking at how governments manage the economic cycle, we are bound to conclude that it is institutional structures, themselves the result of long-term historical processes, and not political coalitions, or partisan strategies for that matter, that account for the specific economic strategies nominally announced by governments.

THE ARGUMENT OF THE BOOK

Demand-management solutions geared to controlling the business cycle stop short, however, of exhausting the stock of available policies to govern the economy. Economic growth and economic competitiveness depend mainly on the supply conditions of the economy, that is, on the level and nature of the factors of production – fixed and human capital.[20] Accordingly, governments of all political orientations have resorted, in a systematic way and well beyond pure demand-management policies, to supply-side, or structural, economic policies,[21] that is, to policies that shape the provision of production factors or inputs and that, in so doing, help to determine the long-run natural rate of output of the economy.

With some rare exceptions, however, scholars have paid scant systematic attention to the political determinants of supply-side economic strategies. In a well-known article, Przeworski and Wallerstein (1986) claim that, on purely theoretical grounds, it is possible to conceive different political alternatives in the management of the supply side of the economy – contrarily to what happens in the area of demand policies.[22] Martin (1979) was probably the first to offer a – pathbreaking – empirical analysis of supply-side economic strategies and partisan politics. Still, his analysis was constrained to a single case study, that of Sweden through the midseventies. Those few who have later ventured on a more general exploration of supply-side issues have insisted on the dominant role of institutional factors over partisan agency. Katzenstein (1985) refers to them as part of policy packages designed by open economies to compensate for exogenous shocks. Hall (1986) relates different industrial strategies in France and England to particular state traditions and institutions. In a more explicit analysis of supply-side economic policies, Garrett and Lange (1991) have linked their nature to the presence of social democratic corporatist structures.[23] Yet, as argued in detail in Chapter 2, neither the organization of the domestic political economy nor a growing internationalization of the economy should be expected, on theoretical terms (tested in Chapters 3 and 4), to play any significant role in constraining governments in the definition of supply-side economic strategies.[24]

Both the quantitative and the qualitative evidence gathered in this book show that parties and partisan preferences have a key impact on the selection of the set of policies directed to shape the supply side of the economy. Left-wing parties attempt to raise directly the productivity of capital and labor through the public sector and government intervention (through more expenditure on infrastructures and education and, sometimes, through the creation of a public business sector). Social democratic policymakers expect that, by increasing the productivity of workers (particularly those initially less endowed), of productive sectors, and of regions, this sort of expenditure will, in the first place, boost the overall efficiency of the economy and its competitiveness and, in the second place, lead to higher wages and a more equal income distribution. Conservative parties expect that, given a system of perfect market competition and the appropriate economic incentives, capitalists will invest in a way that will maximize their private individual and hence, in the absence of externalities, the social rate of return. Similarly, workers will make the proper consumption and investment decisions to maximize their overall income flow – either borrowing or forgoing present consumption to invest in the acquisition of higher skills. Accordingly, conservative governments reject any sort of public capital formation policies and encourage the private provision of physical and human capital. Since private investment is financed by savings, and savings in turn depend on the level of profits, conservative governments are determined to keep taxation low and non-distortionary to avoid reducing private resources.

As shown in Chapter 2, the partisan selection of distinctive supply-side economic strategies takes place in response to particular political–economic trade-offs that differ sharply from the unemployment–inflation trade-off on which the partisan business cycle model is built. In their search for growth, partisan governments are confronted with a pointed employment–equality trade-off. Lowering taxes and decreasing social protection to boost profits, investment, and competitiveness may cause more inequality at home. Yet an excessive commitment to public transfers, for the sake of maintaining social cohesion, may lead to a faltering economic performance. The growing integration of world markets and the unstoppable technological changes of the last two decades have altered the demand for parts of the production factors of the advanced economies and, in particular, lowered the wages of the most unskilled workers. Sharpening then the trade-off between employment and equality, they have brought to the fore, with flaring intensity, the question of how to affect the structural conditions of the economy. In these circumstances, partisan forces, which already embraced very different supply-side strategies in the past, should be expected to propose clear-cut divergent solutions in the future.

Before proceeding any further, two final points are in order. First, the book mainly examines the relationship between parties and economic policies. It does not posit a strict correlation between government partisanship and specific economic outcomes (e.g., necessarily predicting more inequality under a conservative government) in the way the partisan business cycle model does for the unemployment–inflation trade-off. By affecting the supply of production factors, governing parties do certainly have a fundamental impact on the economy. Nevertheless, they intervene in economies that have a given history and institutional structure. Thus, to predict the final economic outcomes, it is important to take stock of both the governmental economic strategies and the initial conditions (the quality of the input factors) under which those policies were launched. This would clearly exceed the goals and the scope of this volume. Still, the book offers the tools, particularly in Chapter 2, to develop these kinds of explanations. Chapter 10 also hints at the ways in which it should be possible to derive particular outcomes from the interaction of initial conditions, governmental policies, and institutional structures.

Second, it is worth emphasizing that this book limits itself to examining the major economic strategies available to governments, their consequences, and their political underpinnings. The book does not advocate one particular economic strategy over another. There is considerable agreement among economists that a more highly skilled labor force implies a higher productivity rate, more rapid growth, and probably less unemployment.[25] The political dispute that this book explores, however, concerns precisely the means that should be employed to achieve them. Uncertainty about which is the best strategy as well as pure redistributive conflict provide the framework within which partisan forces and electoral coalitions continue to clash in the political arena.

PLAN OF THE BOOK

To examine the nature and the consequences of partisan agency on economic policymaking, in particular with regard to supply-side economic strategies, and hence the role of partisanship in the political economy of advanced nations, the book is organized by deploying several strata of evidence: first, of an analytical kind and, afterward, of an empirical nature – both statistical and historical or qualitative.[26]

Chapter 2, which fleshes out the theoretical core of the book, develops a highly stylized model to characterize the economic structure of all advanced countries – centered on a sharp employment–equality trade-off – and presents empirical evidence in its support. It then examines the political sources of economic policymaking. Employing the initial assumptions about partisan goals introduced in the present chapter, Chapter 2 derives the alternative economic strategies pursued by conservative and social democratic governments and discusses the potential role of domestic institutions and the international economy on the conduct of economic policy. It concludes with an examination of the electoral dimension of each economic strategy; its purpose is to offer a more elaborate framework (than the one implicit in the initial assumptions adopted about the motivations of parties) for understanding the relationship between electoral politics and economic policymaking.

The following chapters are organized to explore – in empirical terms – the set of hypotheses raised by Chapter 2. Chapters 3 and 4 bear the burden of confirming the validity of the partisan model for supply-side economic strategies through a set of statistical analyses. The previous discussion of the nature of supply-side economic strategies dictates the set of indicators that should be examined for that purpose. To measure the sources of direct provision of production factors, Chapter 3 examines, first, the public provision of fixed capital formation and, second, the level of public spending on human capital formation, in the form of both general education and vocational training. To measure the indirect provision (by the state) of input factors, and examine the more general issue of public control of ownership, Chapter 4 looks at the nature of governmental strategies toward the public business sector. Finally, to determine the extent to which parties shape tax and regulatory schemes in order to alter (or free up) the saving and investment behavior of private agents, Chapter 4 also examines the structure of the income tax (in particular, its rates). The model is tested with data from all OECD countries with over one million inhabitants,[27] mostly for the period that extends from 1960 to 1990.[28]

The quantitative analysis of Chapters 3 and 4 is followed by the historical examination of the political and economic strategies pursued by two cases that are very dissimilar in terms of partisanship and policy outcomes: the Spanish Socialist government and the British Conservative government in the 1980s. The Spanish case is an ideal illustration of a left-of-center strategy built over a long period of time, heavily constrained in its macroeconomic policy, but able to pursue supply-side policies that deliver timely electoral successes. The British example provides a clear-cut opposite example: the case of a longstanding conservative government capable of turning around the previous model of economic management in favor of a deregulated market economy. The in-depth analysis of these two countries corroborates the plausibility of the results gathered in the statistical chapters. That is, the two cases confirm the nature and overall cohesiveness of the supply-side strategies that each government, from different ideological positions, pursued. The analysis also shows how the clear convergence in macroeconomic policies that ideologically opposed governments experienced (imposed on them by the institutional structure of their countries and high economic integration in Europe and the world market) was not matched with regard to policies directed to shape the supply side of the economy. Finally, the two cases provide a chance to examine the relationship between supply-side strategies and policies to manage the short-term economic cycle (although some evidence on this question is presented in Chapter 3, it remains rather sketchy). Overall, the analysis of the two cases offers a way to uncover the political processes that link partisan preferences to particular policy outcomes.[29]

Nonetheless, the selection (based on the results of Chapters 3 and 4) of two very dissimilar cases is done, above all, to achieve a more fundamental purpose: to examine the underlying electoral dynamics of each economic strategy and, consequently, to throw more light on the variable of partisanship, which, according to our quantitative and qualitative evidence, so heavily affects the choice of economic strategy. The book aspires, therefore, to bridge what normally appears in the discipline as two separate literatures: the study of political economics and the analysis of partisan and electoral politics. Confirming the theoretical analysis in the last section of Chapter 2, the two cases show, first, that, as implied in the initial set of assumptions employed in this book, partisan governments elaborate their economic strategies to respond to the underlying demands of their core electoral constituencies. Second, the two cases make apparent how parties actively design their economic policies to organize and sustain winning electoral coalitions. Finally, both cases give evidence on the rather stringent electoral dilemmas that parties face in choosing the proper levels of public investment, social spending, and taxation. Taken together with Chapter 2, the case studies offer, then, a deeper understanding of the nature of parties, as organized coalitions of interests around ideas, than the one entailed by the strict assumptions put forth at the beginning of the book.

The book devotes two chapters to each country. The first chapter of each case study (Chapters 5 and 7 respectively) examines, first, the ideological stance of each party, its internal evolution leading to electoral victory, and the initial electoral coalition that supported the party. It then briefly surveys the macroeconomic strategies of the government (and the ideas and internal coalitions that sustained them). Each chapter, however, is mainly built around the successful development of the supply-side economic strategy of each government, especially after the constraints of the economic recession cleared away and each cabinet was able to implement its strategy gradually. The second chapter of each case (Chapters 6 and 8) examines the explicit political strategy that underlay the process of economic management and how each government attempted to secure and expand its electoral base. It then studies the set of political limits that each strategy endured: a constant popular demand for extending social benefits, the need to reconcile this demand with the resistance of key centrist voters to further tax increases, and, in the case of the Socialist government, the strained relations with the union movement. In the light of these constraints, it is possible to understand the electoral effects of each economic strategy and the immediate policy choices that each government had to face in the economic downturn of the early 1990s. Chapter 9 takes stock of the lessons learned in the case studies and engages in an extended analysis of the exact relationship between electoral politics and partisan policies, buttressing the evidence gathered for Britain and Spain with more circumscribed information on other European countries such as France, Sweden, and Germany.

To conclude, the successive analytical, statistical and historical sections of the book should be understood as operating in two interrelated ways. On the one hand, both the statistical part and the case studies of the book perform what may be considered their "standard" function. They are jointly used to judge the reasonability of the successive theoretical claims of the book: the existence of an employment–equality trade-off, partly resulting from exogenous shocks and particular institutional arrangements; the development of divergent partisan responses to it; and the formation of specific electoral coalitions behind each party. On the other hand, while testing these propositions, the book has been structured to advance from very stylized assumptions in the first chapters to progressively more historical and "complex" arguments, which in turn have to be seen as informing the initial hypotheses.

2

POLITICAL PARTIES AND THE STRUCTURAL CONDITIONS OF THE ECONOMY

In Chapter 1 I emphasized that, contrary to the findings of the current theoretical literature and contrary, as well, to popular wisdom, political parties, understood as coalitions of interests and ideas, play a rather pivotal role in the economic-policymaking process and in the evolution of the economy. More precisely, I pointed out that, although they are constrained by the configuration of domestic institutions and the international economy in regard to macroeconomic policymaking, all governments have substantial autonomy to affect the production factors or structural conditions of the economy in line with their ultimate partisan preferences. Broadly speaking, social democratic governments primarily mobilize the public sector to shape the supply side of the economy – in order to reconcile growth and equality. Conservative governments believe instead in employing market mechanisms to optimize the savings and investment rates and thus maximize economic growth.

To shed light on the nature and consequences of these economic strategies, and to pave the way for the statistical and historical analysis undertaken in the rest of the book, this chapter starts by developing a stylized model of the political economy of advanced nations. The second section then provides empirical evidence on the economic trade-offs revealed by this model (essentially between unemployment and economic inequality), that all advanced countries face. The third section examines the alternative economic strategies that different parties will embrace, depending on their initial preferences (presented in Chapter 1) toward the distribution of income, to manage the supply side of the economy. This is followed by discussions of the possible, yet relatively minor, constraints – of either a domestic or an international kind – that might affect each partisan structural economic strategy. The chapter concludes with an analysis of the political–electoral dimensions that underlie each economic strategy. Starting with a simple model that represents a naive class-based model of voting, it then elaborates a more complex model where the vote (and, therefore, economic policies) is a result of the distribution of incomes and assets in the population, shifts in those incomes, the competitive strategies of parties, and the electoral institutions within which parties compete.

PRODUCTION FACTORS, SOCIAL WAGE, AND THE ECONOMY: THE INITIAL MODEL

Consider an economy where the initial cumulative distribution of skills among the population resembles the one represented in Figure 2.1 by curve F. Here, the vertical axis depicts the level of skills any worker may have – from unskilled (0) to very skilled (θ). The cumulative distribution of the population of the country (in relative terms, from 0 to 100) is represented by the horizontal axis. Thus, for example, in Figure 2.1, 25 percent of the population has a level of skills of θ' or less (say, a fifth of the skill level of the most qualified worker, θ); the skills of the median worker are slightly over θ''; and only 25 percent of the population has skills over $\tilde{\theta}$.

In this economy the level of skills determines the level of disposable income each worker enjoys. For example, a worker that has skills θ' will earn a *gross* wage (i.e., a wage before taxes) θ'. Imagine now that there is a minimal guardian state, that is, a state whose functions are limited to the provision of national defense and public order. A tax t will have to be levied on each person's gross income to finance these services. As a result, all workers will experience a reduction in their wages. For example, the worker with skills θ' and a gross wage θ' will eventually have a *net* wage ($\theta' - t$). The resulting distribution of net wages across the population is represented in Figure 2.1 by curve Y. Notice that, due to the fact that the state is small in size, this post-tax income distribution Y (which, again, comes from subtracting a tax t from each gross wage θ) closely matches the skill distribution F.

This economy presents a natural rate of unemployment U. This unemployment can be assumed to be frictional – a result of those workers that have left (or have been laid off from) their jobs and are searching for new opportunities – and to affect all the population randomly.[1] It can also be thought of as affecting only the most unskilled workers. For the sake of simplicity, this latter instance is the one represented in Figure 2.1.

Finally, it is reasonable to assume the existence of what may be called a "socially determined minimum income" – that is, a socially accepted income "floor" below which individual disposable incomes should not be allowed to fall. This socially determined income floor, or, for purposes of brevity, a "social wage" (SW) is determined by the government. The social wage, SW, is the amount of cash and goods to be given to the least advantaged workers (generally those that are jobless): unemployment benefits, income supplements, and other social trans-

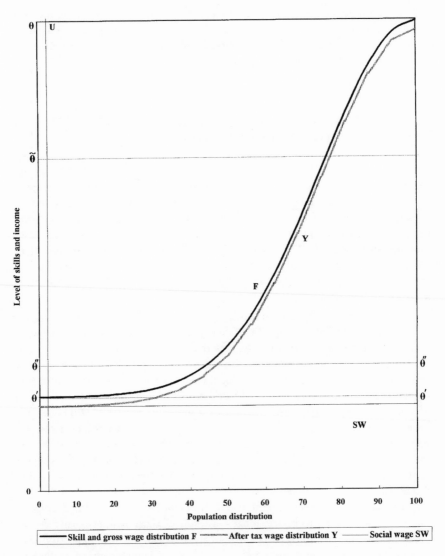

Figure 2.1. The initial set-up

fers (such as free medical care, subsidized housing) for those cases in which a
given worker is jobless. In Figure 2.1 the social wage has been set at the level of
the net wage earned by the least skilled worker.[2]

The consequences of the social wage on economic performance and the income distribution are readily apparent. Imagine that an economy like the one
depicted in Figure 2.1 – with the skill distribution *F*, the social wage *SW*, and
a very low rate of unemployment *U* – is suddenly affected by a relatively lasting

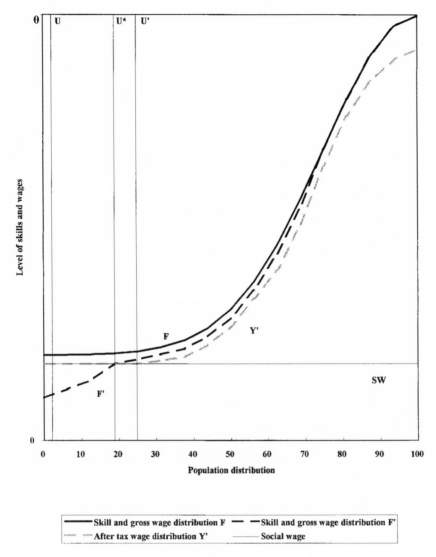

Figure 2.2. The effects of an exogenous shock

economic downturn. In this circumstance, the relatively unskilled workers are more likely to suffer unemployment than the relatively skilled workers. The effects of this lasting economic crisis (and the discussion that follows) are depicted in Figure 2.2.

As a result of the economic shock, unemployment increases to U', around 25 percent in Figure 2.2. All those laid off receive unemployment benefits (equal to SW) that are lower than their previous wage.[3] A short economic crisis – lasting, say, one year – has marginal consequences on the unemployment rate. As the economy recovers, the unemployed should still find jobs paying more than the social wage. The unemployment rate shifts back from U' to U. If the economic crisis lasts longer, however, the already low skills of the unemployed erode over time, simply because they are unable to practice them. The depreciation of the skills of part of the workforce can be represented as a downward shift in the distribution of skills from F to F'. For all the unemployed (the fraction of the workforce to the left of U'), the probability of finding a job similar, in terms of skills, to the one they lost declines steadily. Accordingly, the unemployed will earn less income than before in any job they may get.[4] In fact, a substantial number of the unemployed (the fraction to the left of U^*) end up with skills useful only for jobs providing wages lower than the social wage. Even when the economy fully recovers again, workers with skills below the social wage will prefer to stay unemployed until they can again find a job paying a salary above the social wage.[5] As a result, unemployment may fall from U', but it will remain at U^* – around 18 percent of the workforce in the example depicted in Figure 2.2. It should be noticed, however, that although unemployment may remain high, income inequality does not increase in equal proportion – it may even decrease after taxes are paid and transfers allocated. The distribution of net wages moves only slightly, from Y (in Fig. 2.1) to Y' (in Fig. 2.2). In this last distribution, for all the population to the left of U^* the net wage (equal to SW) is very similar to the one they received when they worked. The richer segment of the population (in the right-hand side of the figure) actually suffers an erosion in its net wage as a result of new taxes to support the unemployed.

A similar situation develops as a result of two kinds of structural transformations: first, technological shocks such as the introduction of microcomputers or computerized machine tools, and, second, increased exposure to low-labor-cost foreign competition. In both cases there is a fall in the domestic demand for very unskilled workers (at least at wages equal to those paid before the structural transformation took place). The skills curve shifts here too from F to F'. Even under a period of economic expansion, unskilled workers either see their wages collapse or face substantial layoffs. With depreciated skills, their incentives to accept the social wage (instead of merely adjusting to a leaner wage) increase rapidly. Similarly, firms will have no interest in hiring them at wages above SW. Over time, unemployment will also stabilize at U^*.

It is worth emphasizing at this point how this model sheds light on the interactive effects of a given skill distribution and the social wage on economic performance and therefore unveils the policy alternatives available to parties and governments to solve the problems of loss of output, long-term unemployment, and economic equality.

Economic performance is determined, on the one hand, by the nature of the domestic productive structure. Although the latter concept was restricted to the quality of skills in Figures 2.1 and 2.2, it also comprises the size and quality of capital or, in other words, infrastructure and machinery.[6] All these factors determine, in the first place, the average domestic level of productivity and, indirectly, the average wage level. A highly (in average terms) skilled population will be able to compete in the world market through a high value-added strategy and, as a result, will be able to maintain high standards of living. An unskilled workforce will have to compete by keeping labor costs low. The quality of input factors determines, in the second place, the pattern of wage distribution and dispersion.[7] A wide distribution of skills leads, other things being equal, to substantial wage inequalities. The narrower the range of skills of the workforce, the less unequal the distribution of income will be. Finally, the input factors affect the level of unemployment: the more unskilled the workforce is, the higher the rate of unemployment will be.

On the other hand, economic performance and economic equality depend on the level at which the social wage, defined as a floor determined by the state and under which the disposable income of any worker should not fall, has been set. The social wage tempers the distributive consequences of increasing unemployment or a depreciation of skills – induced by either an economic shock or a technological transformation in the economy. Nonetheless, although the social wage (loosely) preserves a certain equality of income across social sectors over time, it constitutes a very limited tool to further equality in the medium run. A high social wage will induce higher levels of unemployment in the following way. As soon as the government raises the social wage to an income level above the market-determined wage earned by the least skilled worker (say, in Fig. 2.1, above θ'), the pool of workers whose skills are below θ' will have an incentive to stop working. Given that their market-determined wage is lower than the social wage, they will prefer to be unemployed. Moreover, an equalization strategy based purely on raising the social wage leads to the subtraction of resources from the national pool of savings and investments due to the higher taxes needed to finance the social transfers going to the unemployed. It therefore hampers growth – and hence the basis to pay for the social wage. In short, the effects of an increase of the social wage unveil, in a sharply stylized fashion, the dilemma that governments face.[8] Due to the potential negative effects of the social wage on the level of unemployment and output, even those governments interested in achieving a more equal income distribution have a strong incentive to sustain a relatively low social wage (or at least a social wage equal to the wage of the least skilled worker). Notice, finally, that pure expansionary policies to smooth the business cycle and sustain full employment will be insufficient to equalize social conditions, since even with no unemployment the wage gap between skilled and unskilled workers will remain basically unchanged. In addition, these policies will not be sufficient to provide full employment, if unemployment is determined by the supply conditions of the economy. As a result, any policymaker interested in furthering income equality needs to look for an economic strategy that goes beyond both the pure management of the business cycle and consumption transfers.

EMPIRICAL EVIDENCE OF THE TRADE-OFF

The way in which the quality of skills (and fixed capital) and the social wage affect, separately and in interaction, economic performance has always forced governments to choose among different policy strategies (discussed below) to affect the supply side of the economy. Yet the phenomena modeled above – the hysteretic effects of long-term unemployment, technological shocks, and increased foreign competition – have been the most distinctive events experienced by the OECD economies at least since the late 1970s. By shifting downward the relative price of parts of the labor force, they have undoubtedly intensified the pressure on governments to choose between distinct alternative strategies to shape the supply side of the economy.[9]

Until the 1970s the set of skills enjoyed by most workers was satisfactory for the technological requirements of the period. Moreover, almost all the tradable sectors of the advanced industrialized nations experienced rather weak competitive pressures from less developed nations. In short, the workforce could be thought of as a relatively skilled one. The rapid industrialization of several developing countries, the fall in transportation and communication costs, and a shift toward more advanced technologies from the late 1970s on led to an erosion, in relative terms, of the skills of a portion of the workforce in the industrial world.[10] Such a relative decline of skills (in comparative terms) implies that most of the advanced nations have moved from a situation similar to the one depicted in Figure 2.1 in the 1960s to one that is closer to the situation represented in Figure 2.2 in the 1990s. Accordingly, the trade-off between unemployment and inequality has worsened dramatically. A high and unchanged social wage has led to rising unemployment: unemployment rates have jumped in European Union countries from less than 3 percent before 1973, to 5 percent in the late 1970s, and then to almost 10 percent in the late 1980s. But lowering the social wage (or keeping it at very low levels) results in a substantial increase in the degree of inequality.

In order to offer empirical evidence on the employment–equality trade-off, the first two subsections below show that the level of unemployment is a function of both the level of skills of the workforce and the social wage in place. The last subsection then offers evidence that a reduction in the social wage to drive unemployment down may come at a considerable cost in terms of economic equality.

EDUCATION AND UNEMPLOYMENT

Figure 2.3 and Table 2.1 provide empirical evidence on the joint impact of human capital and the social wage on the unemployment rate. Figure 2.3 plots all OECD countries according to their average standardized unemployment rate from 1982 to 1990 and to how well educated the whole workforce was in 1991 (the only year for which comparable data are available). The level of education is measured by the proportion of the labor force between fifteen and sixty-four years

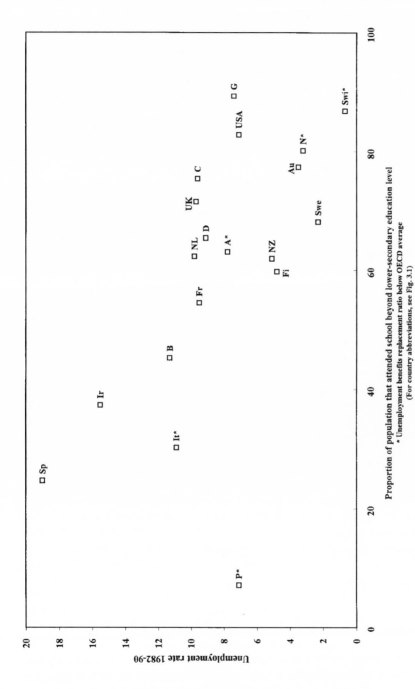

Figure 2.3. *Unemployment, education, and unemployment benefits in OECD countries*

Proportion of population that attended school beyond lower-secondary education level

* Unemployment benefits replacement ratio below OECD average

(For country abbreviations, see Fig. 3.1)

Table 2.1. *Unemployment, education, and unemployment benefits in OECD countries in the 1980s*

	AVERAGE UNEMPLOYMENT RATE 1982-90	
INDEPENDENT VARIABLES	MODEL 1 [a]	MODEL 2 [b]
Constant	12.960* (2.685)	18.110* (1.847)
Percent of population with more than lower secondary education (1991)	-0.130* (0.038)	-0.162* (0.024)
Unemployment benefits (1979-85) [c]	0.117** (0.067)	0.135* (0.039)
Organizational power of labor [d]		-7.190* (1.442)
R^2	0.454	0.875
Corrected R^2	0.386	0.846
Number of observations	19	17

[a] Australia, Austria, Belgium, Canada, Denmark, Finland, France, Germany, Ireland, Italy, the Netherlands, New Zealand, Norway, Portugal, Spain, Sweden, Switzerland, UK, USA.

[b] Australia, Austria, Belgium, Canada, Denmark, Finland, France, Germany, Ireland, Italy, the Netherlands, Norway, Spain, Sweden, Switzerland, UK, USA.

[c] Unemployment benefits (1979-85): unemployment replacement rate as a percentage of the wage of the average production worker. Source: OECD 1994b. Index goes from 0 to 100.

[d] Index goes from 0 to 1.

Estimation: OLS.
Standard errors in parentheses.
* Statistically significant at .05.
** Statistically significant at .10.

old that has more than a lower-secondary education (lower secondary education studies are normally completed when a child is fourteen years old).

The striking pattern unveiled in Figure 2.3 is confirmed by the regression analysis reported in Table 2.1. In the column for Model 1, I report the effects of education and of a proximate (although somewhat crude) measure of the social wage on the level of unemployment in the 1980s. The level of the social wage is measured as the unemployment benefits received by an average production worker during the first year of joblessness as a proportion of his wage (during 1979–85).[11] Human capital and unemployment benefits jointly account for 45 percent of the variance in unemployment, and for 61 percent if we exclude Portugal. According to this statistical analysis, unemployment decreases a whole point for each 6–7 percentage points of population that have studied beyond lower secondary education. In turn, higher unemployment benefits increase unemployment. Other things being equal, a country with unemployment benefits equal to the whole wage of the average production worker has 11–12 percentage points of unemployment more than a country with no unemployment benefits.

Unemployment also has a cyclical component that depends partly on domestic macroeconomic policies. According to the literature on the political management of the business cycle, reviewed in Chapter 1, the presence of corporatist arrangements allows for the successful implementation of an accommodating or expansionary economic policy (which should reduce unemployment on a permanent basis, that is, without sparking an acceleration of inflation). Accordingly, in the second equation I introduce the index of organizational power of labor, which can be taken as a good proxy for the existence of corporatist pacts.[12] Explained variation jumps to 87 percent (from 64 percent, since in the equation reported in this column, neither Portugal nor New Zealand is included for lack of data on their labor market structure). Completely organized labor movements – of the kind prevalent in Scandinavian countries – indeed drive unemployment down by 7 percentage points. Still, structural factors, such as the quality of human capital and the social wage, present very stable coefficients and keep playing a crucial role.

STICKY VERSUS CYCLICAL UNEMPLOYMENT

By looking at the behavior of unemployment in several countries over a long period of time, Figure 2.4 offers further evidence on the negative effects of a high social wage, for a given distribution of skills, on the levels of total employment. As emphasized repeatedly, as the level of the social wage goes up, more workers become insulated from the structural changes that affect the economy, and unemployment is disconnected from the output cycle. In countries with a high social wage, the economic cycle affects only in part the unemployment rate for the following reason. Whereas economic downturns always raise the level of unemployment, in countries with high social wages economic recoveries only lead to a marginal decline of the number of jobless. Workers who, as a result of a prolonged spell of unemployment or a technical change, now have skills useful only for jobs that pay less than the social wage will prefer to stay unemployed and receive the social wage. As a result, unemployment turns out to be sticky – it hovers around the level that was reached in the last economic crisis.[13]

In countries with a low social wage, few workers have the option of remaining unemployed. Once the economic recovery is over and jobs become available, workers rush to accept them, even if they pay less well than the jobs they had before the economic downturn. Unemployment matches the business cycle and fluctuates around the natural rate of unemployment of that given economy. Figure 2.4A shows the evolution of the unemployment rate in two "flexible" labor markets, the United Kingdom and the United States, from 1971 to 1995. In both cases unemployment shot up in the early 1980s from relatively low levels. It was over 12 and 9 percent in the United Kingdom and the United States

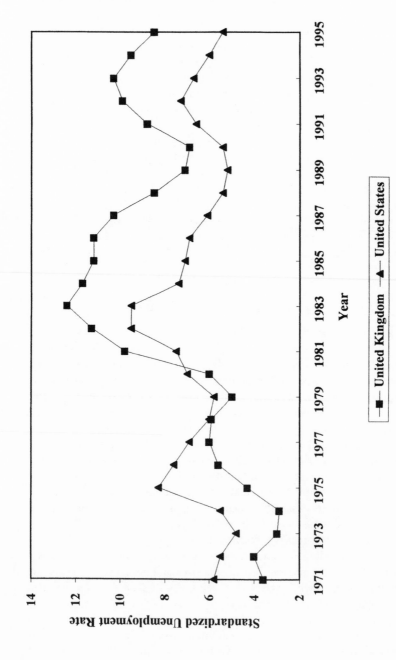

Figure 2.4A. The evolution of unemployment in "flexible" labor markets, 1971–95

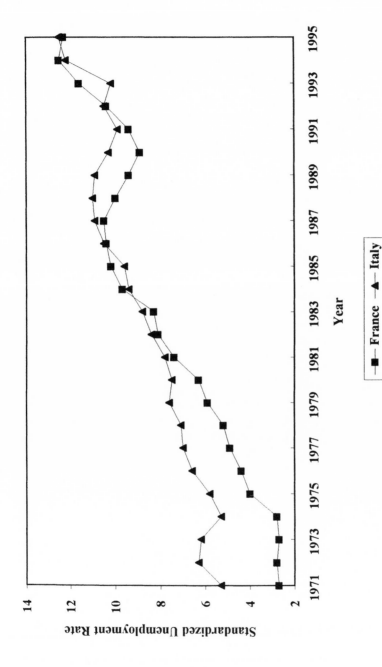

Figure 2.4B. The evolution of unemployment in "rigid" labor markets, 1971–95

Standardized Unemployment Rate

Year

■ France ▲ Italy

respectively by 1983. It declined rapidly in the United States. Its reduction was slower – yet sustained over time – in Britain, once the reforms approved by the Thatcher government started to affect the economy. Unemployment increased again at the end of the decade but by the second quarter of 1995 was almost back to its pre-economic downturn rate in both countries.

Figure 2.4B provides evidence for the same period of time for two rigid labor markets – France and Italy – that suffer from a "sticky" rate of unemployment. Compared to the flexible countries, unemployment rose less dramatically in the early 1980s but it only stabilized by the mid-1980s. In spite of the boom of the following years, it declined by only 2 percentage points. It increased again with the new downturn. By 1995 both countries had unemployment rates at twice the American rate and 50 percent higher than the British rate.

INEQUALITY ACROSS NATIONS

According to the model just developed, the counterpart to the generation of more jobs has been more wage inequality in the last two decades. This conclusion is confirmed when we look at Figure 2.5, which shows the relationship between the annual average percent change in private sector employment (per inhabitant) from 1979 to 1990 and the evolution of wage dispersion (measured as the percent change in the ratio between the wage earned by a worker in the ninth decile and the wage earned by a worker in the first decile) from 1980 to 1990 in thirteen OECD countries.[14] The wider the dispersion of wages, the higher the extent of income inequality. As expected, the generation of jobs (in the private sector) is inversely related to the preservation of wage equality.[15] In countries where the private sector has been particularly dynamic, such as the United States and the United Kingdom, income inequality has increased. In countries where strict labor regulations have resulted in sticky unemployment, such as France, Germany and Italy, income inequality has in fact declined.

ALTERNATIVE SUPPLY-SIDE ECONOMIC STRATEGIES

EQUALIZING CONDITIONS THROUGH SUPPLY-SIDE ECONOMIC STRATEGIES

Since a social and economic strategy that relies on the provision of a social wage leads to a rigid trade-off between the goals of equality and efficiency, or redistribution and growth, social democratic governments (i.e., governments interested in equalizing social and economic conditions) are forced to consider an alternative solution that avoids subsidizing unemployment and distorting the market but that can raise disposable incomes. This solution consists in upgrading the skills of all or most of the population (and the quality of the fixed investment

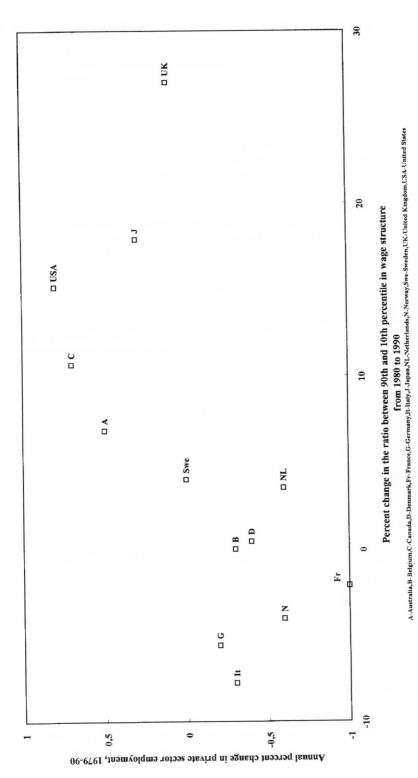

Percent change in the ratio between 90th and 10th percentile in wage structure from 1980 to 1990

A-Australia,B-Belgium,C-Canada,D-Denmark,Fr-France,G-Germany,It-Italy,J-Japan,NL-Netherlands,N-Norway,Swe-Sweden,UK-United Kingdom,USA-United States

Figure 2.5. Employment creation and wage dispersion in OECD countries, 1979–90

as well). By raising the skills of workers, particularly those who were initially unskilled or semiskilled, the government attempts to raise the productivity of the labor force and capital, to increase real disposable income, and to reduce inequality at the same time. After allocating substantial public resources in human capital formation, all workers in general, and the least well-off in particular, should be prepared to engage in tasks that are more productive than those they previously performed. They should then receive significantly higher wages without threatening the competitiveness of the economy. Moreover, as the pool of unskilled people declines, wage inequality and dispersion will necessarily shrink. In short, social democratic governments search for a "virtuous circle" in which higher productivity continues to attract private capital but allows for higher wages and for higher taxes, which are then employed to sustain and increase domestic productivity.

This public capital formation strategy is represented in Figure 2.6. After an exogenous shock, such as the one represented in Figure 2.2, has shifted the initial skill distribution F to F' (leading to unemployment U'), social democrats engage in extensive public spending on human capital formation in order to shift the distribution of skills from F' to the skill distribution F''. A successful shift upward of the skill curve has immediate effects on the distribution of net wages. The distribution of net wages moves from Y' to Y''. Wage differentials shrink substantially and the goal of equality is clearly advanced. It goes without saying that public capital formation policies do also take place before an economic downturn or an exogenous shock has shifted the skill curve from F to F'. In that case, which for the most part corresponds to the economies of the pre–oil shock period, social democrats invest in workers in order to move the skill curve from F to F'' so as to equalize economic conditions – without the pressures of growing unemployment that take place when the skill distribution is F'.

The distributive effects of increasing worker skills may be similar to those that come from establishing a high social wage. But equality is achieved without having to incur the costs of paying vast sums of unemployment benefits. With most workers endowed with relatively high skills, few people will have the incentive to forgo a job to receive the social wage (even if the latter is rather high). If this strategy is successful, unemployment should stay low – back to U in the hypothetical situation drawn in Figure 2.6. Notice too that engaging in a strategy of raising the skills of workers is not incompatible (in principle) with the maintenance of a high social wage. Social democrats do not renounce maintaining or even raising the social wage. The purpose of their strategy, however, is to minimize its use.

Nonetheless, the deployment of a public capital formation strategy does not come without costs. On the contrary, it requires heavy taxation, basically on the better-off social sectors, to pay for various types of interventionist schemes. This reduces the after-tax disposable income of the most skilled workers substantially – from, say, the net wage distribution Y' to Y'' in Figure 2.6. More important, this need for additional taxes imposes two key dilemmas on any social democratic

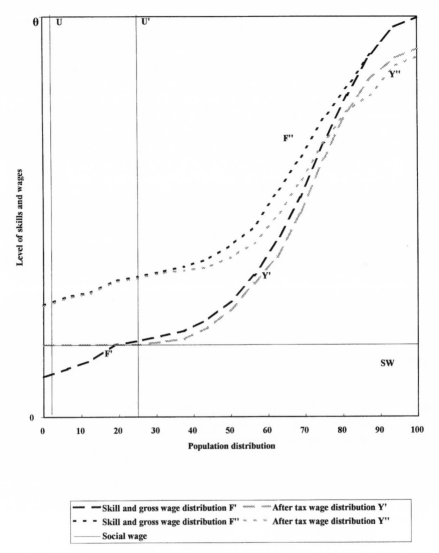

Figure 2.6. Equalization through the public supply of skills

government. The first one involves a mainly economic question: the extent to which heavy taxes (as well as public capital formation schemes) may distort the workings of the economy. The second one revolves around the purely political or electoral issue of how social democratic parties are to build a broad and stable political coalition to implement their preferred economic strategy over time despite the likely opposition of voters to increased taxation. I turn to the first problem in the following subsection, in the context of analyzing the preferred strategy of a nonsocialist cabinet. I take up the discussion of the second dilemma in this chapter's section on the electoral dimensions of economic policymaking.

A MARKET-BASED GROWTH STRATEGY

While interventionist supply-side economic strategies are deemed to be both efficient and fair by social democratic governments, conservative cabinets reject them because they have uncertain results; involve the mismanagement of a substantial amount of resources; distort the smooth operation of markets; and require heavy taxes that will fall especially on the core conservative electoral constituencies. Conservative policymakers contend that, given a system of perfect market competition and the proper incentives, workers will automatically strive to acquire higher skills, either for themselves or for their offspring. Workers as well as firms should be expected to make the proper consumption–investment decisions to maximize their overall income flow (according to their own preferences). A declining stream of income caused by a relative depreciation of their present skills (resulting from an exogenous shock of the sort described above) should naturally induce workers to intensify their training and their education in general, in many cases with the active help of business or other private organizations. As workers gain in skills, their incomes will proportionally increase and a "naturally given" equalization process will ensue. As stressed before, conservatives do not oppose a process of income equalization per se, but they expect it to occur hand in hand with economic growth without any need to resort to state-led redistributive schemes.[16]

An economic strategy that relies on market forces and on establishing the proper incentive structure to spur a virtuous circle of private investment requires keeping the social wage low – that is, equal to the wage of the least advantaged worker. This strategy, represented in Figure 2.7, implies lowering the social wage in response to an exogenous shock that decreases the demand for the least skilled workers and shifts the skill curve downward.

In Figure 2.7 an exogenous shock shifts the initial distribution F (represented in Figs. 2.1 and 2.2) to F'. As discussed previously, unemployment rises to U' (at the trough of the economic crisis). As the economy recovers, it then declines to U^*. It should remain there if both the current social wage and the distribution of skills (F') do not change. The distribution of net wages takes the form of Y'.

Conservatives do not react by pumping extra resources to shift F' upward – the policy of social democratic governments. They attempt instead to lower the social wage from SW to SW' (the level of the least advantaged worker in F'). New taxes are in this way avoided. Above all, with the social wage now at SW', workers to the left of U^* have an incentive to search for jobs. With the social wage now at SW', unemployment will decline to its natural rate (U) again.

As a result of this economic strategy, income equality will suffer, at least in the short- and the medium-run. As shown in Figure 2.7, the distribution of net wages will move from Y' to $\hat{Y}$. That is, to the left of U^*, net wages are below

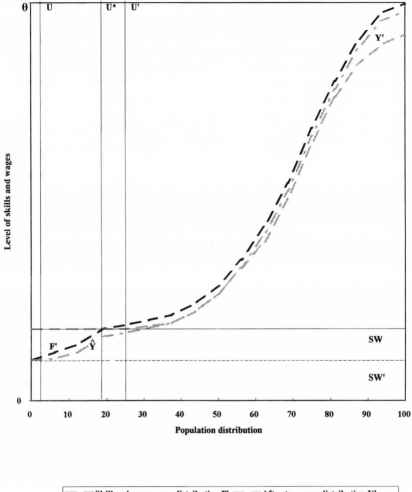

Figure 2.7. A market-based employment strategy

SW, matching the distribution of skills *F"*. It is important to emphasize that the resulting inequality is a mere by-product of choosing the *appropriate* policy to maximize growth (and therefore disposable incomes) in the long run – that is, the policy for which a conservative government understands that there is no alternative course of action available. Higher inequality is never an intended outcome of any conservative government. It is merely the result of policymakers preferring, for efficiency reasons, growth through private investment rather than growth through a public capital formation strategy. If growth were not to suffer from pursuing more equality, all policymakers would probably prefer more income equality than less. Still, as I pointed out before, conservatives expect that workers themselves will invest time and resources to acquire the skills necessary to increase their income in the long run. This will enable the wages at the bottom of the scale to rise and wage differentials will, therefore, shrink over time.

THE POTENTIAL EFFECTS OF DOMESTIC INSTITUTIONS

Now that we have examined the two ideal strategies partisan governments may employ to shape the supply conditions of the economy, we are in a position to explore the conditions under which parties choose to implement them – or, in other words, we can now examine what room is available for pursuing their true policy preferences.

Recall that the domestic institutional conditions within which governments operate, as well as the international economy, have a fundamental impact on the capacity of parties to manage the economic cycle. Certain institutional frameworks – those with encompassing unions and central banks subjected to the central government – lend themselves well to expansionary strategies of a social democratic nature. Other institutional systems – those characterized by decentralized labor markets – are particularly amenable to orthodox anti-inflationary policies. In the absence of the "right" institutions, and unless governments engage in the costly strategy of altering existing institutions, parties are like boats sailing against strong winds, continually being pushed away from the economic policies they would prefer to implement.

This section therefore turns to the task of examining the potential impact of different institutional equilibria on the capacity of parties to pursue their preferred supply-side economic strategies. Two different models are discussed here. The first subsection explores the impact of different wage-bargaining systems (alone and in interaction with partisanship). The second subsection examines those approaches that focus directly on the impact of different institutional frameworks on the supply of input factors. As I pointed out at the beginning of this chapter, the inquiry is done here in theoretical terms, which are fully tested in the following chapters.

WAGE BARGAINING REGIMES AND ECONOMIC POLICIES

Depending on the overall organization of labor and capital, particularly in regard to their wage bargaining regime, the literature distinguishes, in a highly stylized manner, between coordinated and decentralized labor markets. In coordinated labor markets, social actors (usually the labor movement) are structured within strong and widely encompassing organizations, with high levels of affiliation and with centralized decision-making procedures. With such an organization, workers hold a high degree of political leverage. They are capable of sustaining nationwide, coordinated systems of wage bargaining. And they have a strong incentive to moderate their wage claims since excessive wage aggressiveness translates into a loss of total employment, which, due to the sheer size of the union movement, threatens to affect all its members equally. By contrast, decentralized labor markets have weak unions and business organizations. Wage bargaining in these settings is conducted in a decentralized manner – indeed close to the neoclassical model of the labor market. Nationwide wage agreements are next to impossible to reach and sustain.

As briefly discussed above, the structure of the labor market has significant effects on the partisan manipulation of the business cycle. Helped by the presence of a centralized, encompassing union movement, capable of delivering voluntary wage restraint, social democratic parties can pursue expansionary policies without having to bear their inflationary consequences.[17] On the contrary, a decentralized labor market facilitates the anti-inflationary policies of right-wing governments.

Union assent is not a *necessary* condition, however, to realize interventionist supply-side policies. Labor cooperation is only needed to ensure that expansionary macroeconomic policies do not produce an acceleration of inflation that wipes out any gains in employment. Yet, contrary to what part of the literature seems to maintain, fully interventionist economic policies can be developed even in countries in which labor markets are decentralized.[18] Left-wing governments can raise taxes, expand the public business sector, and contribute heavily to capital formation without obtaining voluntary wage restraint. To sustain this strategy, socialist policymakers only need a solid electoral majority. While they engage in strong public capital formation strategies, balanced monetary and fiscal policies can be developed to achieve the economic stability which they otherwise might not get from unions because of the lack of wage coordination. As a matter of fact, deprived of the option of expanding the economy to lower unemployment, social democratic governments in decentralized economies have a greater incentive to pursue aggressive supply-side policies than socialist cabinets in corporatist regimes.

As will be made clearer from the empirical analysis carried out in Chapter 3, the historical experience of the last decade confirms this theoretical point. Through the late 1970s social democratic governments and corporatist arrangements went hand in hand in most countries. Such "social democratic corporatist regimes" generally resulted in highly interventionist supply-side policies; the Swedish implementation of the Rehn–Meidner model provides the most elaborate and best explored case.[19] Accordingly, by just looking at that historical period, it is difficult to disentangle empirically whether highly organized unions or social democratic parties or both explained the development of extensive public programs in capital formation. In the 1980s social democracy gained power in several

Southern European countries, where unions are weak and fragmented and hence unable to sustain corporatist pacts. The fact that governments engaged in ambitious public investment strategies in those countries confirms, therefore, the key role partisanship plays regardless of the presence of neocorporatist structures.

ECONOMIC INSTITUTIONS AND ECONOMIC COMPETITIVENESS

According to a more recent body of research, the supply conditions of the economy – skills and flows of knowledge and information across companies – as well as the production strategies of companies hinge on the institutional framework of the domestic economy, that is, the economy's set of "institutional 'conventions' or formal or informal institutional rules and understandings" (Soskice 1995, 1). More specifically, this literature depicts two stylized economic regimes, coordinated and decentralized economies, and links them to rather distinctive production profiles. These two institutional frameworks partially overlap, especially geographically and historically, with the wage bargaining regimes described in the previous subsection. But they are distinguished by a wider range of institutional traits and affect the supply side of the economy in ways that have little to do with the macroeconomic logic of either corporatist or decentralized wage-setting systems.

"Coordinated market economies" are regimes characterized by the existence of dense, stable, and organized linkages among the main economic agents that result in the adequate supply of skills and collective goods needed to engage in high value-added competitive strategies. Germany is typically used to exemplify this sort of economy.[20] Banks and companies maintain strong links, which make the former willing to offer long-term financial help beyond business cycle fluctuations. Companies keep strong ties and a tight cooperative relationship with labor. Here a "tacit contract" takes place between labor and business (Soskice 1991). In exchange for promises of long-term employment and a certain control of firms' decisions, unions maintain cooperative relationships with management and monitor workers to reduce shirking within the firm. Individual workers commit themselves to perform adequately both at school and at work. This "tacit contract" is underpinned by a rather rigid labor law and wage bargaining system. Given that the law makes redundancies extremely costly to firms, and that restructuring plans that involve layoffs are closely scrutinized by unions, companies prefer investing in workers to increase their productivity over time rather than dismissing them as soon as there is an economic downturn (and rehiring them again with the following economic recovery). Poaching by other firms is in turn prevented by the structure of wage agreements. Wage settlements are collectively established, encompass all companies, and are characterized by rather rigid wage schedules. Firms therefore have little leeway to offer significantly higher wage packages than other companies to lure workers trained elsewhere. Firms are also prevented from poaching by the powerful employer associations to which they belong. Operating under such an institutional regime, companies have the proper incentives to invest time and resources in training their workforce. The probability that their own employees and other companies will free ride on them is extremely low. As a result, the supply of skills will be abundant and the population will be highly qualified.

In a "decentralized" economy (such as the United States, which is the paragon of this model) both business associations and unions are weak. Labor markets are decentralized and only weakly regulated. Labor mobility is high. Firms rationally adjust to the business cycle through layoffs. In the absence of institutions that would curb the short-term, hyperrational behavior of firms, companies have no incentives to invest in human capital in a sustained way. Even when they are interested in training employees, companies are reluctant to do so, calculating that other firms in the same industry or sector will attract them, through higher wages, once they have been fully trained. As a result, the economy suffers from a suboptimal provision of skills, the job force is poorly trained, and firms have to restrict themselves to follow low-labor-cost production strategies.

How do these regimes affect partisan politics? According to the most radical strand of the literature on institutional coordination, the production profiles of each country, strictly determined by their respective institutional frameworks, can be changed hardly at all through state intervention. Due to the way in which skills and long-term capital are created, a well-trained labor force and stable financial channels cannot be generated simply by massive public spending and intervention. In-firm training (to create a highly skilled labor force) or company–bank financial deals (to sustain long-term competitive strategies) involve using a particular sort of information that companies will be reluctant to share with public authorities – since governments could always be tempted to use it against firms in some other context or at a later time. Consequently, according to this literature, public intervention cannot do much to change historically determined institutional equilibria.

Such a theoretical claim is difficult to sustain. Different institutional settings may affect the quality of the input factors of the economy – and therefore the severity of the employment–equality trade-off.[21] But they neither determine a priori any supply-side strategy nor preclude governments from pursuing the alternative supply-side economic policies presented throughout this book. A coordinated institutional setting is not the only possible mechanism to provide for different types of human and fixed capital. It is true that part of the training process takes place at the plant or firm level. And that in-firm training particularly prospers when it comes embedded in particular institutional frameworks. But most human capital that is necessary to engage in productive activities consists in *generic* (rather than specific) assets. The provision of generic assets is done through settings such as the school system, which are almost disconnected from firms and in-firm training.

The empirical results of Table 2.1 and Figure 2.3 showed, in a rather sharp manner, that generic skills (measured as the completion of lower secondary education, a measure that excludes vocational training) are good enough to reduce substantially the levels of unemployment in advanced countries. More than half of the difference between the Spanish rate of unemployment (around 20 percent) and the Swiss rate (around 1 percent) comes from the extraordinary gap in generic skills that exists between the two countries. As a result, most skills can be provided without relying on the coordination of business. As a matter of fact, because of the highly volatile world economy – an economy in which competitiveness grows more acute and where patterns of demand from customers change quickly – generic skills (such as wide knowledge and the general capacity to interact with peers) may be becoming even more important than company-specific skills to fight unemployment.[22] Finally, even with regard to company-specific skills, based on in-firm training, it is unclear why public agencies cannot step in, if they are willing to do so, through mechanisms that avoid the informational problems referred to by the literature on institutional coordination. The Swedish labor market policies set up by the social democratic government in the 1960s are a pertinent example.

In short, as shown in this book, solutions to the problems of inequality and unemployment have been engineered regardless of the degree of institutional coordination in the country. This applies to *all* economic strategies. Social democrats can try to invest heavily in people's skills. Conservatives can reasonably expect that, once the government has established the appropriate legal framework, individuals will find ways to improve their education and that they will set up the proper structures to respond to demands for more education. This will take place even if there are no coordinating mechanisms operating in the economy.

THE POTENTIAL EFFECTS OF INTERNATIONALIZATION

In investigating the sources of economic policymaking, the literature has come as well to recognize the powerful constraining effects that the international economy has on any attempt to manage the economic cycle. On the one hand, with increasing trade openness, a higher portion of domestic demand is satisfied abroad. As a result, internally engineered expansionary policies risk propelling imports up, increasing trade deficits, and eroding economic competitiveness. On the other hand, the higher the levels of capital mobility, the lower the autonomy policymakers have to shape fiscal and monetary policies. In an open economy with a fixed exchange regime, interest rates will converge worldwide (at levels determined by international price-setters, such as the United States or, in Europe, Germany). Only fiscal policy can affect domestic demand (since monetary policy is geared toward sustaining the currency). Still, fiscal policy is constrained by the performance of the current account in the long run. With floating exchange rates, domestic monetary expansions are possible in the short run through currency depreciations, but the effects are likely to be quickly outweighed by the increasing cost of imports and a wage push that neutralizes the gains of the depreciation.

Trade integration has grown considerably over time. Total exports and imports combined represented an average of about 40 percent of gross domestic product (GDP) in advanced countries in the 1960s. Thirty years later, they amount to over 60 percent of GDP. Due to the systematic removal of national barriers to cross-border capital flows, capital mobility across borders has accelerated even more rapidly.[23] These two trends have naturally worked to narrow the latitude for national macroeconomic management. Recent notorious cases of ill-fated macroeconomic management, such as several corporatist attempts in the late 1970s (Scharpf 1987, 1991) or the French experiment of 1981–83 (Sachs and Wyplosz 1986; Hall 1986), have dramatically highlighted the scarce autonomy remaining for politicians in the post–Bretton Woods era. As a matter of fact, recent systematic research shows that, already in the 1960s, expansionary policies were hardly employed by social democratic politicians, who happened to hold power mainly in the smallest and most open European economies (Garrett 1994).

Supply-side economic strategies are instead designed, to a great extent, with an eye to solving the competitive challenges imposed by the growing internationalization of the domestic economy. The dilemma posed by the choice between the public training of the labor force and the lowering of labor costs partly derives from, or is exacerbated by, increasing competition from emerging markets abroad. Both a high-tax-rates–*public*-investment strategy and a low-tax-rates–*private*-investment strategy are geared toward ensuring high levels of capital formation, boosting productivity rates, and furthering the international competitiveness of the domestic economy. Both strategies attempt, in the face of substantial (and increasing) capital mobility, to increase the net rate of return to capital. A market-based growth strategy is organized accordingly to lure investment by reducing taxes and labor costs. A public-sector-led strategy is instead designed to broaden the wedge between taxes and gross profits by deliberately increasing productivity. Higher productivity should then dissuade capital from fleeing the country even in the presence of high marginal tax rates.[24] Insofar as both strategies are successful in attracting private capital, keeping a high rate of capital formation, and securing strong growth rates, either of the two can be sustained over time. It is worth emphasizing again that, although both strategies aim at maximizing growth, they differ in their redistributive consequences: economic conditions may be more equal under a social democratic regime but at the cost of a heavier tax burden (especially on the most advantaged sectors of society). Accordingly, the requirements of an internationalized economy do not necessarily constrain the choice by countries of one strategy over the other. In other words, increasing trade openness does not mechanically lead to any cross-national convergence in policies in this sphere, in the way it does in the area of macroeconomic management. Convergence, if it takes place in the future, will instead be due to political causes (a change in the actors controlling the government) or to instrumental factors (the conviction that one of the strategies is inherently flawed and is unable to respond adequately to the pressures of competitiveness and technological change).

ECONOMIC STRATEGIES AS ELECTORAL STRATEGIES

As emphasized in Chapter 1, according to the assumptions of the partisan model, which provide the initial foundations of this book, political parties adopt different economic strategies due to the latter's redistributive consequences. In the political business cycle literature, the distributional effects of different combinations of unemployment and inflation lead left-wing and right-wing cabinets to choose different macroeconomic policies. Similarly, the first part of this chapter has shown that governments run by different parties adopt divergent supply-side economic strategies to foster growth because they have different effects on the welfare of all social sectors. In short, economic strategies respond to the concerns of the particular electoral constituencies that support the party in power. This section examines in detail the electoral dynamics behind the formulation of economic policies in order to achieve three interconnected purposes. It aspires to develop a more complex model of electoral preferences (and their interaction with economic policies) than the rather simple one employed so far to describe the link between voters and governmental selection of alternative supply-side economic strategies. It emphasizes the fact that, besides responding to voters' preferences, economic policies are employed to build electoral coalitions. Finally, it highlights the electoral tensions that may beset each economic strategy – and that have indeed grown more relevant with the worsening of the employment-equality trade-off in the last two decades.

The stylized model of the political economy of advanced nations presented in the first part of this chapter can be employed again fruitfully as a *benchmark* to examine the electoral dimension of the economic policymaking process. In the initial assumptions employed in Chapter 1 (as well as in this chapter), social democrats are said to poll the vote of relatively unskilled workers or, to use broader terms, of those who are relatively lacking in (all sorts of) assets.[25] Conservatives are instead assumed to receive most of their support from relatively more qualified workers (or from voters that are asset-holders).[26] Again, as pointed out before, mainly because they obtain their support from different constituencies, partisan governments engage in different economic policies. This electoral cleavage can be incorporated into the political–economic model introduced in this chapter. This is done in Figure 2.8. Figure 2.8 represents what the literature on voting behavior defines as a "class-based" model of electoral behavior or, more precisely, what has been described as a "naive theory of class politics" (Kitschelt 1994, 40–47): blue-collar workers vote socialist, and middle-class voters vote nonsocialist.[27]

This initial model offers a first approximation to the policy equilibria that

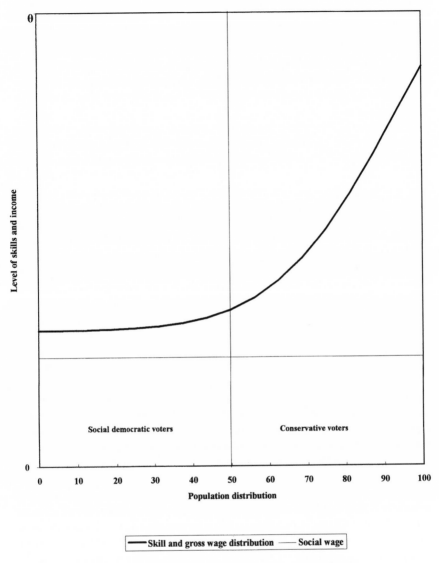

Figure 2.8. The initial model and the distribution of electoral preferences

are likely to prevail in each country. As can be easily deduced from Figure 2.8, the electoral success of each party and the ultimate policy adopted (e.g., the degree to which a conservative government can lower the social wage) will depend on the profile of the distribution curve of skills (assets) and of the social wage. In a country where the skills curve is rather steep, that is, where most voters have few assets, conservative parties may be more hesitant about lowering the social wage. Under the same conditions, however, it is easier for socialists to garner a stable coalition around progressive tax rates and high levels of public investment. By contrast, the more skilled the population, the less political appeal public investment programs may have (unless the public investment programs are the mechanisms that generate and sustain the high-skills equilibrium that characterizes the population).[28]

PARTIES AS BUILDERS OF ELECTORAL COALITIONS

Figure 2.8, however, only represents a given *initial* distribution of skills, assets, and (potential) electoral preferences. It would be simplistic to see such a distribution as a *fixed* structure that determines the vote and to interpret politics as a set of electoral events in which parties merely try to win over the median voter.[29] The electoral and economic strategies of each partisan government have to be conceived instead in a dynamic sense: as attempts to mold the preferences of voters in order to build broad electoral coalitions and parliamentary majorities.

As emphasized by Przeworski and Sprague in their pathbreaking analysis of social democratic electoral politics, political parties do not just represent given preferences but "forge collective identities, instill commitments, define the interests on behalf of which collective actions become possible, offer choices to individuals and deny them" (1986, 9). Przeworski and Sprague stress that the organizational level of parties and unions and the presence of other distinctive political cleavages account for much of the fortunes of electoral socialism. But they do not specify the political appeals and kinds of policy commitments that (social democratic) parties must employ to shape preferences and therefore to fashion a winning coalition.[30] We must turn to Esping-Andersen's work linking particular welfare-state regimes to specific electoral coalitions (Esping-Andersen 1985) to find an appropriate theoretical foundation for Przeworski and Sprague's fundamental insight. According to Esping-Andersen, the construction of a universalistic welfare state allowed social democracy to manufacture a broad electoral coalition across classes in Scandinavia. As a matter of fact, this argument can be put in more general terms. Policies are the key instruments employed by parties and partisan governments to build and sustain an electoral majority. They are used as bargaining cards – indeed, as bundles of side-payments – to weld together partly conflicting interests. In some cases policies have even more radical consequences: they shape preferences.[31]

Economic policies (jointly with redistributive policies in the strict sense) are used to promote partisan identities and hold together winning electoral coalitions in the following way. Social democratic parties see their public investment strategy as a way to create a broad electoral coalition that will include blue-collar workers (their most natural constituency) and parts of the middle class through the following mechanisms. High taxes to build up fixed and human capital are expected to increase the productivity of the workforce and thus allow for higher wages without endangering the competitiveness of the economy and the rate of investment by private capital. Since these higher wages will benefit, above all, blue-collar workers, they will reinforce these workers' support for the social democratic government. Moreover, if, as a result of extensive public capital formation policies, productivity and wages rise for all social sectors, the economic conditions of middle-class voters will also improve and convince them to support the social democratic cabinet. In other words, although in the short run the need for high tax rates mainly depresses the disposable income of the relatively qualified work ers, public investment policies are expected to benefit both the unskilled and the skilled workers in the long run. A strategy of public capital formation is therefore formulated as the proper means to retain the allegiance of key middle-class voters to the social democratic party. With higher productivity rates, it will be possible to finance (without inducing any economic inefficiencies) a generous welfare state. As pointed out by Esping-Andersen, universal welfare policies will then reinforce the political hegemony of social democracy around a broad cross-class electoral coalition.

The same logic applies to right-wing parties. Conservative governments develop their (private) investment strategy to secure and expand their basis of electoral support in the following way. Low taxes and a low social wage are expected to attract private investment and accelerate the rate of economic growth. With taxes lower and the disposable income of relatively educated voters higher, support for the conservative government will increase among its natural constituency. Nevertheless, economic growth will raise incomes across the board and gradually enlarge the proportion of asset-holders and middle-class voters – in other words, it will shift upward the skills distribution curve. As the natural constituency of conservative voters becomes larger, the probability of a conservative electoral victory (or the adoption of more moderate policies by the Left) will increase. In other words, in the short run a fall in the social wage may create social havoc and even threaten the electoral support of the party in power. But in the long run a private-investment–low-tax strategy is expected to benefit all social sectors. Thus, a conservative economic strategy can successfully maintain a broad coalition of middle-class sectors and increasingly affluent industrial workers. Again, a particular organization of the welfare state – stressing the role of private savings and the importance of individual effort and choice – is likely to reinforce a nonsocialist majority.

ELECTORAL DILEMMAS OF SOCIAL DEMOCRATIC AND CONSERVATIVE GOVERNMENTS: THE POLITICAL CONSEQUENCES OF EXOGENOUS SHOCKS

Even when supply-side economic strategies work (particularly in the medium run) to the advantage of the natural constituencies of each party, in the deployment of each strategy governments face important electoral dilemmas that may jeopardize their level of political support and the success of their economic plans. Supply-side economic measures may involve altering the present and future levels of the voters' welfare in substantial and, often conflicting, ways. For example, raising the rate of public investment implies a promise to increase future incomes at the expense of present consumption (since taxes are higher and public transfers lower than they could be). Similarly, lowering the social wage increases the level of inequality in the short run in exchange for higher incomes in the long term. Since structural economic policies may temporarily hurt the welfare of voters (or specific segments of voters), it may be difficult for the party in government to hold together the rather broad coalition that it needs to remain in office. As discussed in the previous subsection, supply-side economic strategies are opportunities to build a social democratic electoral coalition encompassing the heterogeneous interests of unskilled manual workers and semiqualified white-collar employees – or, on the contrary, to organize a conservative majority based on the latter and on well-paid managerial cadres. But it is important to emphasize that the initial heterogeneity of those interests (that gets resolved through a successful economic strategy) may, at the beginning, frustrate any attempt to develop coherent economic policies.

In implementing their preferred economic policies, both social democrats and conservatives have always faced the kinds of electoral dilemmas I describe in this section. But, as pointed out shortly below, the changes in the relative demand for unskilled and skilled workers that OECD nations have recently experienced have only increased the heterogeneity of the interests of voters and therefore intensified the electoral dilemmas confronted by all partisan governments as they develop their supply-side economic strategies.

For the sake of understanding these electoral dilemmas, any governmental strategy to shape the supply conditions of the economy can be described as the composite of two separate policy decisions: first, a decision about the rate at which voters should be taxed – that is, the tax rate t; and, second, a choice of the proportion or ratio (δ) according to which tax revenues will be distributed between public investment (δt) and public transfers ($[1 - \delta]t$).[32] Consider now the dilemmas that affect social democrats and conservatives respectively.

Social Democratic Electoral Dilemmas

At the time of deploying their "optimal" long-run strategy, all social democratic governments are confronted with two dilemmas. The first dilemma concerns the level of taxes. Excessive taxes may both alienate the centrist electorate and endanger the rate of private investment. Low taxes will prevent the government from deploying its preferred strategy and spur discontent among leftist voters. The second dilemma involves the actual allocation of tax revenues. An investment rate that is too high may have electoral costs since it reduces present public transfers for the sake of productivity increases in the future. Still, as emphasized before, a combination of high taxes and little public capital formation is economically lethal for socialists.

An excessively high tax rate may, in the first place, threaten private investment and cause capital to exit (endangering the social democratic economic strategy). The extent to which the tax level may threaten the long-run growth rate (by forcing capital to exit) depends on the options capital has (i.e., whether there are more profitable places to invest) *and* on the way the government decides to allocate the tax revenues. According to an interventionist model of the optimal supply-side policy, high levels of public investment increase the productivity of capital and labor and therefore raise the net rate of return to capital. As a consequence, the higher the amount of tax resources the government applies to public capital formation, the higher the tax rate the government should be able to establish.[33]

Thus, a social democratic government is interested in spending most tax revenues on capital formation. But the second policy decision social democrats confront, the selection of the rate of public investment (a decision that affects in turn the tax rate), is also shaped by political considerations. Whenever any government decides to increase the rate of public capital formation (in order to increase future consumption), it is reducing the level of public transfers and thus asking electors to forgo present consumption. Public investment may make economic sense in the medium run, but it can affect the electoral support of the socialist party in the short run, especially among those voters who are the least skilled. Although unskilled workers profit from investment spending, they will demand high levels of social spending until the effects of capital formation are noticeable. Naturally, to avoid losing the support of unskilled workers, a socialist government could accommodate both high capital spending and high social spending by raising the tax rate. But, again, a tax rate that is too high may push middle-class (relatively skilled) voters toward the conservative camp and therefore frustrate the social democratic economic strategy altogether. In short, the two political dilemmas that emerge in respect to the tax rate and the public investment rate are subtly connected because they involve mastering potentially conflicting electorates.

The electoral dilemmas inherent to a social democratic economic strategy were rather mild before the structural shocks that have affected the advanced countries since the late 1970s. Growth was fast. Good jobs and acceptable wages were available to rather unskilled workers. Unemployment was low. Under such conditions, it was politically easy to finance social transfers and investment programs: since tax rates could be kept at reasonable levels, substantial parts of the middle class voted for left-wing parties. The recent shift in the relative demand for (and wages of) unskilled and skilled workers has aggravated the electoral dilemmas confronted by social democratic governments.[34] A fall in the demand for unskilled workers presses socialist cabinets to step up the rate of public investment. But introducing new taxes to pay for more capital spending (to compensate workers for an exogenous shock) endangers the support for the socialist government among relatively skilled voters. To avoid new taxes and still finance its investment policies, the socialist cabinet can approve a reduction of the social wage. But this solution carries substantial electoral risks. Unskilled workers, who are now threatened by the prospects of unemployment to a greater extent than in the postwar period, are likely to respond to any cut in social spending by abandoning the socialist party. They may abstain. They may shift to radical leftist parties. Or, as apparent in countries like France, they may turn toward a radical right-wing party that attributes the current deterioration of their economic conditions to excessive foreign competition and that promises them protectionist policies and the expulsion of all immigrant workers.

Conservative Electoral Dilemmas

The electoral dilemmas faced by a conservative government are extremely similar to those confronted by a social democratic cabinet. Broadly speaking, conservatives wish to reduce taxes. The capacity of the conservative government to cut taxes is limited over time, however, by the extent to which it is able to reduce public spending in both public investment and social transfers. Unless the conservative cabinet is willing to run a public deficit, tax cuts will have to be matched by spending cuts, at least in the medium run. In turn, the government's ability to cut taxes depends on the level of public support for each governmental spending program.

In general, public capital formation programs are easier to dismantle. They are primarily geared toward the less skilled workers and the less developed regions and sectors, which are likely to constitute a minor part of the electorate. Moreover, the inherent uncertainty about the future benefits of a strong public capital formation strategy diminishes such a strategy's electoral appeal even among its potential beneficiaries. Accordingly, a reduction in public investment in exchange for tax cuts may be welcomed by the majority of the population. As the British and American experience of the 1980s seems to suggest, social transfers (such as health spending or pensions) are, on the contrary, harder to trim. Especially if public transfers have a universal nature (i.e., if they benefit the working and the middle classes equally), conservatives may be unable to reduce welfare spending. Excessive cuts risk generating mounting opposition from the middle segments of the electorate and therefore an almost certain electoral defeat for the conservative government. But, on the other hand, if the conservative cabinet is unable to cut spending and taxes, voters with the greatest skills and assets may start defecting to radical libertarian parties.

Because they have increased the disparity of incomes and the heterogeneity of interests of the electorate, the structural shocks of the last two decades have jeopardized the conservative basis of support in the same way that they have threatened the historical social democratic coalition with fragmentation. The decline in the demand for unskilled workers has raised the volume of expenditure on unemployment benefits and curtailed the tax base. Any increase in the tax rates to pay for this new expenditure is likely to trigger a backlash from the relatively well-off segments of the electorate. Conservative parties feel pressed to reduce public expenditure to please their core constituencies. Excessive spending cuts, however, may push middle-income sectors toward leftist parties. But, again, overly moderate tax reductions may boost the support for libertarian parties to the right of the traditional conservative forces.

Notice the ways in which the stylized model (and its underlying arguments) just developed accommodates, in a historical way, several explanations – sometimes presented as conflicting in the specialized literature – about the electoral behavior of advanced countries: class-based and sector-based models of voting. Figure 2.8 captured the initial, static distribution of political preferences across voters. It closely represented the (naive) class-based models of voting that have been put forward to describe the electoral scenario of the first postwar period. At least until the 1960s, socialist and conservative parties drew their support from very different social classes. As emphasized above, those electoral coalitions were kept together through specific economic and social policies. Figure 2.9 depicts in turn how the new structure of political competition after an exogenous shock, such as the one affecting the industrialized world in the last years, alters the distribution of relative skills and incomes: the demand for unskilled workers falls; by contrast, the demand for educated workers, and therefore their wages, rise. As a result of an increasing disparity of incomes, interests become more heterogeneous or polarized. In other words, relatively homogeneous classes fragment into several social segments and economic sectors. Figure 2.9 conforms with a recent literature that, pointing to the decline in class-based voting in advanced democracies, has come to stress instead the growing importance of sectoral cleavages – such as those that pit high-skilled workers in internationally competitive firms against low-wage workers in sheltered sectors – and sector-based voting patterns.[35] Under these new conditions, parties have a harder time accommodating the voters' preferences in broad and stable coalitions through coherent economic policies. Before the structural shocks of the last two decades, sector-based preferences were in part less salient (the blue-collar working class was larger and more homogeneous) and in part more manageable (the trade-off between investment, social spending, and taxes was less acute). Although the interests of voters were partially conflicting (they had to be since voters occupied different positions in the social ladder), parties could reasonably expect to build class-based coalitions through their social and economic policies. After the technological and trade shocks of the last twenty years, sectoral divides have grown in intensity. The electorate around the median voter has grown more volatile: more taxes (to sustain the welfare state) or too radical spending cuts (to attract private investment) make this electorate equally uneasy. Right-wing voters may shift to libertarian forces if the progress in reducing taxes is too slow. Trade issues increasingly pit unskilled, low-wage workers against highly qualified, new middle classes. The most unskilled workers, whose position is now increasingly precarious, threaten to vote for radical-left parties or play with the idea of supporting protectionist, anti-

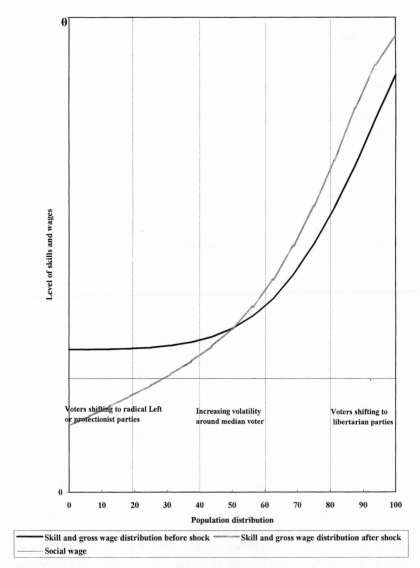

Figure 2.9. The political consequences of an exogenous shock

immigration right-wing parties if traditional left-wing recipes (investment and free trade) no longer work effectively.

In short, as a result of rather dramatic structural shocks, political parties may be experiencing more difficulties in organizing sufficiently broad coalitions to govern and effect change. Increases in the heterogeneity of interests and the extent of sector-based voting, however, do not necessarily translate into new parties and a different party system. Again, it would be too naive to read off policies and partisan programs mechanically from voters' preferences. Parties build as much as represent electoral interests. As emphasized above and shown in the rest of the book, parties employ bundles of policies to build majority coalitions. Under the fire of protectionist demands from part of its own constituency, the French Socialist Party seemed close to collapse in the mid-1990s. But the Swedish and Spanish Socialist Parties were still able to hold together a broad electoral coalition around the central idea of free trade and domestic compensation. Austrian Christian Democrats have lost most of their blue-collar sector to the Freedom Party in the last elections. But German Christian Democracy has succeeded in keeping the allegiance of its working-class electorate intact.

Besides policies, parties can count on two other broad instruments to gather a majority coalition. First, parties benefit from having a strong internal organization. As already emphasized by Przeworski and Sprague, a well-oiled party machine with high affiliation levels and strongly mobilized cadres, or an encompassing union movement, will certainly help social democratic parties, for example, to convince workers of the need to pursue public capital formation strategies – in spite of the high costs in terms of short-term consumption – and therefore to keep their political allegiance.

Second, the success of parties in securing an electoral victory depends on the "structure of political opportunities" within which politicians compete for power (Strom 1990), that is, the rules for attaining office and the electoral strategies of other parties, which jointly lead to a specific party system. First, a highly permeable electoral system (where electoral rules, party finance, and access to mass media make the entry of new parties inexpensive) is likely to produce more competition from fringe parties, more fragmented party systems, and more fractured coalition cabinets. Under such circumstances, and unless the party in power relies on a well-organized electoral machine, capable of canvassing the vote effectively, formulating its most preferred long-term economic policies should be more costly electorally. Second, the presence of other political cleavages besides the traditional economic left–right one (such as a religious divide or a postmaterialist dimension), and the use other parties make of them, equally affect the government's ability to build a durable winning coalition. For example, the ability of social democratic parties to hold office alone over a long period of time has been significantly aided by the division of nonsocialist forces in Scandinavia and by an excessively conservative party in Spain. Socialist parties, on the other hand, have not attained the same electoral salience in countries with significant religious cleavages or strong communist competitors.

CONCLUSIONS

This chapter has laid the groundwork for understanding the key role that partisan forces play in the governance of the economy. Using a stylized model of the political economy of advanced nations, it shows that all partisan governments face a substantial employment–equality trade-off that pushes them to go beyond the management of the economic cycle and to develop economic strategies focused on the supply conditions of the economy. Partisan responses to the trade-off differ due to the redistributive consequences of the alternative economic strategies available to governments. As the following two chapters show, social democratic governments, concerned about both achieving growth and equalizing economic conditions, attempt to raise the productivity of capital and labor through public intervention. Conservative cabinets, less worried about equality and wary about taxes, rely, instead, on market mechanisms to raise productivity and promote economic growth.

Partisan responses to the requirements of economic growth can be put in a historical context as well. An increasingly integrated world economy and strong technological shocks have recently changed the demand for (and prices of) parts of the production factors in advanced nations. Unskilled workers have seen their incomes decline. The social wage has now clearly emerged as a barrier to job creation. In short, the employment–equality trade-off has sharpened in all industrialized nations, and the policy solutions that different parties are espousing have become more polarized. As shown in the following two chapters and in the two case studies of the book, the rejection of state-led solutions has only intensified among conservatives in the last two decades. Similarly, left-wing cabinets have embraced even more vigorously their recipes of public investment and intensive human capital formation.

Finally, this chapter has explored the electoral dimension of economic strategies. Although supply-side economic policies are developed to please the core constituencies of the party in power, they are also employed to bind initially heterogeneous interests into broad and winning electoral coalitions. The Left aspires to secure the support of relatively skilled sectors for its program of public investment and universalistic social policies. Conservatives attempt to expand the size of the middle class to win elections. The ability of each political force to organize its most preferred coalition and policy is to a great extent constrained by the actual distribution of skills and assets within the population and by the role of the social wage. A steep income distribution and a large segment of unskilled workers may play to the advantage of socialist parties. Conservative parties probably benefit from sizable middle classes. Moreover, alterations in the structure of incomes, such as those generated by the exogenous shocks of the last two decades, change the conditions under which parties organize broad electoral coalitions. Nevertheless, as shown in the British and Spanish cases, and in the more general discussion of Chapter 9, it is the sets of policies that governments develop, the institutional setting in which parties compete, and the competitive strategies of opposition parties that ultimately determine the success of the party in power.

SUPPLY-SIDE ECONOMIC STRATEGIES FROM A COMPARATIVE PERSPECTIVE (I): PUBLIC INVESTMENT AND THE FORMATION OF HUMAN CAPITAL

As argued in the two first chapters, governments eventually have to choose between two alternative economic strategies to spur economic growth and sustain the competitiveness of domestic firms in the medium run. In one case, governments employ the public sector to raise the level of domestic savings and total investment and boost the productivity of capital and labor. In the other case, they rely on market mechanisms and private agents to maximize the rate of investment and thus foster economic growth. Although equally geared toward improving economic performance, each economic strategy has distinct redistributive effects. Public investment strategies, developed to equalize conditions without forsaking growth, require higher taxes on well-off sectors. Private investment strategies imply a reduction in taxes and in current levels of social protection – particularly when exogenous shocks exacerbate the employment–equality trade-off latent in all advanced democracies. The two strategies accordingly receive the support of different parties and electoral constituencies. Broadly speaking, social democrats and working-class voters rally around active supply-side policies. Conservatives and the middle classes defend privatization policies and tax reductions. We must now turn to the task of empirically testing the model put forward in Chapters 1 and 2.

This chapter is organized as follows. The first section shows how supply-side policy choices have diverged substantially across countries and over time. The data presented dispel a rather widespread belief that there is a unique governmental strategy toward the supply side of the economy. They also contradict the hypothesis that in the last few years countries have converged toward the same set of policy solutions, mainly as a result of increasingly integrated markets. The rest of the chapter (jointly with Chapter 4) tests in a comprehensive manner the political factors that lie behind the choice of specific structural strategies.

AN EMPIRICAL GLANCE AT NATIONAL INVESTMENT STRATEGIES

The character of any supply-side economic strategy derives from the way in which governments manage the following policy instruments:

1. Direct public spending on fixed capital formation
2. Direct public spending on human capital formation (to enhance the skills of the population), either generically (through education) or specifically (through training programs targeted at particular populations)
3. The "indirect" provision of production inputs through public firms (that can be used to increase the quality of infrastructures, fixed business investment, or the workforce)
4. Tax and regulatory schemes to alter (or free up) the saving and investment behavior of private agents

An interventionist economic strategy is based on high levels of direct public investment, a sizable public business sector, and high taxes (especially on upper-income brackets) to pay for these supply-side economic policies. A "laissez-faire," or market-based, economic strategy entails minimizing public spending on investment, selling public firms, and maintaining taxation low and nondistortionary to encourage private investment. Table 3.1 gives a summary of both ideal strategies.

The role played by the public sector in each of these policy instruments has varied widely across OECD countries and over time. Figure 3.1 reproduces data on public fixed capital formation by the general government (i.e., direct public investment in the public budget) as a percentage of total investment for the late 1960s, late 1970s, and late 1980s. Public investment by the general government averaged around one-sixth of all investment in all OECD countries in 1970. Although two decades later it had declined somewhat, it still represented around a seventh of total investment.[1] Cross-national variation has always remained remarkable. The difference between the strongest and the weakest investors has consistently amounted to at least 10 percentage points of total investment (from almost 25 percent in Sweden to 14 percent in the United States in the late 1960s and from close to 19 percent in Spain to less than 9 percent in Belgium and the United Kingdom in the late 1980s).

Figure 3.2 displays the levels of investment by state-owned companies for the same periods (for those countries where the information is available). Com-

Table 3.1. *Overall economic strategies of parties and corresponding policy instruments*

	ECONOMIC STRATEGIES	
	Market-Based	Interventionist
POLICY INSTRUMENTS		
Gross Fixed Capital Formation	Low rate of public investment	High rate of public investment
Human Capital Formation	Relies on private sector	High levels of public spending
Public Business Sector	Small or negligible	Large
Tax Policies	Low tax rates	High tax rates
		Regulatory mechanisms to foster investment

parisons across countries and over time should be done carefully because some data are missing for several countries and national definitions of public firms are not uniform. Gross fixed capital formation by public firms has fluctuated around a seventh of total investment during the last three decades. Cross-national differences in fixed investment by state-owned firms have been even higher than for direct public investment and have tended to grow over time. Capital spending by public companies represented more than a sixth of total investment in Australia and Britain in 1970, close to or over a fifth of total investment in Austria, Portugal, and Norway in 1980, and again in these countries and Greece in the late 1980s. But it was below 6 percent of total investment in Japan, Britain, and the United States in 1988.

In 1970 total public gross fixed capital investment (the sum of capital investment by the general government and the public business sector) averaged almost 30 percent of all investment in OECD countries – or 6.8 percent of GDP. Two decades later it still represented over a fourth of all investment – or 5.9 percent of GDP. Across countries, total public fixed capital formation stretched from over 40 percent of total investment in the United Kingdom to less than 20 percent in the United States in 1970 and from 40 percent in Norway to less than 15 percent in the United Kingdom and the United States in 1990.

A detailed analysis of the figures also shows that change has been pervasive over time in many countries – in different directions. Britain led all OECD countries in terms of public investment in the 1960s only to fall to the last position (jointly with the United States) two decades later. Meanwhile Norway has moved from the OECD average rate of public investment in 1970 to the

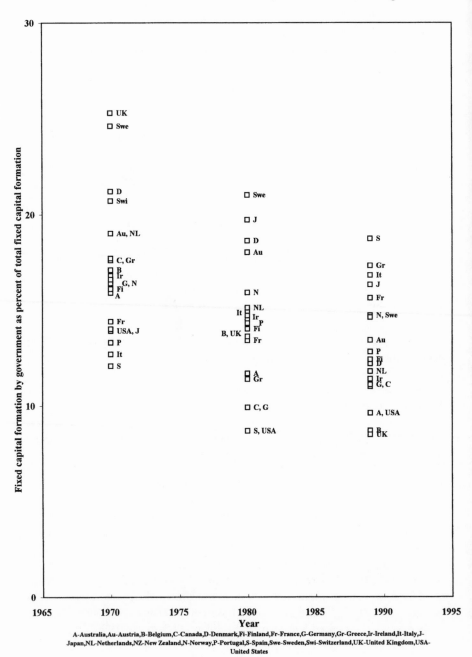

Figure 3.1. Fixed capital formation by the general government in OECD countries, 1970–90

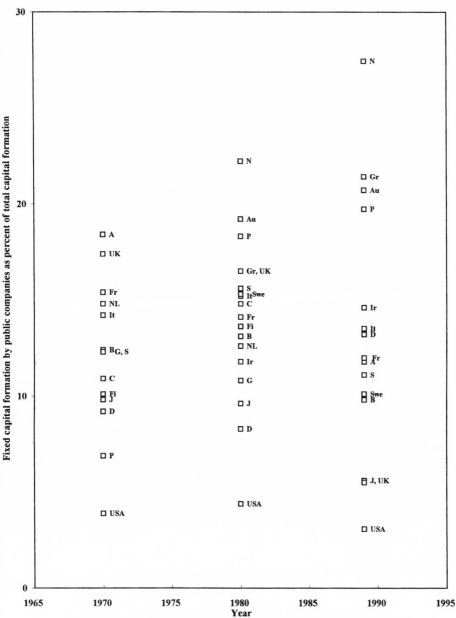

A-Australia,Au-Austria,B-Belgium,C-Canada,D-Denmark,Fi-Finland,Fr-France,G-Germany,Gr-Greece,Ir-Ireland,It-Italy,J-
Japan,NL-Netherlands,NZ-New Zealand,N-Norway,P-Portugal,S-Spain,Swe-Sweden,Swi-Switzerland,UK-United Kingdom,USA-
United States

*Figure 3.2. Fixed capital formation by the public business sector in OECD countries,
1970–90*

leading position in 1990, with a public investment rate that is almost two thirds higher than the OECD average. The Spanish state, whose rate of investment was a fifth lower than the OECD average in 1970, spent around 20 percent more than the OECD mean in 1990.

Similar differences appear in the levels of public effort in human capital formation. Figure 3.3 reproduces the percentage of GDP spent on public education in 1970, 1980, and 1988–89 in all OECD nations. Public spending on education ranged from around 8 percent of GDP in Canada and Sweden to 2 percent of GDP or less in Southern European countries in 1970. Public expenditure on education has slowly converged over time (the standard deviation for OECD countries declined from 1.9 points in 1970 to 1.2 points in 1988–90). Nonetheless, there were still strong cross-national differences in the late 1980s. While Norway, Denmark, and Sweden spent more than 7 percent of their GDP on public education, Germany spent only 4.2 percent and Greece about 2.8 percent.[2]

Figure 3.4 shows the levels of public expenditure on active labor market policies, a second source of human capital formation. Public spending averaged 0.7 percent of GDP in the second half of the 1980s. Yet, more than doubling the OECD mean, the Swedish and Irish governments were allocating 1.8 and 1.5 percent of their GDP respectively to manpower policies. At the other extreme, the Japanese and Swiss public sectors spent less than 0.2 percent of their GDP on such programs.

Finally, Figure 3.5 represents the effective personal income tax rates paid by high income earners in both the the late 1970s and the late 1980s.[3] In the late 1970s, while the effective tax rate was over 72 percent in Sweden and over 60 percent in Denmark, it was only 18 percent in Spain and 17 percent in Switzerland. During the 1980s nominal tax rates were reduced across the board in all countries without exception. From 1980 to 1990, top tax rates fell an average of 14.3 points (from 63 percent to 48.7 percent) in all OECD countries. Nonetheless, the structure of national income tax systems did not necessarily converge toward less progressive schemes in real terms. Progressivity increased through fiscal drag in some cases (e.g., in Spain). In other countries, cuts in top tax rates were accompanied by even deeper cuts in low rates and a substantial reduction in past deductions and tax loopholes. As a result, during the 1980s the average *effective* tax rate declined slightly, from 41 to 39 percent. Cross-national variation remained almost unchanged. It stretched now from over 65 percent in Denmark to 20 percent in Japan and 17 percent in Switzerland. During that decade change within particular countries also proved to be remarkable. In New Zealand, the United Kingdom, and Japan drastic tax reforms reduced the effective tax rate by at least a fifth. But the French, Greek, and Spanish effective tax rates (on upper-income brackets) experienced substantial increases – over 20 percent in relative terms – and moved close to or above the OECD average.

The striking divergence observed in the levels of public fixed capital formation, spending on education and labor market policies, and tax rates confirms

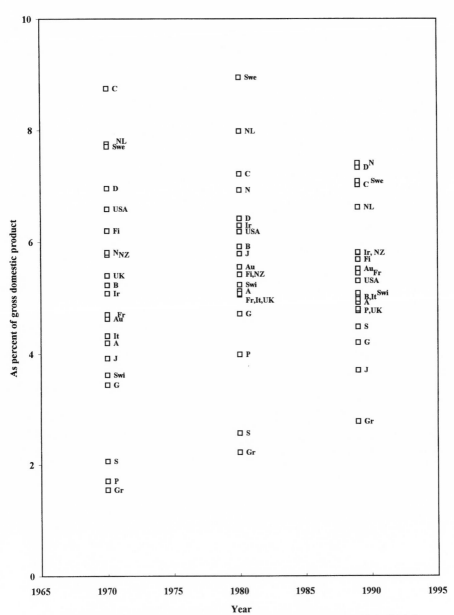

Figure 3.3. *Public expenditure on general education in OECD countries,*
1970–89

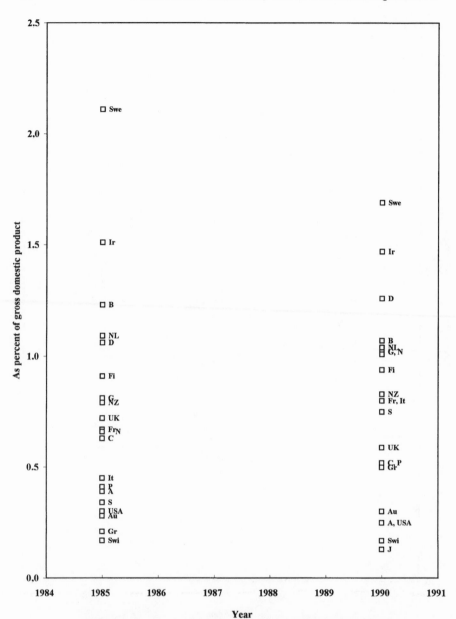

Figure 3.4. Public expenditure on active labor market policies in OECD countries, 1985–90

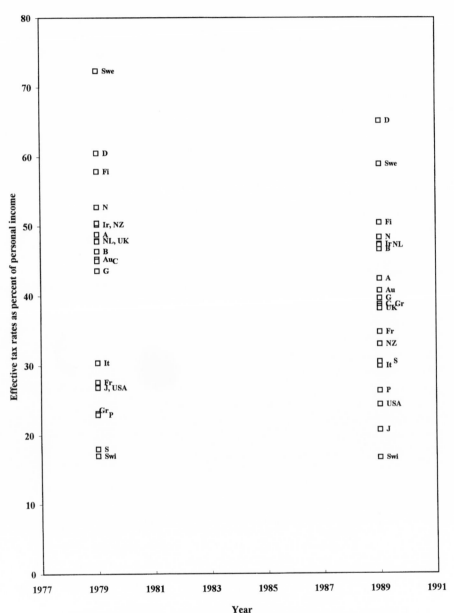

Figure 3.5. Effective tax rates on personal income in OECD countries, 1979–90

the theoretical expectations raised in Chapter 2. There is no unique governmental strategy followed by all nations with regard to the supply side of the economy and the provision of the production inputs. A related conclusion is that neither economic conditions common to all countries at the international level (such as, say, economic shocks) nor potentially dominant economic ideas or instrumental models (e.g., the extended perception among academic elites in the last decade or so that publicly owned businesses are damaging to economic growth) can explain the choice of supply-side economic strategies. What then are the factors that explain why certain countries rely on the public sector while other nations stress the virtues of markets? I turn now to the task of systematically answering this question. In the next section I introduce the analytic methods employed for that purpose. In the following sections I explore in detail the impact of parties (as well as other plausible explanations) on the selection of direct investment policies. The size of the public business sector and the structure of tax rates are examined in Chapter 4.

HYPOTHESES AND METHODOLOGY

As I anticipated in Chapter 1, this book holds partisanship to have a profound impact on how governments formulate their economic strategies. But this claim, I rushed to add, remains a clear matter of contention among researchers for multiple reasons. Consequently, any satisfactory inquiry into the causes underlying the selection of any economic strategy must include an exploration of the potential effects of factors other than the partisan control of the cabinet.[4] In the examination of the choice of each policy instrument, I consider, besides the effect of the partisan composition of the government, the following possibilities:

1. Political and institutional factors:
    a. The domestic structure of the economy, that is, the degree of explicit coordination of labor (and business), alone or in combination with a specific political coalition in office. This explanation, as I emphasized in Chapter 1, has gathered strong support to account for the patterns of economic policymaking in contemporary democracies.[5]
    b. The internal structure of the cabinet in office; that is, the extent to which the cabinet is internally fragmented or heterogeneous, a condition which is alternatively said to moderate policies or diminish the effectiveness of governments.
    c. The degree of political centralization in each country.
2. The potential effects of economic development (in two different ways: levels of per capita income and the weight of the primary sector in the whole economy) to test whether different economic strategies respond to different structural needs (determined by the complexity of the economy).
3. The position of each domestic economy in the international economy, mea-

sured by the country's relative exposure to trade and the level of financial integration, since it may be that more economic openness pushes governments to practice more interventionist policies to raise the productivity of workers faster.[6]

4. Specific short-term economic conditions (budget deficits and the growth rate) as well as long-run growth (to see whether instances of secular decline or expansion have any influence on policy decisions).

To explore adequately the impact of partisanship, and of all the other variables, on the nature of the economic strategy, I rely on the simultaneous comparison of all OECD countries with more than one million inhabitants, mostly for the period from 1960 to 1990, always subject to the constraints imposed by the availability of data.[7]

To manage the vast array of data collected and to determine which explanation makes most sense, I have relied on the technique of regression analysis. To reduce, however, the intrusiveness of complex statistical techniques, I present the results in their simplest form. Moreover, in most cases I use simulated results to shed light on the results obtained through regression analysis. The simulations consist in using the coefficients in the regressions to calculate the extent to which economic policies vary when the partisan composition of governments changes while all other circumstances (such as, say, the level of economic development) are held constant.

THE PUBLIC PROVISION OF FIXED CAPITAL

THE EFFECT OF PARTISANSHIP, DOMESTIC INSTITUTIONS, AND ECONOMIC INTERDEPENDENCE

In regard to (direct) public investment, or, more technically, public spending on gross fixed capital formation, we probably have the most standardized and systematic data among all the quantitative evidence available to examine supply-side policy instruments. Almost all of the national accounts of OECD countries have reported the volume of public fixed capital formation since at least the early or mid-1960s.[8] This broad panel of data allows me to test all of the competing hypotheses mentioned above in a rigorous way. It is also well suited for exploring the short-term dynamics of supply-side economic strategies and, in particular, as we will see shortly, the latter's relationship to policies geared strictly toward managing the business cycle.[9] Results are shown in Table 3.2.

It is clear from Table 3.2 that lagged investment explains the bulk of the variation. Policies only change incrementally. The results confirm, however, our theoretical expectations. Full control of the cabinet by the socialist party during one year adds 0.2 percentage points of GDP to public investment – a rather sizable effect.[10] Notice that a whole decade under a socialist government raises

TABLE 3.2. *Political determinants of fixed capital formation strategies: a cross-national time-series analysis of public investment as a percentage of gross domestic product, 1963-90* [a]

INDEPENDENT VARIABLES	GROSS FIXED CAPITAL FORMATION AS PERCENT OF GDP
Constant	0.500*
	(0.114)
$(PI/GDP)_{t-1}$	1.115*
	(0.046)
$(PI/GDP)_{t-2}$	-0.217*
	(0.045)
Socialist control of government [b]	0.200**
	(0.104)
Organizational power of labor [b]	0.119
	(0.101)
Socialist control of government x Organizational power of labor	-0.228**
	(0.137)
Growth rate in previous year	0.018*
	(0.008)
Socialist control of government x Growth rate in previous year	-0.009
	(0.016)
Balance of budget in previous year	0.009
	(0.006)
Socialist control of government x Balance of budget in previous year	0.031*
	(0.013)
Trade openness	-0.0011
	(0.0009)
Financial integration	-0.00000
	(0.00015)
Real GDP per capita (every $1,000)	-0.0233*
	(0.0063)
R^2	0.916
Adjusted R^2	0.911
Number of observations	466

[a] All OECD countries with over 1 million inhabitants except New Zealand and Switzerland, for which no data on general government fixed capital formation are available, and Turkey, Greece, and Portugal, for which there are no data in the "organizational power of labor" index (based on Cameron 1984) used here.

[b] Index goes from 0 to 1.

Standard error within parentheses.
* Statistically significant at .05 or less.
** Statistically significant at .10 or less.

public investment by 2 percentage points of GDP – or approximately two-thirds above the OECD average in public capital spending and close to two standard deviations of the sample.

Figure 3.6 conveys even more clearly the key role of partisanship. Based on the coefficients of the regression in Table 3.2, the evolution of public investment (as a percentage of GDP) is simulated from 1965 to 1990 under two alternative scenarios: a socialist government and a conservative administration throughout the period, both with a starting per capita income in 1960 of $4,000 (in 1985 prices) (the OECD average at that time), the OECD annual average growth, the OECD annual average budget balance, and an initial public investment rate of 3.5 percent in 1960.[11] Both cases show public investment declining over time, a trend consistent with the pattern observed in Figure 3.1. Public investment peaks under the two cabinets in the early 1970s. It then falls precipitously through the mid-1980s. Higher economic development over time does not account for the bulk of this decay in investment. Growing at the OECD average annual rate, a country with a per capita income of $4,000 in 1960 would reach a per capita income of $11,000 in 1990. This implies a fall of 0.16 percentage points in the rate of public investment – around 10 percent of the average decline that actually took place from 1965 to 1990. As shown shortly, the downward slopes of Figure 3.6 are related to a generalized reduction in the rate of annual growth and particularly to an increase in budget deficits after the first oil shock. Within a pattern of decline, public investment rates keep differing widely depending on the party in power. In 1965 a socialist government spent 4.9 percent of GDP on public investment, 0.6 percentage points more than a conservative cabinet or a sixth more in relative terms. This divergence sharpened over time. In 1990 an average socialist cabinet spent slightly below 4 percent of GDP on public investment. But a conservative government spent only 3 percent of GDP. As a result the average "social democratic" rate of public investment was 20 percent higher than the "conservative" rate. In short, partisanship turns out to matter more, rather than less, over time – at least in relative terms.

Parties determine the level of public investment regardless of the dominant domestic institutional structure. The organizational power of labor is not statistically significant in Table 3.2. The interaction of a socialist government and heavily organized unions has, in fact, a negative effect on public investment.

To explore the actual effect of partisanship and levels of labor organization, in Table 3.3 I simulate the annual increase in public investment as a percentage of GDP for different values of partisanship and labor strength. In strongly corporatist countries, public investment increases, other things being equal, at an annual rate of 0.1 percentage points of GDP, regardless of the party in office.[12] In countries that are only mildly corporatist, and particularly in countries where labor is completely unorganized, the rate of public investment strongly covaries with the party in office – surging when socialists are in office. Notice, finally, that the increase in the rate of public investment under a socialist government

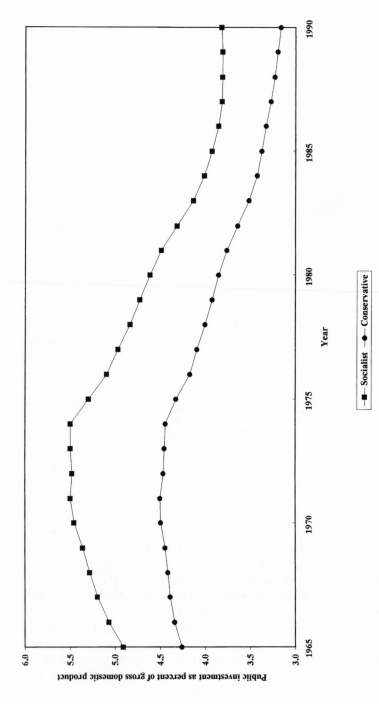

Figure 3.6. Partisan governments and public investment, 1965–90: a simulation

Table 3.3. *The interactive effects of partisanship and the organization of labor on the rates of public capital formation*

		ANNUAL INCREASE IN PUBLIC GROSS FIXED CAPITAL FORMATION AS PER CENT OF GDP		
		Degree of organizational power of labor		
		None	Medium	Complete
	100	+0.200	+0.146	+0.091
Proportion of cabinet posts held by socialist parties	50	+0.100	+0.103	+0.105
	0	+0.000	+0.059	+0.119

Results are derived from results in Table 3.2. Budget balance and annual growth rate have been set at 0.

Extent of organizational power of labor: None (0 in score of labor organization), Medium (0.5 in index of labor organization), High (1.0 in index of labor organization).

is twice as high in noncorporatist than in corporatist countries. This actually suggests that, deprived of a corporatist arrangement to sustain expansionary policies and reduce unemployment, socialist parties are more likely to launch aggressive public investment programs.

Finally, notice that economic interdependence has no clear-cut impact on the rate of public investment. Both trade openness and capital mobility present negative coefficients in Table 3.2, but they are negligible and not statistically significant. The interactive terms of these variables and partisanship also present results that are not significant from a statistical point of view (this is not reported in Table 3.2).

ARE PUBLIC CAPITAL FORMATION STRATEGIES A FORM OF DEMAND MANAGEMENT?

Increasing public investment has been traditionally considered a straightforward manner of boosting the economy and reducing unemployment. In the 1930s, long before Keynesian ideas percolated into the policymaking sphere, governments of all political orientations resorted to financing more public works to reduce joblessness. So far the evidence shows that social democratic cabinets (which are in principle more prone to expand the economy than conservative governments) spend more on investment programs. Does this mean that intensive public spending on capital formation is merely part of countercyclical demand-management policies, or does it mean that it is a response to a long-term commitment to transform the supply conditions of the economy?

Table 3.2 shows that all governments behave in a procyclical manner. The rate of public investment moves with economic performance. For each point of output growth, all governments increase public investment by 0.018 percentage points of GDP the following year. Conversely, they cut public investment when the economy contracts. The interactive term Socialist Control of Government × Growth Rate in Previous Year (−0.009) suggests that socialist governments follow slightly less procyclical policies than conservative cabinets: that is, the evolution of the economy has a lower impact on their rate of public investment than it has on the decisions of a nonsocialist cabinet. Still, since the coefficient of the interactive term is not statistically significant, any conclusions about different left-wing and right-wing responses to the evolution of the business cycle must remain tentative.

More strikingly, partisan responses diverge widely depending on the stance of the public budget. Although the coefficient of the parameter Balance of Budget in Previous Year is not statistically significant, it indicates that, regardless of the ideological sign of the government, a budget surplus (deficit) boosts (shrinks) the level of public investment: each point of the budget balance changes public investment by 0.009 points of GDP. The degree of budget imbalance has, however, a particularly powerful effect on the policy decisions of a socialist cabinet. Socialist governments develop public investment policies contingent on the latter's sustainability. The interactive term Socialist Control of Government × Balance of Budget in Previous Year, which is statistically significant, shows that a socialist cabinet increases public investment by 0.031 percentage points of GDP more than a conservative government for each percentage point of budget surplus. Conversely, a budget deficit depresses the public investment rate under a socialist government rather rapidly. As anticipated in the theoretical discussion, left-wing governments care strongly about balanced budgets: since balanced budgets are a way to build up public savings (and thus boost the overall rate of domestic savings and investment), they take priority over increasing the public investment rate in the agenda of socialist policymakers.

Figures 3.7 and 3.8 show the key role that fiscal deficits and, in a more limited way, declining growth rates have played in the evolution of public investment rates across OECD countries over the last three decades. Figure 3.7 simulates the evolution of public investment from 1965 to 1990 under both a socialist and a conservative government in two different circumstances: in the first one, I use the OECD average annual budget balance, which was slightly in surplus until 1973 and then experienced an average deficit of 2.8 percent of GDP; in the second one, I calculate what would have happened if the budget balance had been kept at the average surplus of the prestagflation crisis (0.3 percent of GDP) *after* 1973.[13] Figure 3.7 shows vividly that most of the fall in public investment taking place across all OECD countries (apparent in Figure 3.1) has derived from a worsening budget balance. In the 1960s, when most governments enjoyed budget surpluses, investment rates were high. Once public budgets began to deteriorate, mostly as a result of sluggish growth, all governments cur-

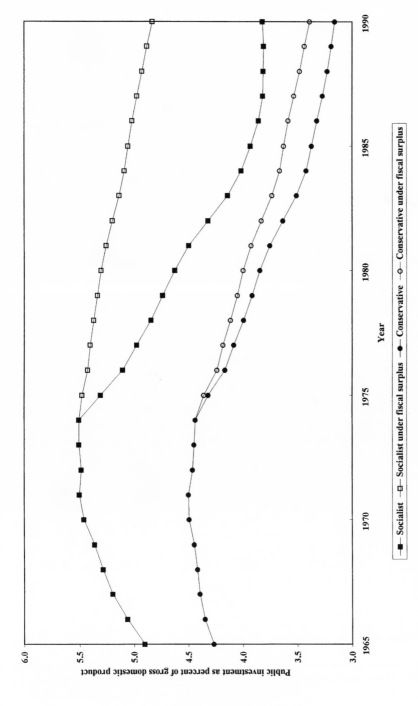

Figure 3.7. Partisan governments, the budget balance, and public investment, 1965–90: a simulation

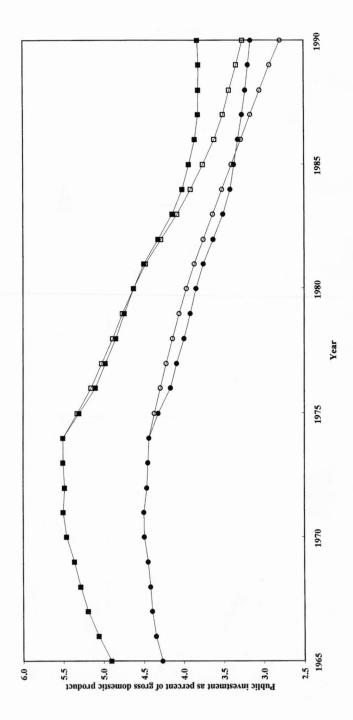

*Figure 3.8. Partisan governments, growth rates, and public investment,
1965–90: a simulation*

Legend: ■— Socialist — □— Socialist and high growth after 1973 — ◆— Conservative — ○— Conservative and high growth after 1973

X-axis: Year (1965, 1970, 1975, 1980, 1985, 1990)

Y-axis: Public investment as percent of gross domestic product (2.5, 3.0, 3.5, 4.0, 4.5, 5.0, 5.5, 6.0) tailed capital spending. All governments preferred fiscal discipline to high investment rates. Social democratic cabinets continued to invest at comparatively high rates but were held back from investing more by public deficits: had they been able to run a surplus through 1990 they would have spent two-thirds more on public investment than conservative governments.

Figure 3.8 simulates the effect of growth on public investment from 1965 to 1990 under both a socialist and a conservative government, again under two different circumstances: first, with the OECD average annual growth rate, which was over 5 percent of GDP until 1973 and averaged 2.6 percent afterward; then, with an average growth rate at the level of the pre-1973 crisis (5.2 percent of GDP) all the time.[14] The fall in growth rates does not explain the fall in investment. With higher growth rates, public investment would have been slightly higher in the 1970s. But, in the long run, a consistently higher growth rate would have boosted the level of economic development, causing public investment to decline.[15]

Two main conclusions can be derived from this inquiry on the political determinants of public investment. First, partisanship plays a key role in explaining the size of public capital formation, independently of the presence of corporatist arrangements. It is true that before the stagflation period, and corresponding to the hegemony of socialist parties mainly in Scandinavian countries, a regime of public investment appeared under corporatist arrangements. But, after the 1970s, all socialist parties that came into office in Southern Europe developed strong investment policies, without any pressure from unions, which were much weaker and less organized than their Scandinavian counterparts. In short, partisanship alone rather than any sort of corporatist arrangement explains the existing variation in supply-side strategies. As a matter of fact, socialist parties governing in decentralized countries seem more likely to rely on public investment than social democratic cabinets in corporatist nations.[16]

Second, the decision to engage the state in the provision of fixed investment is mostly based on supply-side policy considerations. Public investment is always conditional on balanced budgets and reasonable growth rates. More public investment is undertaken by social democratic governments only after the finances of the state have been balanced (either through higher taxes or as a consequence of an upturn in the business cycle). Large public deficits, incurred to achieve a temporary boost in consumption, are abhorred by social democratic governments because they threaten to erode public savings and therefore the overall rate of domestic savings. This, in turn, affects the investment rate in a way that upsets the core of a social democratic supply-side economic strategy. A leftist strategy based on "spending one's way out of the crisis" may occasionally happen (as indeed took place in several countries in the late 1970s; see Hall 1986; Scharpf 1987) but is exceptional. Long-term economic growth, allocated in a redistributive manner, takes precedence over short-term, demand-management policies.

HUMAN CAPITAL FORMATION (I): PUBLIC EXPENDITURE ON EDUCATION

In the theoretical discussion presented in Chapter 2, increasing the skills of the labor force was presented as the most distinctive supply-side measure social democratic parties implement to overcome the dilemmas that technological change and international competitiveness impose on them. Human capital formation takes two forms. It may entail spending on general education to increase the generic skills of the whole population. It may also involve specific programs to retrain given segments of the population such as the unemployed. I examine public expenditure on education in this section. The following section considers the second, more targeted form of human capital investment – that is, active labor market policies.

The lack of a complete and consistent data series on public expenditure on education and on population makes it impossible to reproduce the panel data analysis presented above for public gross fixed capital formation. Instead, I engage in a cross-national analysis of the volume (and evolution) of current public expenditure on education as a proportion of GDP in 1970, 1979–80, and 1988–89.[17]

A great deal of public spending on education is driven by "demand" factors – mainly the demographic structure of the country. A country with strong population growth will tend to spend more on education than another nation with a more mature demographic profile, all other things being equal. To capture the role of demographic factors in public spending on education, I develop an index, the "public effort of education," which results from dividing the proportion of GDP spent on current public education by the percentage of the population that is twenty years old or younger. Thus, for example, in 1980, Ireland and Italy spent 6.3 percent and 5.1 percent of their GDP on education respectively. Yet, given that the Irish population under twenty years of age was 40.7 percent of the whole population and the Italian proportion was 31.2 percent, the actual spending effort per school-age person in both countries was identical. In both cases the "public effort of education" turned out to be 0.15 points.

Table 3.4, part A, reproduces the extent to which socialist control of government as well as the organization of the labor movement explains the level of the public effort in education in 1970.[18] For the following decades, I examine the impact of partisanship (and other political and institutional variables) on the change in the public effort in education. These results are reported in Table 3.4, parts B and C.

Partisan control performs well as an explanatory variable in the 1960s. More than 40 percent of the variation in the public effort in education in 1970 is explained by the partisan nature of the government.[19] The impact of partisanship remains stable (and its coefficient statistically significant) when I introduce a measure of the proportion of the population actively employed in agriculture in

1965 (Table 3.4A, Model 1). This variable, which controls for the level of economic development, seems particularly appropriate here to control for the level of demand for education since the population engaged in agricultural tasks seems less prone to participate in the educational system.[20] Full control of the cabinet by a socialist party implies 0.123 percentage points more of GDP spent on education (for each percentage point of population under twenty-one years) than under a conservative government. This, in turn, means that for a country where 30 percent of the population is younger than twenty-one, the difference between a socialist and a nonsocialist cabinet amounts to 3.7 percentage points of GDP. Given the strong correlation between social democracy and corporatism in the 1960s, it is natural that both the existence of encompassing, well organized unions (Table 3.4A, Model 2) and the interaction between social democratic governments and union power (Table 3.4A, Model 3) are strong predictors of the level of public effort in education in 1970.

Neither partisanship nor the organizational power of labor plays any explanatory role in the evolution of the level of public expenditure on education in the 1970s (Table 3.4B). Their coefficients are positive and show a relatively sizable effect (implying that both variables increase public spending on education by almost 20 percent in both cases) but they are not statistically significant.

Partisanship is, however, a key variable for understanding the change in the public effort in education after the stagflation period. As reported in Table 3.4C, socialist control of government is a significant variable from a statistical point of view. Once we control for the effect of the initial level of public effort in education at the beginning of the decade and the proportion of the population employed in the primary sector, the statistical analysis shows that a socialist government expands the level of public effort in education by 46.8 percent in less than ten years (Model 1). Assuming, for example, that the level of public effort in education was 0.20 points in 1980, ten years of socialist government would put it at 0.25 points, all other things being equal. With 30 percent of the population younger than twenty-one, this would mean an increase from 6 to 7.5 percent of GDP in public spending on education. The organizational power of labor has, by contrast, no impact on the evolution of public money spent on education, alone or in interaction with government partisanship (Models 2 and 3).[21]

To clarify the size of the effect of partisanship on the levels of public education, I report in Table 3.5 a set of simulations based on the statistical results presented for Model 1 in Table 3.4A–C. In the simulation table, I calculate what would have been the level of public spending on education as a percentage of GDP in 1970, 1980, and 1989–90 if during the entire decade previous to each date (1960–69, 1970–79, and 1980–89 respectively) either a socialist or a conservative party had been in power. To calculate the percentage of GDP spent on education (since the regressions are done on the index of public effort in education), I assume that the proportion of the population younger than twenty-one is the OECD average: 33.8 percent in 1970, 31.4 percent in 1980, and 26.9 percent in 1989. Similarly, I assume that the proportion employed in the primary

Table 3.4. *Political determinants of public spending on education*

A. *Political determinants of public spending on education in 1970*

	PUBLIC EXPENDITURE ON EDUCATION (AS PERCENT OF GDP) / PERCENTAGE OF POPULATION UNDER 21 IN 1970		
INDEPENDENT VARIABLES	MODEL 1	MODEL 2 [a]	MODEL 3 [a]
Constant	0.155* (0.022)	0.143* (0.025)	0.157* (0.021)
Socialist control of government 1960-69 [b]	0.123* (0.036)		
Organizational power of labor [b]		0.091* (0.034)	
Socialist control of government 1960-69 x Organizational power of labor			0.130* (0.036)
Percent of active population employed in agriculture in 1965	-0.0015** (0.0008)	-0.0008 (0.0010)	-0.0008 (0.0009)
R^2	0.505	0.339	0.458
Corrected R^2	0.450	0.251	0.385
Number of observations	21	18	18

B. *Political determinants of public spending on education in the 1970s*

	RELATIVE CHANGE IN PUBLIC EXPENDITURE ON EDUCATION (AS PERCENT OF GDP / PERCENTAGE OF POPULATION UNDER 21), 1970 TO 1979-80		
INDEPENDENT VARIABLES	MODEL 1	MODEL 2 [a]	MODEL 3 [a]
Constant	48.842** (27.248)	68.648* (19.994)	69.647* (20.091)
Socialist control of government 1970-79 [b]	17.850 (17.963)		
Organizational power of labor [b]		17.054 (14.979)	
Socialist control of government 1970-79 x Organizational power of labor			19.011 (16.160)
Public effort in education in 1970	-202.145** (128.807)	-280.496* (103.535)	-268.881* (97.682)
Percent of active population employed in agriculture in 1978	0.797 (0.916)	-0.970 (0.836)	-1.017 (0.837)
R^2	0.418	0.348	0.352
Corrected R^2	0.316	0.208	0.213
Number of observations	21	18	18

Table 3.4. *Political determinants of public spending on education (continuation)*

C. *Political determinants of public spending on education in the 1980s*

INDEPENDENT VARIABLES	MODEL 1	MODEL 2 [a]	MODEL 3 [a]
	RELATIVE CHANGE IN PUBLIC EXPENDITURE ON EDUCATION (AS PERCENT OF GDP / PERCENTAGE OF POPULATION UNDER 21), 1979-80 TO 1988-90		
Constant	71.599* (30.370)	40.010 (42.654)	52.059 (48.143)
Socialist control of government 1980-89 [b]	46.834* (21.082)		
Organizational power of labor [b]		7.581 (23.481)	
Socialist control of government 1980-90 x Organizational power of labor			22.560 (36.710)
Public effort in education in 1980	-351.215* (126.904)	-260.664** (179.975)	-306.965 (194.630)
Percent of active population employed in agriculture in 1988	-0.623 (1.336)	3.431 (2.602)	2.854 (2.803)
R^2	0.533	0.442	0.453
Corrected R^2	0.451	0.323	0.336
Number of observations	21	18	18

[a] There are no data for Greece, New Zealand, and Portugal in the "organizational power of labor" index (based on Cameron 1984) used here.

[b] Index goes from 0 to 1.

Estimation: OLS

Standard errors in parentheses.
* Statistically significant at .05 or less.
** Statistically significant at .10 or less.

sector is the OECD average: 17.7 percent in 1965, 10.7 percent in 1978, and 7.9 percent in 1988.

In 1970, two countries with a similar proportion of school-age members of the population (33.8 percent, the OECD average in 1970) and the same percentage of persons employed in the primary sector (17.7 percent, again the OECD average in 1965), but governed by distinct partisan coalitions would differ strikingly in terms of the level of public spending on education. After a social democratic cabinet from 1960 to 1969, the state would be spending 8.5 percent of its GDP, slightly above the Swedish case in 1970. Following a nonsocialist administration during the same period, the state would be spending 4.3 percent of GDP on education, approximately the German case in that year.[22]

Table 3.5. *Partisanship and public current expenditure on general education (as percent of GDP) in 1970, 1980, and 1989-90: a simulation*

GOVERNMENT 1960-69	PUBLIC SPENDING ON EDUCATION IN 1970	GOVERNMENT 1970-79	PUBLIC SPENDING ON EDUCATION IN 1980	GOVERNMENT 1980-89	PUBLIC SPENDING ON EDUCATION IN 1989-90
Socialist	8.5	Socialist	9.8	Socialist	8.7
				Conservative	4.8
		Conservative	8.4	Socialist	8.6
				Conservative	5.2
Conservative	4.3	Socialist	6.0	Socialist	7.5
				Conservative	5.1
		Conservative	5.3	Socialist	7.0
				Conservative	4.9
OECD average	5.0		5.6		5.4

Results are derived from the following regressions: Table 3.4A, Model 1; Table 3.4B, Model 1; Table 3.4C, Model 1.

In each simulation I hold constant the proportion of population under 21 years using the OECD average (33.8 percent in 1970, 31.4 percent in 1980, and 26.9 percent in 1989) and the proportion of persons employed in the primary sector using as well the OECD average (17.7 percent in 1965, 10.7 percent in 1978, and 7.9 percent in 1988).

The next two columns simulate the effect of partisanship during the 1970s taking as the initial point of departure the two hypothetical education-spending figures of 1970. As a result, the table shows four possible outcomes for 1980: a continuous socialist government from 1960 to 1979, a socialist government in the 1960s followed by a conservative government in the 1970s, a conservative cabinet followed by a socialist cabinet, and a permanent conservative administration from 1960 to 1979. The results should be interpreted cautiously given that the coefficient of partisanship (for the 1970s) is not significant from a statistical point of view. Nevertheless, two things are noticeable. First, in spite of a slight fall in the size of both the younger cohorts and the primary sector, there is a general upward drift in public spending, particularly if such spending was low in 1970. Even conservative governments inheriting modest levels of spending boosted education expenditure sizably. Second, the increase in the level of public spending on education continued to be higher under socialist administrations.

To calculate the level of public spending for 1989–90, I repeat the procedure carried out for 1979. I consider how the four initial levels in 1980 evolve under different governments. As a result, I present eight distinct combinations for 1989–90. The results have to be interpreted against the background of a significant decline in young age cohorts, which has been driving down public expenditure on education in all countries. Still, socialist governments beginning with high levels of expenditure refrained from cutting it further; the simulation shows that, other things being equal, they ended up spending over 8 percent of GDP on education in 1989–90. In countries with low public education spending in 1980, socialist governments raised public expenditure on education to 7 percent of GDP or more by 1989. In contrast with the 1970s, during the 1980s nonsocialist governments not only held down public spending as a whole but showed impressive willingness and capacity to reduce education expenditure. In the simulation, expenditure falls to around 5 percent of GDP. As a result, one can notice a slight trend toward more divergent outcomes among partisan governments of different ideological traditions.

HUMAN CAPITAL FORMATION (II): ACTIVE MANPOWER POLICIES

Moving beyond traditional income maintenance programs for jobless people, industrialized countries have progressively introduced active manpower policies to directly retrain the unemployed or to subsidize apprenticeship and other vocational schemes. Systematic measures on manpower policies have been gathered only recently. The OECD provides an almost complete battery of data since 1985, including strict labor market training measures, subsidized employment, and measures for the disabled.

I have regressed the battery of independent variables on two sets of data:

first, on public expenditure on manpower policies as a proportion of GDP in the mid-1980s;[23] second, on the relative change in public expenditure on manpower policies from 1985 to 1990. The results are shown in Table 3.6A–B.

Table 3.6 confirms the same explanatory model found for public investment and public expenditure on education in the 1960s and 1970s. The participation of socialist parties in government during those decades is positively related to the strength of manpower policies in 1985 (Model 1), and controlling again for the proportion of the workforce employed in the primary sector, it explains 22 percent of the dependent variable's variance. The organizational power of labor performs just slightly better (Model 2). Again, we should remember that both variables are strongly correlated for that period (Model 3), underscoring how common social democratic corporatist regimes were through the early 1980s.[24]

If we look, however, at the relative change in public expenditure on manpower policies from 1985 to 1990, it is again partisanship that performs as a key variable (Table 3.6B). Alone, it explains 22 percent of the variance.[25] The parameter of socialist control of government continues to perform well within the more complex models reported in Models 1 and 2. In both of them partisanship is controlled for the initial level of expenditure on manpower policies, the level of unemployment in 1985, and the proportion of workers employed in the primary sector in 1988. The coefficient is rather stable – the socialist control of government in the mid- and late 1980s increased by 10–14 percent the level of public expenditure on manpower policies – and is statistically significant in all cases. The level of public expenditure on manpower policies in 1985 has a negative effect on the size these policies have in the public budget in 1990. For each 1 percent of GDP spent in 1985, public spending is around 5–7 percent lower in 1990. On the contrary, the number of unemployed tends to increase the volume of manpower expenditure – around 0.5–0.7 percent for each percentage point of unemployed – so that, for unemployment at 10 percent in 1985, we should expect labor market policies to be 5 percent higher in real terms in 1990 (see Table 3.6, Models 1 and 2).

To further clarify the role of partisanship, I engage once again in a simulation of the evolution of manpower policies similar to the one done in Table 3.5 for public spending on education. The simulation, carried out using the regressions reported for Model 1 in Table 3.6, is reported in Table 3.7. In both simulations I hold the proportion of the population employed in the primary sector constant at the OECD average (10.7 percent in 1978 and 7.9 percent in 1988) and the level of unemployment at the OECD average (8 percent in 1985).

The simulated result shows that, other things being equal, in the early and mid-1980s public expenditure on manpower policies was almost three times larger after the continuing dominance of a social democratic party (1.3 percent of GDP) than after a conservative government (0.5 percent of GDP). In the second half of the 1980s conservative parties on average contributed to a reduction of expenditure by 0.1 percentage points of GDP, from 1.3 to 1.2 percent of GDP. Social democratic parties instead raised it to 1.4 percent of GDP. In other words, both in 1985 and in 1990, social democratic governments were spending twice the OECD average on active labor market measures.

CONCLUSIONS

The role that the state and private agents play in the supply of physical capital and human capital has varied widely in advanced democracies in the last thirty years. Total public fixed capital formation has consistently ranged from two-fifths of total capital formation (in the United Kingdom in the 1960s and Norway in the 1980s) to about one-seventh of total investment (in the United Kingdom and the United States in the 1980s). Public spending on human capital has ranged from almost 10 percent of GDP (in a country like Sweden) to around a third of that figure in several Southern European countries. Tax rates as well have varied substantially: effective tax rates on high income brackets have always been three to four times higher in the most progressive tax systems than in the least progressive systems. In general, there has been little convergence with respect to supply-side economic policies. Countries have moved apart in terms of public spending on fixed capital, especially in the public business sector, over time. They have only become closer in education expenditure, but this relative convergence has mainly derived from demographic trends.

The level of public investment has been strongly determined by the political or partisan coalition in power, mostly unconstrained by domestic institutional variables or international factors. Left-wing governments have boosted fixed and human capital. Nonsocialist cabinets have consistently sought to minimize the extent of state intervention on the supply side of the economy.

Until the late 1970s, public investment strategies were developed by socialist cabinets within corporatist regimes. Leftist governments, which happened to rule in open and coordinated economies in most cases, launched aggressive public investment schemes and engaged in strong education and manpower policies to both sustain the economic competitiveness of their countries' industrial base and ameliorate social conditions. The commitment of substantial public resources to revamp the supply conditions of the economy was employed to induce the wage restraint from the labor movement needed to sustain expansionary full employment policies on the demand side. Social democratic corporatist regimes thus embodied the joint solution of free trade and domestic compensation that has been described, among others, by Katzenstein (1985).

Public investment, however, is not an exclusive strategy of corporatist nations. In the 1980s, leftist governments, now common in Southern European medium-sized economies, pressed ahead with substantial fixed investment plans and expanded public education and vocational training schemes. Active supply-side policies were developed, however, disconnected from any corporatist practices. Union movements were not coordinated enough in Southern Europe to support noninflationary expansionary policies and to engage in permanent pacts

Table 3.6. *Political determinants of active labor market policies*

A. *Political Determinants of Active Labor Market Policies in 1985*

INDEPENDENT VARIABLES	PUBLIC SPENDING ON MANPOWER POLICIES (AS PERCENT OF GDP) IN 1985		
	MODEL 1	MODEL 2[a]	MODEL 3[a]
Constant	0.550* (0.235)	0.370 (0.283)	0.529* (0.257)
Socialist control of government 1960-79 [b]	0.795* (0.390)		
Organizational power of labor [b]		0.800* (0.345)	
Socialist control of government 1960-79 x Organizational power of labor			0.958* (0.456)
Per cent of active population employed in agriculture in 1978	-0.004 (0.014)	0.007 (0.021)	0.005 (0.022)
R^2	0.228	0.265	0.229
Corrected R^2	0.142	0.167	0.126
Number of observations	21	18	18

B. *Political Determinants of Active Labor Market Policies in 1985-90*

RELATIVE CHANGE IN EXPENDITURE IN MANPOWER POLICIES, 1985-90

INDEPENDENT VARIABLES	MODEL 1	MODEL 2	MODEL 3 [a]
Constant	-1.591 (3.911)	-5.246 (4.281)	-9.107 (5.888)
Socialist control of government 1985-90 [b]	13.911* (4.485)	10.033* (4.820)	
Organizational power of labor [b]			3.628 (7.905)
Level of expenditure in manpower policies in 1985	-7.446* (3.253)	-4.763 (3.461)	-3.141 (4.903)
Level of unemployment in 1985	0.688* (0.314)	0.541** (0.310)	0.351 (0.492)
Per cent of active population employed in agriculture in 1988		0.521** (0.305)	1.485* (0.705)
R^2	0.486	0.565	0.442
Corrected R^2	0.395	0.457	0.270
Number of observations	21	21	18

[a] There are no data for Greece, New Zealand, and Portugal in the "organizational power of labor" index (based on Cameron 1984) used here.

[b] Index goes from 0 to 1.

Estimation: OLS
Standard errors in parentheses.
* Statistically significant at .05 or less.
** Statistically significant at .10 or less.

79

Table 3.7. *Partisanship and public expenditure on active labor market policies (as percent of GDP) in 1985 and 1990: a simulation*

GOVERNMENT IN 1960-79	PUBLIC SPENDING ON LABOR MARKET POLICIES IN 1985	GOVERNMENT IN 1985-90	PUBLIC SPENDING ON LABOR MARKET POLICIES IN 1990
Socialist	1.3	Socialist	1.4
		Conservative	1.2
Conservative	0.5	Socialist	0.6
		Conservative	0.5
OECD average	0.7		0.7

Results are derived from the following regressions: table 3.6A, Model 1; table 3.6B, Model 1.

In each simulation I hold constant the proportion of population employed in the primary sector using the OECD average (10.7 percent in 1978 and 7.9 percent in 1988). To estimate public spending in 1990 I hold constant the level of unemployment at the OECD average (8.0 percent of active population in 1985).

with socialist cabinets. As confirmed by the Spanish case examined later in the book, socialist cabinets in this region, unable to rely on labor movement cooperation and constrained by highly integrated financial and goods markets, embraced relatively tight macroeconomic policies. Deprived of the traditional strategy of social concertation, public spending on capital formation became the only means to reduce unemployment while minimizing inequality. As the analysis of public fixed capital formation done in this chapter suggests, left-wing cabinets actually raise public investment spending substantially more in decentralized economies than in corporatist regimes.

In a way somewhat parallel to the increasing resort by social democrats to public investment – in response to the gradual collapse of corporatist institutions and the sharpening of the employment–equality trade-off – the historical commitment of conservative governments to market solutions has only risen over time. Less generous policies toward public fixed capital formation (whose effects can be appreciated in the simulation of Figure 3.6) and toward public education and vocational training (which according to Tables 3.5 and 3.7 have experienced a real decline under conservative governments in the 1980s) make apparent an ongoing turn toward even more antistatist solutions within the conservative camp. To collect more evidence on this historical shift, we should now examine the evolution of the public business sector and the tax system.

4

SUPPLY-SIDE ECONOMIC STRATEGIES FROM A COMPARATIVE PERSPECTIVE (II): THE PUBLIC BUSINESS SECTOR AND TAX STRATEGIES

A part from providing physical and human capital directly through the public budget, whose political determinants have been explored in Chapter 3, the government may equally choose to shape the supply conditions of the economy by "indirect" means. The state may affect the provision of supply factors through the creation of a public business sector.[1] Also, it may affect the levels of both domestic savings and private investment through tax and regulatory measures.

This chapter starts by examining the political factors that motivated the distinct strategies that OECD nations have been pursuing toward the public business sector since the late 1980s. Besides confirming again the key role partisan forces have played, this first section highlights how increasingly strained economic conditions (since the mid-1970s) broke down an already tepid consensus around postwar industrial policies and generated substantially divergent policy responses across the political space. The second section then explores the evolution of tax policies. In light of the empirical results obtained in both this chapter and Chapter 3, the third section offers a first appraisal of the political dimensions of economic policymaking in advanced nations.

STRATEGIES TOWARD THE PUBLIC BUSINESS SECTOR

Although in the 1960s public firms played, on average, a sizable role in the OECD, the size of the public business sector differed sharply across nations. As a result of the emergence since the late 1970s of an extensive political debate

82

about the role of state-owned firms and their potential privatization, these differences only increased in the following twenty years. Recent studies have estimated that OECD governments raised over $200 billion through the sale of state assets between 1980 and 1991 (Stevens 1992), close to the whole Swedish GDP in 1990 or to all gross fixed capital formation in Germany that year. As shown in Table 4.1, however, the extent to which public businesses were privatized varied widely across OECD nations. The sale of state assets from 1979 to 1992 amounted to 14 percent of the average annual GDP in New Zealand and 12 percent of the GDP in the United Kingdom. But it represented less than 1 percent in half of the OECD countries. And, as a matter of fact, France and Greece launched extensive nationalizations in the early 1980s. Thus, whereas the public business sector in countries like Japan, New Zealand, and Britain had been reduced to a marginal status by the early 1990s, a swollen Norwegian state-owned business sector was controlling a third of all the domestic investment, and Austrian, Greek, and Portuguese public businesses provided a fifth of all investment.

GROWTH SLOWDOWN AND FISCAL CRISIS

The extensive privatization strategies of the last decade have been conventionally attributed to the economic malaise of the 1970s. According to this argument, policymakers began to blame the disappointing economic performance of those years on structural factors and the pernicious effects of an oversized public sector (OECD 1989). From this perspective, a fall in output, investment, and productivity rates to almost half their 1960s level would have sparked a thorough process of deregulation, especially in countries in which there was heavy intervention in the economy. Moreover, growing international competitiveness would have convinced policymaking elites of all ideological orientations to scale back the level of state intervention in order to free private investment, reduce vast inefficiencies, and enable national businesses to regain world markets. As a result, public firms, which were mostly operating in declining industries such as steel or coal, would have become one of the first targets of the reforms implemented to adjust the economy to the challenges of the 1980s. Finally, the privatization of public businesses would have proved attractive as well for budgetary reasons. After two consecutive oil shocks and a significant decline in growth rates strained many governments financially, OECD government budgets deteriorated sharply in a short period of time. From being roughly balanced around 1970, they fell into an average deficit of more than 5 percent of GDP in 1982 (Oxley and Martin 1991). At the same time, the average balance of Western European state-owned companies went from a deficit of 1.4 percent of GDP in 1970 to more than 2.5 percent of GDP in 1980.[2] By selling public corporations, governments could both eliminate a significant source of losses and apply the new revenues to the reduction of public debt without having to resort to unpopular tax increases or spending cuts (Vernon 1988; Vickers and Wright 1989). In short, growing

Table 4.1. *The scale of privatizations in OECD countries, 1979-92*

Country	ACCUMULATED PRIVATIZATION PROCEEDS AS PERCENT OF AVERAGE ANNUAL GDP OVER THE PRIVATIZATION PERIOD	AVERAGE GROWTH RATE OF REAL GDP PER CAPITA 1961-79	NET PUBLIC DEBT IN 1980-85
New Zealand	14.1	1.2	n.a.
United Kingdom	12.0	2.3	47.4
Portugal	7.5	5.1	n.a.
Japan	3.0	6.6	26.5
France	1.6 [a]	3.7	16.8
Greece	1.5 [a]	5.7	41.2
Italy	1.4	4.2	96.3
Sweden	1.4	2.8	15.4
Netherlands	1.0	3.1	41.6
Spain	0.9	4.6	18.4
Austria	0.9	3.9	47.3
Canada	0.6	3.5	30.5
Germany	0.5 [b]	3.2	22.2
Australia	Less than 1 %	2.5	47.3
Belgium	0.0	3.7	111.2
Denmark	0.0?	3.0	35.2
Finland	0.0	3.8	0.6
Ireland	0.0	3.6	102.0
Norway	0.0	3.8	-19.0

TOTAL OF
SOLD ASSETS (1990 prices) $ 200 Billion

	ESTIMATE OF ASSETS NATIONALIZED AS PERCENT OF GDP		
France	5.0	3.7	16.8
Greece	5.0	5.7	41.2

[a] Nationalizations during the same period are not included.

[b] Only through German unification (October 1990).

Source: *Economist Intelligence Unit Country Reports; OECD Economic Surveys; OECD Economic Outlooks*; Reason Foundation (1986-92) and Stevens (1992).

worldwide economic and financial constraints and the internationalization of the economy would have led policymaking elites across the industrialized world to embrace a program of thorough deregulation and privatization.

DIVERGENT PARTISAN RESPONSES TO STRUCTURAL CHANGES

The economic slowdown of the 1970s (and its related budgetary problems) brought back to the fore the substantial inefficiencies generated by public firms, partly eroding the electorate's support for state interventionism. Nonetheless, explanations that mechanically link the sale of public assets to either economic decline or budgetary constraints do not resist a close empirical scrutiny. First, even though the stagflation crisis hit all developed nations with almost equal harshness, privatization strategies were far from pervasive. Moreover, there is no evidence that privatization was undertaken only by bad economic performers. Table 4.1 compares the volume of assets sold from 1979 to 1992, the average growth rate from 1961 to 1979, and the level of net public debt in the early 1980s. Several countries suffering long-term economic stagnation, such as New Zealand and the United Kingdom, engineered vast privatization packages. Yet nations like Japan or Portugal, with growth rates well above the OECD average, engaged in sizable sales of state assets as well. As for public deficits, they were not related to the approval of privatization packages. Countries bearing huge levels of public debt, such as Belgium, Italy, or Ireland, sold hardly any public corporations.

The specific responses of each state to the situation of economic turmoil and international integration depended, above all, on the partisan orientation of the cabinet. In the 1960s, right-wing parties, which generally oppose the presence of an extensive public business sector, were dissuaded by the presence of a regime of high growth and low unemployment rates from engaging in massive and politically costly privatization plans. Nonetheless, the growth slowdown experienced in the 1970s and the sharpening of the employment–equality trade-off in the 1980s eroded the incentives that had previously persuaded conservatives to accept interventionist policies. The Tory Party, which until 1970 had resisted the nationalizations approved by Labour but had overturned very few of them, embraced a resolute privatization program as the decline of the British economy accelerated.[3] Similarly, in the mid-1980s, the French Right, part of which had previously supported a state business sector, carried out policies to discipline unions and improve the long-run performance of the economy which included selling most public firms.

Decisions to curtail, maintain, or expand the public business sector directly affect the allocation of investment and the creation of employment in any domestic economy. They have substantial redistributive effects across economic sectors, regions, and social groups. Accordingly, while right-wing parties adopted a program of extensive privatizations in the face of the growth slowdown of the

1970s, most socialist cabinets remained committed to the existence of a public business sector (or even to its enlargement) as a way to ensure high levels of public spending on capital formation, particularly for the less advantaged workers and regions.[4]

The role of parties and their preferred economic strategies is forcefully conveyed by the evidence presented in Table 4.2. Table 4.2 classifies the strategy pursued toward the public business sector by all governments in all OECD nations with over one million inhabitants from 1979 to 1992, according to the partisan composition of governments and their degree of internal unity or cohesion.

Following Alt's concept of political regime (Alt 1985), a government is here defined as a cabinet with the same party composition (even if there are new elections or the prime minister changes but remains from the same party), unless the government loses the majority support of parliament (or gains it after having had minority support). Two examples suffice to make the definition clear. The British Conservative government since 1979 is considered as one government (in spite of several parliamentary elections and two different prime ministers). The Spanish Socialist administration is defined as one government from 1982 through 1993, because in 1993, the Socialist Party, though still forming the administration alone with the same prime minister presiding, lost its parliamentary majority.[5]

Mostly according to the volume of sold assets and, for some borderline cases, according to the nature and purpose of privatizations, I have coded the strategy followed by each government toward the public business sector into one of the following five categories:

1. All cases that have involved the selling of assets with a value of over 5 percent of the average annual GDP at the time of the privatization have been classified as *large privatizations*. The sales by the British government (for which cumulative asset sales amounted to 12 percent of the average British GDP from 1979 through 1992), Portugal, and New Zealand meet this criterion.

2. I consider as *medium privatizations* those processes that have led to the sale of public assets ranging from over 1 percent to 5 percent of GDP. The cases fitting this category are Japan, where sales amounted to 3 percent of GDP; the French government of Chirac in 1986–88; and the Greek Conservative administration of the early 1990s, where total asset sales were 1.5 percent of GDP.

3. The cases classified as *small privatizations* sold assets that amounted to 1 percent or less of GDP. Although the privatization proceeds under the Italian coalition in charge from 1983 to 1991 slightly exceeded this figure, this case should be considered under the category of small privatizations given that very few sales had any significant size and that, taken as a whole, they hardly dented the huge state holdings.[6] A similar point should be made regarding all the public assets sold under the Swedish social democratic cabinet in the 1980s: here the privatization proceeds came both from selling small companies that were not central to the strategic purposes attributed to the core of the public business

sector and from letting some private capital enter certain enterprises without forfeiting public control over them.

4. Most governments have witnessed no changes at all (*status quo* situation). Among them I include some cases of very limited public-asset sales (the Spanish and the Austrian cases) that, like the Swedish case, included both the privatization of companies marginal to the core of the public business sector and the granting of limited entry to private capital without giving up public control. As stated by the OECD in a recent survey on the Spanish economy, "these sales do not reflect a privatization policy along the lines followed in other OECD countries over the last few years [but] they are rather the corollary of a new industrial strategy aimed at concentrating the activities of INI [the main holding of the Spanish state] on certain industrial sectors only, thereby reaping the benefits of specialization and meeting the challenge of increasing competition" (OECD 1988, 38). As a matter of fact, in those countries, even as limited sales were taking place, new public corporations were being set up and a sizable investment effort was being made to strengthen the public business sector in general terms.[7]

5. Finally, in the category of *nationalizations*, I include those implemented by the French and Greek Socialist Parties in the first half of the decade.

The set of possible strategies toward the public business sector is displayed along the vertical axis of Table 4.2. Along the horizontal axis, I have distinguished between cabinets with and without a significant leftist presence, and among unified (one- or two-party governments with parliamentary majority) and divided (and minority) cabinets.

Table 4.2 shows that, excluding New Zealand and Sweden, Left and Right have behaved along partisan lines. All unified conservative governments have privatized most or part of the public business sector. Among unified left-wing governments, excluding New Zealand, one pressed for spectacular nationalizations (the other nationalization strategy was implemented by a three-party government in France which included the Communist Party); the rest have preserved the public enterprise sector.[8] The exceptional position of New Zealand in the table suggests that, partisan preferences notwithstanding, structural factors did affect policies developed in the 1980s. From 1961 to 1979, New Zealand experienced an annual growth rate of 1.2 percent, about one third of the OECD average and a sixth of the Japanese growth rate for the same period. Such an untenable growth rate prompted the current Labour administration to overhaul in dramatic ways a heavily protected and regulated economy.

Table 4.2 reveals as well that the capacity to generate change is mediated by the degree of internal cohesion of the government. Divided cabinets are unable to reshape the state. By contrast, strong, one-party governments are very likely to follow their preferred policy strategies. Twenty-nine out of the thirty-three governments including more than two parties or in a minority situation have kept the state-owned sector unchanged. By contrast, eight out of eleven nonleftist governments (i.e., where socialists control fewer than 40 percent of all the min-

Table 4.2. *Policies toward the public business sector in the 1980s*

	SOCIALIST PARTIES CONTROL LESS THAN 40 PERCENT OF GOVERNMENT		SOCIALIST PARTIES CONTROL MORE THAN 40 PERCENT OF GOVERNMENT	
	One or two parties with parliamentary majority	More than two parties with majority or minority cabinet	More than two parties with majority or minority cabinet	One or two parties with parliamentary majority
LARGE PRIVATIZATIONS (sold assets: over 5 percent of average GDP)	UK (1979-90) Portugal (1987-)	-----	-----	New Zealand (1984-90)
MEDIUM PRIVATIZATIONS (sold assets: from 1 to 5 percent of average GDP)	France (1986-88) Greece (1990-93) Japan (1985-93)	-----	-----	-----
SMALL PRIVATIZATIONS (sold assets: 1 percent of average GDP or less)	Canada (1984-93) Germany (1982-89) Netherlands (1982-90)	Denmark (1988-90) Italy (1983-91)	Sweden (1982-91)	-----

STATUS QUO (no sales or sales under 1 percent of average GDP approved to rationalize public business sector)			
Canada (1980-84)	Belgium (1980-81)	Denmark (1979-82)	Australia (1983-)
Ireland (1982-87)	(1982-88)	Belgium (1981-82)	Austria (1983-87)
Denmark (1982-88)	(1988-)	France (1988-93)	(1987-)
	Denmark (1990-92)	Finland (1979-82)	France (1984-86)
	Ireland (1981-82)	(1982-83) (1983-87)	Netherlands (1989-)
	(1982)	(1987-90) (1990-)	Spain (1982-93)
	(1987-89)	Netherlands (1981-82)	
	(1989-)	Norway (1986-89)	
	Italy (1980)	Portugal (1983-85)	
	(1980-81)		
	(1981-82)		
	(1982-83)		
	Netherlands (1982)		
	Norway (1981-86)		
	(1989-)		
	Portugal (1979-83)		
	(1985-89)		
	Sweden (1991-)		
NATIONALIZATIONS			
-----	France (1981-84)	-----	Greece (1981-90)

Sources. All countries except Australia and Japan: *Economist Intelligence Unit Country Reports*; *OECD Economic Surveys*; Stevens (1992). For Australia and Japan: *OECD Economic Surveys*; Reason Foundation (1986-92).

Table 4.3. *Political and economic determinants of the strategies toward the public business sector in the 1980s*

	STRATEGY TOWARD THE PUBLIC BUSINESS SECTOR [a]
INDEPENDENT VARIABLES	
Constant	5.442* (0.902)
Socialist control of government [b]	-2.167* (0.052)
Fragmentation index of government [c]	-2.021* (0.671)
Status in parliament [d]	0.917* (0.436)
Annual change in real GDP per capita (1961-79)	-0.620* (0.203)
Log likelihood at convergence	-42.463
Correctly predicted (%)	69.231
Number of observations	52

[a] Public sector strategy: large privatization, 5; medium privatization, 4; small privatization, 3; status quo, 2; nationalization, 1.

[b] It goes from 0 to 1.

[c] It goes from 0 (one-party cabinet) to 1 (extreme fragmentation).

[d] Majority in parliament=1. Minority=0.

Estimation: Ordered Probit

Standard errors in parentheses.
* Statistically significant at 0.05 or less.

isterial posts) holding a majority and including one or two parties have carried out some sort of privatization.

EMPIRICAL TESTING AND SIMULATIONS

A more rigorous testing of the impact of partisanship is reproduced in Table 4.3. Here I estimate the effects of partisan control of office,[9] the internal cohesion of the government,[10] its status in parliament (whether it holds a majority or not),[11] and past economic performance (average annual growth of real GDP per capita from 1961 to 1979) on the strategies pursued toward the public business sector.[12] All these factors prove to have substantial effects on governmental decisions on issues of public control of ownership.[13]

A set of simulations is again developed to convey more clearly how partisanship, the presence of coalition governments, and economic performance lead cabinets to privatize public enterprises.[14] The simulations, based on the results in Table 4.3, are reported in Table 4.4. They include an estimation of the probability of approving at least a small privatization (part A) and of implementing a large privatization (part B) under the following situations. Always assuming a parliamentary majority, I distinguish between one-party, two-party (with an equal share of ministers), and three-party governments. Within each case I then consider three different cabinets depending on their ideological composition: one controlled by a socialist party, one where only half of the ministers are socialists, and a third one with no socialist ministers at all. Finally, I distinguish between low growth rates (annual change of 1 percent), medium growth (at a yearly rate of 3 percent) and rapid growth (5 percent).

I only discuss here the results reported in part A of Table 4.4. Under a conservative government, the likelihood of having some sort of privatization is very high, independent of all other circumstances. The chances of selling state assets are over 50 percent in seven out of nine cases. When past economic performance is good (say, a 5 percent annual growth rate), partisanship loses part of its effect on policymaking, and the degree of fragmentation of the cabinet starts to have a substantial impact. The probability of a privatization drops from 59 percent under a unitary government to 13 percent under a three-party government.

Exactly opposite results are obtained for a socialist government, confirming once more the weight of partisanship. All socialist governments but one refrain from privatizing public corporations. An adverse economic performance puts strong pressure on socialist parties to privatize. The Left privatizes parts of the public business sector (probability, 71 percent) only when the economy has grown at an annual rate of 1 percent before 1979 and there is a unitary government. This result clearly matches the case of New Zealand.

Although the past performance of the economy affects all governments, it influences centrist cabinets most sharply. A centrist government, no matter how fragmented, always approves a privatization package in response to low growth. A stagnant economy gives moderate coalitions the cohesiveness and sense of purpose needed to effect change. When the growth rate is higher than the OECD average, all centrist governments reach a political impasse. Given the costs and the uncertainty of privatizing public corporations, they prefer to muddle through.

The internal structure of governments also affects centrist governments more strongly than it does conservative or social democratic governments. Regardless of economic performance, the chances that centrist governments will privatize are on average more than two times lower if the cabinet includes three parties rather than one. The impact of fragmentation is particularly striking when annual growth has averaged 3 percent. Here privatizing hinges ultimately on the internal cohesion of the government. A unitary government is extremely likely to privatize

Table 4.4. *The role of partisanship, divided governments, and economic performance in the strategy toward the public business sector: a simulation*

A. PROBABILITY OF HAVING AT LEAST A SMALL PRIVATIZATION DEPENDING ON IDEOLOGICAL COMPOSITION OF CABINET, FRAGMENTATION WITHIN CABINET, AND LONG-TERM ECONOMIC PERFORMANCE [a]

Only governments with majority in parliament

Annual change in real GDP per capita

	1 percent			3 percent			5 percent		
	Number of parties in government								
	One	*Two*	*Three*	*One*	*Two*	*Three*	*One*	*Two*	*Three*
Percentage of socialist ministers in government									
0	100	96	91	93	68	55	59	22	13
50	[95]	73	61	[65]	27	17	[20]	3	1
100	71	32	21	24	4	2	2	0	0

B. PROBABILITY OF HAVING A LARGE PRIVATIZATION DEPENDING ON IDEOLOGICAL COMPOSITION OF CABINET, FRAGMENTATION WITHIN CABINET, AND LONG-TERM ECONOMIC PERFORMANCE [a]

Only governments with majority in parliament

Annual change in real GDP per capita

| | 1 percent | | | 3 percent | | | 5 percent | | |
| | | | | *Number of parties in government* | | | | | |
	One	Two	Three	One	Two	Three	One	Two	Three
Percentage of socialist ministers in government									
0	92	66	53	57	20	12	14	2	0
50	[63]	25	15	[18]	3	1	[2]	0	0
100	23	4	2	2	0	0	0	0	0

[a] Based on equation reported in Table 4.3.

Figures in brackets represent cases that are only hypothetical since there cannot be a one-party government where only 50 percent of the ministers are socialist.

(with a probability of 65 percent); a divided government is not (the chances are only 27 percent or less).[15]

TAX STRATEGIES FOR GROWTH

I conclude the analysis of the relationship between supply-side economic strategies and partisan control of office by examining the evolution of the structure of the personal income tax. Conservative governments should be expected to approve low tax rates to minimize any adverse effects on the supply of labor and to encourage high levels of private savings. Leftist governments, instead, will impose high tax rates, especially on upper-income brackets, to finance their interventionist policies.[16]

To determine the impact of partisanship on personal income taxation, I have calculated the "effective tax rate" on high income earners for all OECD countries at two different periods of time: the late 1970s and the late 1980s. An effective tax rate is defined as the actual proportion of the income paid in personal income tax, after all allowances are deducted and the corresponding tax rate has been applied. A high income earner is anyone earning an income five times the wage of the "average production worker" (or APW) as defined by the OECD.[17]

Table 4.5A shows the extent to which the socialist control of government and the organizational power of labor explain the structure of tax rates in the late 1970s. Table 4.5B reports the effect of partisanship (and the organizational power of labor) on the relative change in effective tax rates from 1980 to 1990.

Partisan control of the government from 1960 to 1975 explains around half of the total variation in the effective tax rates on high-income earners in the second half of the 1970s (Model 1, Table 4.5A). The statistical significance of the variable is high. Full control of government by a socialist party from 1960 to 1975 implies a difference of 41 percentage points in the effective tax rate for incomes five times the APW wage – even when controlling for the level of development (measured as real GDP per capita in 1975).[18] The organizational power of labor, highly correlated to socialist tenure of government during the 1960s and the 1970s, explains tax rates equally well.

Which party governs is also a key variable explaining the evolution of personal tax rates in the 1980s. Socialist control of government alone explains a fifth of the total variance in the relative change in the effective tax rate from 1980 to 1990 (this estimation is not reported here). The effect of partisan ideology remains stable when I control for the initial effective tax rate (in the late 1970s) and the level of per capita income in 1980. This model (Model 1 in Table 4.5B), explains almost 60 percent of the variance in the dependent variable. According to this equation, a socialist cabinet during the 1980s increases the effective tax rate by almost 37 percent. That is, starting with an effective tax rate of, say, 40 percent, in 1990 a socialist government should have raised it to almost 55 percent. The initial level of the effective tax rate is inversely related to the evolution of the tax rate. The result (a coefficient of -0.886) implies that for each percentage point of the tax rate in 1980, one should expect a decline in the effective tax rate of almost 1 percent in the following decade. That is, other things being equal, an initial tax rate of 20 percent would fall to 16.5 percent; an initial tax rate of 50 percent would decline to 27.9 percent. Finally, the results for Model 1 show that the level of per capita income also has a negative effect on the effective tax rate: for each $1,000 (in 1980), the effective tax rate declines 2.2 percentage points during the 1980s.

Model 2 reports the effects of the organizational power of labor. As shown in Chapter 3 for investment policies, the power of unions ceases to be related in any particular way to the supply-side strategies developed in the 1980s.

In order to clarify the effects of partisanship on the effective tax rate, I report in Table 4.6 a set of simulations based on the statistical results presented for Model 1 in Table 4.5B. In the simulation table, I calculate the level of the effective tax rate on a high-income earner in 1990 depending on the initial effective tax rate in 1980, the level of economic development, and the party in power.

The simulation includes two different situations in terms of per capita income in 1980 ($5,000 and $10,000), in turn divided into four different initial effective tax rates (20, 40, 60, and 80 percent). For each of these eight hypothetical points of departure I estimate the impact of partisanship on the evolution of the effective tax rate. The table should be read in the following way: in a country with a per capita income of $5,000 and an effective tax rate of 20 percent in 1980, the tax rate in 1990 is 30.4 percent if a socialist party governed from 1980 to 1990 and 23.0 percent if the government was controlled by a conservative party.

The ideological sign of the government has a striking impact on the evolution of tax rates. Under a socialist government, the effective tax rate in 1990 tends to be between a third and two-thirds higher than under a conservative cabinet – the result depends on the initial effective tax rate. The simulation also shows that each party aims at a certain stable outcome. Socialist governments are satisfied with an effective tax that oscillates between two-thirds and three-fourths of top personal incomes. Whenever they inherit very low tax rates, they press for radical change. As rates increase, they engage in sustained but more incremental increases. Conservative governments seem to settle for effective tax rates (on top personal incomes) between 30 and 40 percent.

It is also worth emphasizing that, in relative terms, the differences between parties become somewhat sharper as the level of per capita income increases. But, on the other hand, the higher the level of per capita income, the lower the tax rates. For example, the highest tax rate under a socialist government in the rich country (with $10,000 of per capita income) is 70 percent. In the poor country, it is almost 79 percent. This may imply that in poorer nations there are stronger pressures for redistribution than in more developed countries.

Table 4.5. *Political determinants of tax progressivity*

A. *Political Determinants of Tax Progressivity in 1979-80*

EFFECTIVE TAX RATE ON INCOME FIVE TIMES THE AVERAGE PRODUCTION WORKER'S WAGE

INDEPENDENT VARIABLES	MODEL 1	MODEL 2 [a]	MODEL 3 [a]
Constant	30.096* (6.579)	32.928* (9.016)	41.007* (9.336)
Socialist control of government 1960-75 [b]	41.283* (9.300)		
Organizational power of labor [b]		35.067* (8.135)	
Socialist control of government 1960-75 x Organizational power of labor			40.434* (10.493)
Real GDP per capita in 1975 (every $1,000)	-0.034 (0.085)	-0.426 (1.029)	-0.719 (1.106)
R^2	0.550	0.554	0.498
Corrected R^2	0.526	0.494	0.431
Number of observations	21	18	18

B. *Political Determinants of Tax Progressivity in 1988-90*

RELATIVE CHANGE (FROM 1980 TO 1990) IN THE EFFECTIVE TAX RATE ON ANY INCOME FIVE TIMES THE SALARY OF AN AVERAGE PRODUCTION WORKER

INDEPENDENT VARIABLES	MODEL 1	MODEL 2 [a]	MODEL 3 [a]
Constant	43.804* (15.546)	58.744* (20.503)	59.417* (20.503)
Socialist control of government 1980-90 [b]	36.991* (15.398)		
Organizational power of labor [b]		7.185 (19.013)	
Socialist control of government 1980-90 x Organizational power of labor			10.761 (23.107)
Effective tax rate on high incomes in 1980	-0.886* (0.274)	-0.768** (0.424)	-0.748* (0.355)
Real GDP per capita in 1980 (every $1,000)	-2.246** (1.284)	-3.370* (0.551)	-3.403* (1.552)
R^2	0.590	0.416	0.419
Corrected R^2	0.512	0.291	0.295
Number of observations	21	18	18

[a] There are no data for Greece, New Zealand and Portugal in the 'organizational power of labor' index (based on Cameron 1984) used here.
[b] Index goes from 0 to 1.

Estimation: OLS
Standard errors in parentheses.
* Statistically significant at .05 or less.
** Statistically significant at .10 or less.

Table 4.6. *Effective tax rates in 1990: a simulation*

EFFECTIVE TAX RATES IN 1990 UNDER THE FOLLOWING CONDITIONS

	Per capita income of $5,000		Per capita income of $10,000	
Efffective tax rate in 1980	Socialist government 1980 to 1990	Conservative government 1980 to 1990	Socialist government 1980 to 1990	Conservative government 1980 to 1990
20	30.4	23.0	28.1	20.7
40	53.6	38.9	49.2	34.3
60	69.8	47.6	63.1	40.6
80	78.9	49.4	70.0	40.4

Values of effective tax rates in 1990 are derived from the equation reported in Table 4.5B. Model 1.

CUMULATIVE RESULTS

We are now in a position to describe the political conditions that underlie the different economic strategies that OECD nations have embraced to maximize growth and the competitiveness of their firms. First, we must conclude that the partisan composition of governments is a key predictor of supply-side economic strategies (i.e., strategies intended to modify the long-run growth rate of the economy), *both* before the stagflation period and afterward. Second, as a result of increasing economic interdependence, supply-side economic strategies have become over time the key policy dimension along which partisan forces differ. Finally, the intensification of an employment–equality trade-off in all advanced countries has increased both the importance of structural strategies and the extent of divergence in the supply-side measures adopted by different political parties in power.

Although all governments, regardless of their ideological position, are equally committed to economic growth, they end up formulating, mainly for redistributive reasons, different economic strategies to promote it. To protect the least well-off and increase equality, left-wing parties encourage the intervention of the public sector in the economy. They systematically boost taxes to finance public policies; claim for the state an important role in the provision of physical and human capital, either directly, through the public budget, or indirectly, through a public business sector; and set up regulatory schemes to affect the saving and investment decisions of private agents. Right-wing parties, instead, trust in the capacity of the private sector to supply the volume of production inputs optimal to sustain growth; cut taxes; and, if necessary, lower the social wage.

The empirical evidence gathered here and in Chapter 3 shows that a whole decade under a socialist government implies around 2 percent of GDP (or around 10 percent of total investment) more in public fixed capital formation – a rather sizable figure since it represents around two-thirds of the OECD average in public gross fixed capital formation.

Left-wing governments also have a strong impact on human capital formation. Imagine a country in which 30 percent of the population are age twenty or younger. In 1970, and after ten years of socialist government, public spending on general education would amount to 7.7 percent of GDP. Under a conservative government, it would total only 3.7 percent of GDP. After the 1970s, a decade in which the partisan composition of government had no clear-cut effects, parties influenced the levels of public human capital formation again. In a country with a high level of public expenditure on education, say, 7.7 percent of GDP, a socialist party, governing from 1980 to 1990, would expand it even more – to 9.5 percent of GDP. A conservative cabinet would drive it down from 7.7 percent of GDP to 6.2 percent. In a country with low levels of public spending on education, say, 3.7 percent of GDP in 1980, a socialist government would bring expenditure up to 6.2 percent of GDP in 1990. A conservative government would raise it, but only slightly, to 4.5 percent of GDP. Similar strong partisan effects can be detected for vocational training policies.

Higher public investment rates do not take place merely as a result of a general strategy of higher spending developed by socialist parties. Across OECD countries, the levels of public fixed investment in each country are not correlated to total government spending in any period. Although the expenditure on human capital formation is partially correlated to general government spending (which is not strange, given its volume and its welfare component), its change over time is not related to the change in total government spending. In other words, public capital formation policies are not the residual outcome of larger policies or derivations of more generic preferences in favor of a bigger public sector.[19]

Partisanship has also had a strong impact on the public control of the business sector – an issue that came to the fore of the political agenda in the 1980s mainly as a result of the renewal of conservative programs in response to the stagflation crisis. Although the degree of internal cohesion of the cabinet played a decisive role in the actual size of the privatization process, the sale of public corporations took place almost invariably under right-wing cabinets during the 1980s. It was very unlikely under socialist governments. Only extreme economic distress, such as that experienced by New Zealand, pushed leftist governments to dismantle the public business sector.

Finally, partisan tenure of office has visibly affected taxes and the use of regulatory schemes to shape savings and investment decisions. For conservatives, low income tax rates have always been essential to promote growth. For socialists, high taxes are instrumental in financing investment policies. The effective tax rate for high income levels reached over 70 percent in the late 1970s whenever a socialist party had been governing for the previous fifteen years. It stayed, instead, at 30 percent if a conservative party had controlled the government. Similar partisan effects took place in the 1980s. Starting with an effective tax rate of 70 percent in 1980, a socialist government would have maintained it at the same level during the 1980s. A right-wing cabinet would have pushed it down to 40 percent by 1990. With an effective tax rate of 30 percent in 1980, a right-wing cabinet would have reduced it marginally in the following decade while a leftist government would have increased it to 41 percent. Although the evidence is mostly fragmentary (essentially because the calculation of effective rates is hard to do in this case), there seem to have been divergent tax strategies with regard to corporate taxation too. Several studies show that social democratic governments have set very high tax rates on corporate profits jointly with extensive investment incentives to channel the latter into productive activities. Conservative governments have, instead, preferred to minimize tax rates on corporate income altogether (Przeworski and Wallerstein 1988; Swank 1992, 1993).

When the empirical evidence of Chapter 3 and of this chapter is considered jointly with the literature on the political management of the business cycle (see Chapter 1), it is possible to conclude that partisan politics play a key, although asymmetrical, role in the process of governing the economy. On the one hand, the short-term management of the economy according to partisan preferences is strongly constrained by the institutional structure of the domestic economy and the extent of economic interdependence. Decentralized labor markets ease the adjustment costs of macroeconomic discipline. Coordinated economies provide the proper preconditions for left-wing cabinets to sustain noninflationary countercyclical policies. Moreover, macroeconomic policy autonomy is inversely related to trade and financial integration. On the other hand, differences over the proper policies to affect the supply side of the economy have constituted (and constitute) the central political divide setting apart different political parties in advanced nations.

These findings can be put in a more historical perspective. During the first part of the postwar period, public intervention on the supply side of the economy and demand-management techniques came hand in hand under socialist cabinets, then mostly governing in corporatist countries. In response to the oil shocks of the 1970s, the Left, now in power in several weakly coordinated economies, intensified its commitment to the use of countercyclical policies.[20] But, as several attempts at demand management failed repeatedly by the end of the decade, Keynesianism came under intense fire. Substantially more interdependent economies, high interest rates among world interest-rate setters such as the United States and Germany, and weakening corporatist institutions impelled most leftist governments to set aside most of their penchant for expansionary policies and to embrace anti-inflationary targets.[21] Public sector interventionism was gradually left as the main area in which socialist cabinets differed from conservative cabinets. Even during periods of monetary and fiscal discipline, like the early 1980s, the Left continued to view (and employ) the state as a central agent to overcome market failures, sustain national competitiveness abroad, equalize conditions, and ameliorate the social effects of competitive markets. Conversely, conservative parties tried to free the market from any kind of dirigisme.

When we look at the evolution of supply-side economic strategies from a historical point of view, there are clear signs that the importance that each partisan force attaches today to its own kind of investment strategy has intensified over time. The collapse of demand-management techniques has pressed more governments to choose between public investment schemes (to avoid subsidizing unemployment) and deregulatory measures (to prevent tight macroeconomic policies from having inordinate employment costs). Above all, as the cases explored in the following chapters convey in a forceful way, the fall of demand for unskilled workers – experienced in the last fifteen years in the advanced world – has squarely confronted governments with the need to choose between less social protection and more public capital spending. Left-wing governments have responded by calling for more public investment and larger education and vocational-training programs and by defending, in some cases, the strategic role of public firms in an increasingly competitive world economy. Mirroring the experience of the Left, supply-side issues have remained relevant, or indeed grown in relevance, among the Right in the last fifteen years. The stagflation crisis and the following exogenous shocks have revealed to conservative parties the costs of maintaining a generous social wage and have prompted radical reforms in several countries. The tax reform movement of the 1980s is a clear example. Massive privatization programs are another one.

THE TASK AHEAD: THE COMPARISON OF BRITAIN AND SPAIN IN THE 1980S

The current literature on the political determinants of the business cycle is mostly content with assuming as given the differences in party preferences concerning macroeconomic management and says little about how to derive the goals of parties from the distribution of voter preferences, material resources, and positions in the political and economic structures of advanced countries. For the sake of simplicity, this book has adopted a similar point of departure. But the powerful connection we have found between the choice of economic strategy and partisanship leads us necessarily to examine the ideological and electoral basis of each partisan government and the political and electoral dynamics that lie behind the development of every economic strategy. Do economic policies actually respond to different redistributive demands from distinctive economic sectors? Which particular electoral constituencies are behind each partisan government? Do instrumental ideas play any role in building those electoral coalitions? How do parties in government keep together what inevitably are broad-based coalitions? What is the electoral and policy impact of the shifts in the demand for unskilled and skilled workers? To what degree do parties respond to long-term interests and strategies against short-term electoral calculations?

The Spanish Socialist government and the British Conservative cabinet of the 1980s have been chosen to explore these issues. Their cabinet stability and, as a matter of fact, their divergent responses to similar dilemmas (they are extreme cases in the OECD sample of that decade) make them especially suited to explore the validity of the hypotheses drawn in the last section of Chapter 2. In the chapters that follow, I map out the social sectors that supported each political project and the programmatic and policy appeals made by both governments. I describe how those different electoral constituencies responded to the policy choices made by the two cabinets. And I particularly dwell on the electoral calculations of each government – in reaction to or, in many cases, in anticipation of voters' attitudes – and how they affected the policymaking process. Chapter 9 crowns all this historical analysis with a comparative approach that includes pointed references to other European cases.

The analysis of Spain and the United Kingdom confirms that clear-cut redistributive politics indeed drive most of the divergence of partisan responses to the employment–equality trade-off, in line with the initial assumptions of this book (and of most literature on political economics). A public investment strategy responds to the pressures and needs of the core constituencies of social democrats:

working-class and lower-middle class sectors. By contrast, lowering taxes and the social wage result from the pressure of traditional conservative party voters: middle classes and, especially in Great Britain, propertied voters. Hence there is some truth to what I referred to as a naive model of class politics predicting that the electoral strength of each party will depend, at least in part, on the size of each class and the distribution of skills in the polity.

Nevertheless, the cases (jointly with other countries brought into the discussion in Chapter 9) also show that political parties and their policy strategies are not mechanical representations of particular economic sectors or classes. Parties run on programmatic appeals that mobilize certain interests and that serve them in particular ways. In the wake of a sharp fall in their wages, unskilled workers can equally vote for a social democratic project of more public capital formation or for a radical anti-immigration and anti-free-trade party. Middle classes can become attached to the social democratic project of a universal welfare state. But they may equally support trimming social spending.

Economic policies are the tools employed by parties to organize and sustain broad electoral coalitions. The González government shows that socialist parties expand public capital spending and social benefits to compensate the most unskilled workers for their acceptance of the consequences of a market economy and free trade. These measures, jointly with the universal character of the welfare state, are expected to attract, in turn, skilled blue-collar workers and parts of the middle class. The Thatcher government believed that strong growth – resulting from less state intervention and lower taxes – would enlarge the middle classes and therefore the core constituencies of the Tory Party. A new structure in the provision of goods and services (such as housing) would equally strengthen the conservative electoral basis. Moreover, in some instances, policies turn out to be not only the instruments of the bargaining process through which cross-class coalitions are built but ways of generating truly new constituencies. For instance, the aggressive creation of public sector employment by Scandinavian left-wing governments (or the extension of pensions and unemployment benefits by the Spanish Socialist Party) has generated a new (and very solid) basis of support for social democracy. As emphasized in Chapters 9 and 10, these results point to a more complex conception of parties than simple representatives of particular economic sectors or bundles of sectors. Political parties seem to lie, instead, at the intersection of material interests, instrumental policies, and political projects.

Finally, the British and Spanish cases show the kinds of policy and electoral dilemmas that governments face in the context of a sharp employment–equality trade-off and the ways in which they respond or adapt to them. The Spanish (and any social democratic) strategy of public capital formation required repressing social transfers (which alienated unions and left-wing voters) and raising taxes (jeopardizing the support of middle classes). In Britain, deregulation and spending cuts, advocated to restore a full-employment economy, were partly contained in order not to alienate key moderate voters. The policy and electoral trade-offs both governments were confronted with had important (and often unintended) consequences for voting patterns and the economy: the electoral basis of the Spanish Socialist Party went through a considerable realignment; the Tory government could only barely tame public expenditure and suffered growing levels of internal strife (and policy paralysis) beginning in the early 1990s. As the employment–equality trade-off intensifies, more nations are being gripped by the same set of conflicting pressures that affected Spain and Britain – in some cases with even more dramatic consequences, such as the emergence of powerful extreme right-wing parties in Austria, Belgium, and France.

Before turning to the cases, it should also be noted that the detailed historical examination of both economic experiences has some other important benefits besides showing the electoral dynamics of economic policy. It corroborates the overall statistical results of this chapter and Chapter 3 and foregrounds the unity (and internal consistency) that each economic strategy had in each country (which is to some degree missed in the econometric analysis of separate policy instruments). Moreover, when set against each other, both cases provide powerful evidence of what amounts to a growing divergence (rather than a commonly held perception of convergence) in the supply-side solutions that partisan governments are embracing in the post–Cold War era.

For each case, I start by providing an account of the evolution of economic policy, which draws connections with and fleshes out the quantitative evidence of this chapter and Chapter 3, as well as the current theoretical work on the politics of macroeconomic management. I then turn, especially in the second chapter of each case, to the analysis of the political and electoral processes that underpin the formulation of economic policy.

5

THE SOCIAL DEMOCRATIC PROJECT: MACROECONOMIC STABILITY AND STATE INTERVENTION IN SPAIN

As a result of a prolonged economic crisis beginning in the mid-1970s, the European political scenario went through an unprecedented shift of electoral fortunes in the early 1980s. While Northern European conservatives seized most cabinets, in Southern Europe the Left experienced an unprecedented wave of electoral victories. In 1981 the French and the Greek Socialist Parties secured strong parliamentary majorities. In 1983 the Portuguese Socialist Party rejoined the government, and the socialist Bettino Craxi was appointed prime minister in Italy. The Spanish Socialist Party – Partido Socialista Obrero Español (PSOE) – proved, however, to be the most successful one in the electoral arena. Elected to office in October 1982 with an impressive majority and a lead of 21 percentage points over the conservative opposition, it governed alone until 1993 and, in a minority cabinet with external support from moderate regionalist parties, until 1996.

The Spanish Socialist government provides an excellent opportunity to examine the development of full-fledged left-wing economic policies, particularly in an era of high financial and trade interdependence. The failure of the French expansionary policies initially pursued by Mitterrand and swelling public and trade deficits convinced the Spanish Socialist cabinet of the need to avoid any countercyclical measures to fight unemployment. Unable to rely on weak and divided trade unions, the Spanish government willingly embraced a strategy of macroeconomic discipline as the best means to attract investment and open Spain to the world economy throughout the decade. In the eyes of the government, however, the increasing economic interdependence of Spain dictated granting the public sector an active role in the transformation of the structural conditions of the Spanish economy and in the expansion of its input factors. The sluggish performance of the Spanish economy in recent years – most apparent in the

extremely high rate of unemployment and the widening income gap with other
advanced nations – had derived from the very weak supply conditions of the
economy. Savings and fixed capital formation had declined by a third since the
first oil shock. A sizable part of the workforce was badly trained and could only
engage in unskilled jobs. Unless the growth rate, the productivity, and the overall
competitiveness of the Spanish economy were significantly boosted, the welfare
state and the redistributive plans of the PSOE could prove impossible to implement.

To revamp the supply side of the Spanish economy, the Spanish Socialist
government developed a long-run fiscal policy in two steps. Gradual tax increases
and moderate spending cuts in subsidies and social programs were employed to
reduce the public deficit and to raise the level of public savings. Once the budget
deficit was under control, public spending was geared to expand the formation
of fixed and human capital. Public firms played an important, yet more subdued,
role in the PSOE's strategy. Aware of the dubious consequences of the French
nationalizations program, the González government focused on the rationalization of most of the public sector until the mid-1980s. As the world economic
cycle experienced an upturn, several key public corporations were then used to
supplement direct public investment policies and to open up foreign markets for
Spanish businesses.

The Spanish case corroborates the statistical analysis of Chapters 3 and 4
(as well as the findings of the political business cycle literature). Constrained
by the international economy, the Socialist cabinet adhered, like most other
nations, to stable macroeconomic policies. Nonetheless, it relied on the active
involvement of the public sector in the supply of input factors. Moreover, the
analysis of the Spanish case allows us to interpret the policy instruments examined separately in the previous chapters as part of an overall economic strategy – of a social democratic nature in this instance. Above all, this chapter
establishes the basis for the detailed examination of the political and electoral
dimensions of a social democratic supply-side strategy in Chapter 6. However,
the present chapter already offers important insights on the electoral calculations of the González government: besides describing its sources of electoral
support, it discusses how the evolution of the business cycle, by altering the severity of the employment–equality trade-off, affected the pace of the public investment strategy.

This chapter is organized as follows. The first section examines the adoption
by the PSOE of a social democratic plank and describes the initial electoral
coalition that supported it in 1982. The second section briefly dwells on the
macroeconomic side of the PSOE's policies, showing the constraints suffered by
social democratic parties in noncoordinated economies in an era of economic
interdependence. The rest of the chapter turns its attention to the core of the
Spanish (and, indeed, any) social democratic project: the state-led transformation
of the supply side of the economy.

THE CONSTRUCTION OF A SOCIAL DEMOCRATIC ALTERNATIVE

After becoming the largest party of the Left during the Second Republic, balloting around a sixth of all voters, the PSOE almost disappeared during the Franco regime, supplanted in terms of both organizational capacity and membership by the Spanish Communist Party (PCE). A new generation of young militants mostly drawn from Madrid, the Basque Country and Andalusia, however, revived the PSOE in the early and mid-1970s. In 1974 Felipe González replaced a Civil War exile as party secretary-general. In the following two years the number of militants quadrupled to eight thousand and the PSOE steadily gained in political influence.

Influenced by the radical leftism in vogue in Europe in the 1970s and the effervescence of the Spanish transition to democracy, the PSOE approved a militant program in December 1976 calling for sweeping nationalizations and the construction of a classless society. Nonetheless, as the first democratic elections approached, the PSOE readily moved toward the political center. The 1977 electoral manifesto limited the PSOE's demands to the elaboration of a democratic constitution, a tax reform, the extension of the welfare state, and targeted nationalizations (Gillespie 1989). The PSOE ran a strong campaign emphasizing the moderate, authoritative leadership of Felipe González. To the great surprise of its leaders, the PSOE emerged as the second-largest Spanish party, receiving 29 percent of all valid votes, only 5 points behind the center-to-the-right coalition UCD.

Certainly comparable, in strength and in the social sources of support, to other mainstream center-to-the-left, social democratic parties in Northern Europe, the PSOE drew most of its support from blue-collar workers and from voters who, independent of their objective social class, identified themselves as members of the working class.[1] Moreover, it was heavily supported by the secular pole of society (Gunther, Sani, and Shabad 1988, 234ff.). Nevertheless, the PSOE started to make some inroads among white-collar employees and practicing Catholics.

The relatively disappointing electoral performance of the PSOE in the General Election of March 1979 and in the local elections of April 1979 (in which the Socialist Party actually lost votes in relation to 1977) convinced its leaders to take another step toward the political center. After severe infighting and two national congresses in a year, one of them extraordinary, González forced the party to drop its Marxist label and reinforced the organizational power of the party elite. By the early 1980s, the PSOE had turned into a mainstream social democratic party that, brushing aside its former radical plans for nationalizations and the extension of worker control of companies, favored a deep tax reform, the extension of the welfare state, and the strategic use of the public sector to maximize long-term growth and reduce unemployment (Maravall 1981, pt. 4; PSOE 1982; Gillespie 1989).

The moderate stance inspired by González paid off handsomely again. The acute economic crisis of the early 1980s and the collapse of the center-to-the-right governing coalition eventually gave González the opportunity to capture the political center and to build a broader electoral coalition in the 1982 General Election. The share of the Socialist vote, as a proportion of the whole electorate, almost doubled, from 20.4 percent in 1979 (or 29.9 percent of the valid vote) to 37.7 percent in 1982 (or 47.3 percent of the valid vote).

The PSOE's success derived, above all, from its capacity to form a broad coalition of middle- and working-class voters.[2] The PSOE reinforced its hegemony in its natural stronghold, the industrial working class, where support went up from 35 percent in 1979 to almost 50 percent in 1982. Yet the electoral victory of 1982 was the result of successfully adding white-collar employees in subordinate positions (where support doubled, from 20 percent in 1979 to more than 40 percent in 1982). The extent to which it held its natural electoral base and extended it to voters who had previously supported UCD can be observed by looking at voters' left–right self-locations. The PSOE doubled its support among extreme leftists (from 17 percent to 37 percent) and leftists (from 29 percent to 55 percent). More important, it became the dominant party among those located in center-to-the-left positions, who account for a fourth of the electorate, going from 51 percent to 75 percent, as well as the party that received the most votes from the center, with 29 percent of the vote.

THE SEARCH FOR MACROECONOMIC DISCIPLINE, 1982–89

When the PSOE formed a government for the first time at the end of 1982, Spain had already endured a protracted economic crisis. Unemployment had increased steadily from less than 3 percent of the active population in the early 1970s to 17.1 percent in December 1982. Private investment had declined by almost a third in less than ten years, from 25.7 percent of GDP in 1974 to 18.3 percent of GDP in 1982. After a brief recovery following the first oil shock, by the late 1970s and early 1980s the Spanish economy was growing less than 1 percent annually in real terms. As a result, Spain had suffered a fall in the relative level of per capita income in comparison to the European Community (EC) during the last decade (Pérez and Ruiz 1989).

In spite of the dismal performance of the Spanish economy and of the generic promises made during the electoral campaign that a future Socialist government would engage in expansionary policies, the González government immediately rejected the implementation of countercyclical policies to boost internal demand.[3] The fiasco of the French reflationary attempt just a year before convinced the government that expansionary policies could be attempted by one country alone only at the risk of incurring a high economic and electoral cost (Boyer 1983a, 1983b, 1984; Borrell 1990; PEMP 1985, 1:8; Dehesa 1988, 30).[4] Moreover, the calamitous Labour administration in Britain in the late 1970s also served as a strong warning against expansionary strategies. Finally, those two historical experiences were reinforced by an emerging consensus among Spanish economists that the country's persistently poor economic performance derived from structural factors that could not be solved by merely propelling up internal demand (Rojo 1981; Fuentes 1979; Banco de España 1983, 56ff. and 141ff.; Banco de España 1984, 22ff.).[5]

Emphasizing, instead, price and wage moderation as a precondition for economic recovery, the PSOE government reversed the broadly accommodative monetary policy implemented under the previous centrist government (Poveda 1986; Argandoña 1990; Banco de España 1983) and cut the public deficit by 0.8 points of GDP to 4.8 percent in 1983.[6] Helped by a worldwide downward trend of raw-material and food prices, the government's restrictive stance drove inflation down by about 5 percentage points – to 9 percent – by the end of 1984.

However, domestic demand contracted 1 percent in real terms in 1984. Unemployment reached almost 2.9 million people, or 21.7 percent of the active population, by the end of the year. With parliamentary elections getting closer, the government promoted a broad social pact in order to further its anti-inflationary goals while rekindling the economy. Given the frail state of the economy, the General Workers' Union (Unión General de Trabajadores; UGT), the socialist trade union, was willing to secure a national agreement that could strengthen the position of the PSOE and move the economic policy closer to a "social democratic corporatist" model (Zufiaur 1985; Espina 1991). With the participation of the national business organization (Confederación Española de Organizaciones Empresariales; CEOE), in the fall of 1984 the government and UGT signed a two-year pact, the Acuerdo Económico y Social (AES), that provided for moderate pay increases to reduce inflation to 8 percent in 1985 and 6 percent in 1986. In exchange, the government pledged to commit significant resources for public investment, public employment and unemployment benefits, and accepted tax allowances for low income families and a slight cut in employers' social security contributions. By the second semester of 1984, the economic authorities loosened monetary policy. In the following spring the cabinet approved an overtly expansive fiscal policy to boost private demand. The public deficit worsened by 1.4 points of GDP to 6.9 percent of GDP.

Economic conditions in Spain eventually turned around by mid-1985. Private consumption grew by 2 percent in 1985 – the strongest increase since 1977 – and then by 3.6 percent in 1986. Inflation fell to less than 5 percent by the summer of 1987. In the summer of 1985 Spain entered an expansionary cycle that, after peaking at the end of 1988 (with GDP growing at an annual rate of 5.5 percent in real terms), lasted through the beginning of 1992.

As soon as the economy started to grow, the government, reelected in 1986 with a solid parliamentary majority, abandoned the temporary fiscal impulse engineered in 1985 and emphasized again its commitment to achieving a stable macroeconomic framework to deliver long-term noninflationary growth.[7] The cabinet's determination to sustain a stable and noninflationary macroeconomic framework was bolstered throughout the decade by the increasing economic openness of the Spanish economy and, especially, the integration process into the EC since 1986 (Dehesa 1988, Solchaga 1990). The inflationary costs of an autonomous economic expansion (which were almost certain to happen unless inflation was checked by a social compact guaranteeing moderate wage increases) could only be eased through currency devaluations. Yet a devaluation clashed directly with the European economic and political project, threatened the credibility of the governmental commitment to balanced long-term growth, and jeopardized the capital inflows still essential to sustain Spain's growth rates.

Unlike the French case, in which there was a clear-cut intragovernmental confrontation between those in favor of loosening European ties in order to regain policy autonomy and those promoting fiscal austerity within the EC (Hall 1986, chap. 8), the Spanish Socialist government never doubted the need to sacrifice national sovereignty in the area of macroeconomic management. González had strong political and economic incentives to adhere wholeheartedly to the European project. Joining the EC had overwhelming public support, mostly derived from a general belief linking the integration into Europe to the culmination of the modernization process of the country. With almost 60 percent of all Spaniards consistently endorsing the European project throughout the decade, Spain was only second to Italy in its levels of allegiance to the EC. Moreover, the political and business elites agreed that entering the EC would yield substantial economic benefits to the Spanish economy: a vast market and a place to look for readily available capital. In this context, the González government promptly connected the Spanish membership in Europe to its program of political and social transformation and, crowning a decade of thorough governmental efforts to fight inflation, joined the European Monetary System (EMS) in June 1989.[8]

THE DEVELOPMENT OF A SOCIAL DEMOCRATIC SUPPLY-SIDE STRATEGY

With macroeconomic policy surrendered to the twin goals of low inflation and European integration, the González government was left with only one possible strategy to foster growth and reduce huge levels of unemployment and a widening income gap with other European nations: promoting the transformation of the supply conditions of the Spanish economy and increasing the volume and quality of the Spanish productive factors.

In the words of Antonio Zabalza, then general secretary for Planning and Budgeting, the "great shortage of capital" suffered by the Spanish economy was "seriously constrain[ing] our competitiveness, and [leading], in several ways, to a dramatic reduction of our potential for growth" (1989, 30). It was due to serious supply bottlenecks that the economic crisis had hit Spain more strongly than other countries and that, after the two oil shocks, the unemployment rate was almost double the EC average. Plainly put, "Spain [did] not enjoy enough capital stock to employ all the available labor force" (1989, 35). Moreover, the internationalization of the Spanish economy, furthered by the process of European integration, intensified the need to improve the country's productive factors. Increasingly open markets and growing capital mobility were undercutting the traditional recourse of using exchange rate policies to increase competitiveness. As a result, the cost of production factors as well as their productivity were becoming the fundamental variables that determined the competitive edge of Spanish companies. Finally, the weakness of Spanish input factors had straightforward redistributive consequences too. It contributed decisively to the relative underdevelopment of most areas of the country in relation to the rest of Europe and produced wide income differentials. In 1984, the per capita income in sixteen out of seventeen regions was less than 75 percent the average per capita income in the EC. Moreover, the internal distribution of wealth was strongly unequal. The income level among all Spanish regions diverged widely: the per capita income in the richest regions was more than twice the per capita income in the poorest areas. In short, increasing investment was imperative. Only through investment could the potential productive capacity of the economy be raised, employment created on a permanent basis, and national competitiveness secured over time.

From a social democratic perspective, this diagnosis unquestionably called for granting to the public sector an active role in the expansion of the Spanish productive factors. Since both underdevelopment and, to some extent, unemployment were being defined as secular phenomena that the spontaneous action of markets had aggravated rather than diminished, the public sector should intervene to remedy them and to break up the set of structural bottlenecks that were slowing the economy down and hampering long-term social and economic development (De la Cruz 1986; Zabalza 1988a, 1988b, 1988c; Solchaga 1987, 1988). Massive public spending to enhance the national stock of fixed capital and to improve the quality of the labor force would increase the overall productivity of the private sector and stimulate domestic and foreign investment in search of higher rates of return (Zabalza 1991b). Moreover, this active investment strategy had a purely redistributive dimension. It could be targeted to accelerate the rate of growth in the most-underdeveloped regions (Zaragoza 1989). Similarly, an increased effort in the area of human capital formation had a clear egalitarian function: it was "an important part of a social policy directed to accelerate the vertical ascent of specific social sectors" (Solchaga 1988, 24).

Table 5.1 summarizes the PSOE's supply-side economic strategy (examined in detail in the following sections). The González government raised revenues systematically: 7.7 percentage points of GDP. It contained social expenditures, which increased hardly at all before 1990, and cut subsidies and capital transfers substantially; most revenues were initially used to lower the public deficit and increase the level of public (and hence total) savings. By 1989 the public deficit was 2.8 percent of GDP, or 3.2 percentage points less than in 1986, although a

Table 5.1. *General government expenditure and public capital formation in Spain, 1982-91*

	LEVEL OF EXPENDITURE (AS PERCENT OF GDP)				CHANGE 1982-91 (AS PERCENT OF GDP)
	1982	1986	1989	1991	
Total revenues	32.4	36.1	39.8	40.1	+7.7
Budget balance	-5.6	-6.0	-2.8	-4.9	+0.7
Total capital formation	6.3	8.0	9.4	10.4	+4.1
Fixed capital	3.1	3.6	4.4	5.2	+2.1
Education	3.0	3.8	4.1	4.2	+1.2
Active labor policies	0.2	0.6	0.9	1.0	+0.8
Social expenditure	18.4	18.6	18.7	20.4	+2.0
Pensions	9.2	10.4	10.2	10.8	+1.6
Unemployment benefits	2.6	2.6	2.4	2.9	+0.3
Other social benefits	2.3	1.0	1.3	1.6	-0.7
Health	4.3	4.6	4.8	5.1	+0.8
Public debt interests	1.0	4.0	3.5	4.0	+3.0
Subsidies and capital transfers	5.5	3.6	3.6	3.6	-1.9

Source: Statistical Appendix in Lagares 1992, 162-66, except data for active labor policies, derived from Table 5.3.

sudden increase in social spending in 1990–91 pushed the public deficit up to around 5 percent of GDP. The containment of the public deficit to boost the pool of savings was immediately followed by a systematic public capital formation strategy.[9] Fixed capital formation, that is, spending on basic infrastructures and on transportation, was steadily increased by 2.1 percentage points of GDP up to 5.2 percent of GDP in 1991. Another 2 percentage points of GDP were allocated to both general education expenditure and new manpower programs. A similar and complementary strategy was developed regarding the public business sector. After approving painful restructuring plans and minimal privatizations, in the mid- and late 1980s the government engaged several key public firms in strong investment plans and in opening up new markets abroad.

A SOCIAL DEMOCRATIC TAX STRATEGY

Although government revenues had increased strongly in the late 1970s, boosted by a comprehensive tax reform approved in 1977–78, they had not kept up with the rate of increase in expenditures, driven by a weak economy and the political pressures of the transition process. As a result, taxes had been insufficient to contain a deteriorating public deficit. Accordingly, raising tax revenues was a necessary condition to hold together the González economic strategy of combining a stable macroeconomic policy and the state's direct intervention in capital formation and economic growth.

Driven by its electoral commitments (PSOE 1982, 18ff.; Programa 2000, 1988, 162–63) and economic plans but constrained by a delicate economic situation, the González government designed a two-pronged strategy to raise fiscal revenues. On the one hand, it developed a thorough campaign to combat pervasive fiscal fraud that included enhancing the organizational capabilities of the Ministry of Economy and Finance (Ministerio de Economía y Hacienda 1989; Borrell 1989), making tax evasion a criminal offense, and launching large and politically sensitive antifraud operations. The number of tax returns filed doubled to almost 11 million in less than ten years. By 1990 the national tax base was almost twice that of 1981 measured in constant pesetas. In the same period, the Spanish GDP had grown by 40 percent in real terms.[10] On the other hand, the government raised revenue through fiscal drag,[11] which was then unequally corrected across tax brackets to enhance the progressivity of the tax system – a goal forcefully defended by the PSOE.[12]

After ten years of incremental reform, the tax strategy of the government achieved the two fundamental goals that characterized the Socialist electoral manifesto of 1982. Revenues had surged markedly and the overall progressivity of the tax system had been strengthened.

As shown in Table 5.2, in nine years revenues rose 7.7 percent of GDP (a relative increase of 24 percent), from 32.4 percent of GDP in 1982 to 40.1 percent

Table 5.2. *Evolution of Spanish government revenues, 1982-91*

	AS PERCENT OF GDP			ABSOLUTE CHANGE 1982-91	RELATIVE CHANGE 1982-91
	1982	1986	1991		
Direct taxes	6.6	7.9	11.9	+5.3	+80.3
Indirect taxes	7.9	10.8	9.9	+2.0	+25.3
Social security contributions	13.3	12.8	13.1	-0.2	-1.5
Other	4.6	4.7	5.3	+0.6	+13.0
Total	32.4	36.1	40.1	+7.7	+23.8

Source: IGAE (1993) and own estimations.

in 1991 – therefore putting Spain on almost equal terms with other medium-sized European nations in relation to the size of fiscal revenues.[13] Making good on the promise to enhance the redistributive structure of the tax system, the increase was heavily concentrated on direct taxes. Almost two thirds of the increase derived from higher personal and corporate income taxes (5.3 percent of GDP, or a relative increase of 80 percent). Most of the rest came from consumption taxes as a consequence of the introduction of the value-added tax required by Spain's integration into the EC.[14]

Overall progressivity deepened strikingly in less than a decade. Figure 5.1 displays the effective tax rate, that is, the percentage of the tax base paid to the state after all deductions and allowances have been taken away, paid in 1981 and 1990 for incomes up to Pta 10 million in 1981 pesetas.[15] In 1981, the effective tax rate on an income of Pta 500,000 was 5.4 percent. For an income ten times larger, the effective tax rate was 21 percent.[16] The effective tax rate reached 30 percent only when the income exceeded Pta 9 million. Ten years later, tax rates had gone up for all incomes over Pta 700,000 (also in 1981 pesetas, which would be Pta 1,478,000 in nominal terms in 1990) – that is, for more than 50 percent of all taxpayers. The real progressivity of the tax had increased substantially as well. For an income of Pta 9 million (in 1981 pesetas) the effective tax rate was now around 42 percent.

FOSTERING INVESTMENT AND BUILDING "PUBLIC CAPITAL"

INCREASING PUBLIC SAVINGS

Progress in reducing the public deficit and increasing public savings was slow and more volatile. During the first parliamentary term, the public deficit increased as a result of the expansionary measures approved in 1985. The government was able, however, to tackle some of the underlying structural causes of an excessive public deficit. The budgetary process was rationalized, and the structure of personnel costs clarified. The government enacted a reform of the Social Security system that slashed current benefits and shifted some contributions to employees. As a result, social benefits other than pensions fell 1.3 percentage points of GDP from 1982 to 1986. Finally, subsidies and capital transfers were cut by a third, from 5.5 percent of GDP to 3.6 percent of GDP in the same period (see Table 5.1).

Once the economic climate improved and tax revenues grew accordingly, a considerable proportion of all new tax revenues was directly applied to reduce the deficit – even though that effort compromised the PSOE's political program to enlarge public services and threatened to damage the electoral standing of the government among its supporters.[17] Between 1985 and 1990, 83 percent of all net tax increases (i.e., tax increases minus new public transfers), which grew 4.7

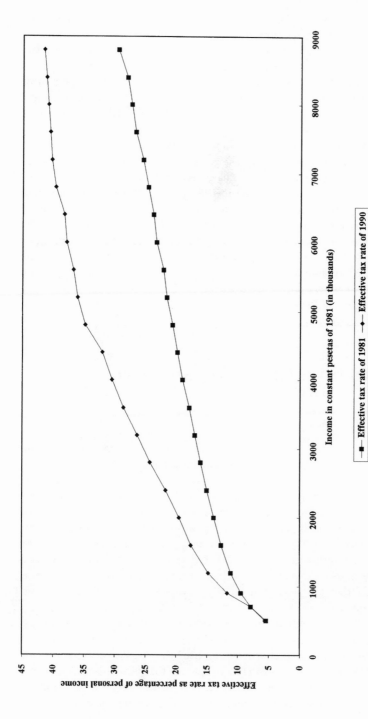

Figure 5.1. *Effective tax rates on personal income in Spain, 1981–90*

points of GDP, were applied to reduce the public deficit (Zabalza 1991c). Public savings increased from −1.4 percent of GDP in 1985 to 2.9 percent in 1989. The government's capacity to raise the level of savings proved, however, to be short-lived. Competing political and social demands on the budget, to be examined in Chapter 6, eventually led to higher expenditures in the late 1980s. As a result, the level of public savings then declined somewhat to 2.0 and 1.6 percent of GDP in 1990 and 1991 respectively.

EXPANDING THE PUBLIC STOCK OF PHYSICAL CAPITAL

Once the economic trough of the early 1980s was left behind and the budget deficit started to decrease, the government decided to press ahead with what would become the core of its supply-side strategy: building what was termed a "national stock of public capital."

Although the volume of public direct capital investment was increased in 1985 and 1986 to sustain a temporary expansionary policy, it was slightly curtailed in 1987 to accommodate a strong cut in the public deficit. After 1988, public investment rose steadily – by almost half a percentage point of GDP every year. In 1991 it reached more than 5 percent of GDP. Although some of this increase was a result of decisions by the regional and local governments (around a fifth), most of it (more than two-thirds) was the result of the ambitious investment strategy approved by the central government.

Most of the public investment spending by the central government was allocated to build or improve those basic infrastructures that were thought to play a key role in linking the country (and especially the less developed regions) to the European market, increasing overall productivity and therefore offering more incentives to private investment, and helping to overcome acute shortages and demand bottlenecks. Accordingly, the government developed a comprehensive set of plans to improve transport and communication networks. The construction and maintenance of roads, railroads, ports, airports, and urban networks represented more than half of the investment assumed by the central government. Another tenth of all the investment was directed to dams and irrigation systems. The rest was mainly employed in education and health infrastructure and, only secondarily, in culture, housing, and environmental protection.[18]

From 1984 to 1991, an ambitious construction program tripled the public highway network from 2,300 to 6,000 kilometers and repaired and improved another 15,000 kilometers of existing roads (García-Blanch et al. 1990; MOPTMA 1993). Total expenditures from 1985 to 1992 reached Pta 1,680 billion (in 1990 pesetas) – close to 0.5 percent of GDP every year. The investment in the Spanish road system was then strengthened with an overall plan for big cities and their metropolitan areas approved in 1990 that was to pour Pta 445 billion in four years into Madrid, Barcelona, Valencia, Málaga, and Seville. New plans (approved in 1987) to streamline the public railway company, modernize equipment, and expand two-way railroads represented Pta 415 billion (in 1990 pesetas), or 10 percent of all investment by the central government (García-Blanch et al. 1990; Sánchez Revenga 1990).[19] Completing the state effort to modernize the transportation system, Pta 220 billion (in 1990 pesetas) was spent to expand the capacity of ports and to renew the Spanish coasts, and Pta 186 billion (1990 pesetas) was spent to enhance both the capacity and the performance of airports from 1985 to 1992.

Public investment in the Spanish water system was equally strong. A total expenditure of Pta 586 billion (1990 pesetas) was used to increase the capacity of dams from 43,540 hm^3 to 51,314 hm^3 from 1985 to 1992. In response to redistributive concerns, 80 percent of all public spending in the expansion of the water system was concentrated in the southern half of the country.[20]

HUMAN CAPITAL FORMATION

Although there is no doubt that the public supply of physical capital was the crux of the investment strategy adopted by González, the provision and upgrading of human capital remained prominent in the economic strategy of the Socialist cabinet. Most of the public effort on human capital formation took the form of increased expenditures on general education. Public expenditure on education, which represented 3 percent of GDP in 1980, was steadily increased to 4.2 percent of GDP in 1991 and then to 4.7 percent in 1994 – an increase larger than those in areas such as health and pensions (Maravall 1992). The Socialist government reorganized primary and secondary education (through legislation in 1985 and 1990), extended free and compulsory education until the age of sixteen (in 1990), and attempted to revamp the university system (through a new law in 1983). Combined with a decline in demographic growth, the rise in educational expenditure meant doubling the amount spent per student in real terms, a vast increase in teacher hirings, and the expansion of enrollments at the secondary and university levels (Puerto 1991).[21] The proportion of fourteen-year-old to eighteen-year-old students attending school increased from 50 percent in 1980 to 70 percent in 1989, and the proportion of nineteen-year-old to twenty-three-year-old students increased from 22 to 33.1 percent.[22] The volume of grants and scholarships was multiplied by 6 between 1982 and 1992, from Pta 12 billion to Pta 71 billion, and the number of beneficiaries went from close to 500,000 in 1987 to more than 800,000 in 1992 (Riviere and Rueda 1993). Finally, the Socialist government attempted to strengthen the system of vocational education (*formación profesional*; FP) by adapting it to the demands of the marketplace and by giving it more status within the overall education system. In ten years, the number of students in FP doubled (CIDE 1992).

Active labor market policies took off later. A first attempt came through the promotion of specific training contracts, approved with the assent of unions at the time of the social compact of 1984–86. From 1984 to 1992, around 10 percent of all hirings corresponded to training and apprenticeship contracts. Although timidly at first, the Socialist cabinet also embarked on active manpower policies narrowly defined (see Table 5.3). In 1983, they totaled 12 percent of all expenditure on labor market policies (the rest consisted of unemployment benefits) and 0.25 percent of GDP. They were mostly focused on a rather disparate set of incentive schemes in the private sector. After the social compact of 1984, their volume more than doubled in a single year, and by 1986 they amounted to 0.64 percent of GDP. By 1991 they had reached 1.03 percent of GDP.[23] Their composition changed as well. Around a third still consisted of applying unemployment subsidies to finance workers' entrepreneurial projects (Espina 1991). Yet by 1987–88 almost a fifth of the expenditure in manpower policies was directed to vocational-training programs. Participation in the so-called occupational vocational education scheme (*formación profesional ocupacional*), created in 1985 to train workers in very specific jobs (in contrast to the general skills provided through FP), would quadruple in a few years to reach almost 350,000 people in 1988 (Corugedo et al. 1991).

THE SPANISH PUBLIC BUSINESS SECTOR

RATIONALIZATION OF THE STATE-OWNED BUSINESS SECTOR, 1983–87

In 1982 the González government inherited what, by European standards, was a sizable public enterprise sector, burdened, however, by a vast financial and managerial crisis. A product of nationalistic policies developed in the 1940s and the 1950s to grant the state a major role in promoting the industrialization of the country,[24] by the early 1980s the Spanish state-owned companies accounted for nearly 10 percent of both national value added and total compensation to employees and for almost 15 percent of all gross fixed capital formation. The level of investment supplied by all public companies was significantly higher only in Austria, Greece, Norway, and Portugal and was similar to that in Italy and the United Kingdom. Although overall rather diversified, the Spanish public enterprise sector played a key role in certain productive areas. As shown in Table 5.4, the state had a dominant stake in mining, heavy industries (such as steel, shipbuilding, and aluminum), oil, electricity, telecommunications, railways, and maritime and air transport. In a fragmented industrial system such as the one prevailing in Spain, moreover, the average Spanish public enterprise was bigger than the average Spanish private enterprise[25] and was significantly ahead in terms of exports.[26]

Both the economic shocks and the democratic transition of the 1970s left almost all state-run businesses in disarray. The historically high profits of the Spanish petroleum public sector (grouped within the Instituto Nacional de Hidrocarburos, or INH, since 1981) waned in just a few years. Entire sectors within the biggest public business group – the Instituto Nacional de Industria (INI) –

Table 5.3. *Spanish public expenditure on the labor market, 1983-92*

	AS PERCENT OF GDP	ACTIVE LABOR MARKET POLICIES		
	UNEMPLOYMENT SUBSIDIES	TOTAL	EMPLOYMENT POLICIES[a]	VOCATIONAL TRAINING
1983	1.94	0.25	n.a.	n.a.
1984	2.12	0.24	n.a.	n.a.
1985	2.60	0.31	0.29	0.02
1986	2.59	0.64	0.57	0.07
1987	2.68	0.70	0.55	0.15
1988	2.71	0.74	0.65	0.19
1989	2.66	0.95	0.73	0.22
1990	3.11	0.96	0.74	0.22
1991	3.78	1.03	0.78	0.25
1992 (provisional)	4.53	0.85	0.64	0.21

[a] Includes all incentives for new hirings (except reductions of social security contributions for training contracts), public employment schemes, and the use of employment subsidies to finance workers' own entrepreneurial projects.

Source: Data from Ministerio de Trabajo y Seguridad Social, reproduced in García Perea and Gómez (1993).

Table 5.4. *Relative weight of the Spanish public business sector in the Spanish economy by selected production sectors, 1985*

PRODUCTION SECTOR	PRODUCTION OF PUBLIC COMPANIES AS A PERCENT OF NATIONAL TOTAL IN 1985
Gas	100.0
Radioactive mineral	71.4
Coal	51.0 [a]
Oil production and transformation	50.7
Electricity	24.8 [a]
Aluminum	73.0
Iron and steel	28.6
Shipbuilding	65.0
Air and sea transportation	34.3 [a]
Railways	100.0
Telephone	100.0
Banking	17.1 [b]
Fertilizers	34.5
Potash	67.7
Paper pulp	65.7

[a] 1986

[b] It includes only proportion of total credit to the economy by the group Instituto de Crédito Oficial (ICO).

Sources: Fariñas, Jaumandreu and Mato (1989), Rodríguez López (1989) and INI (several years).

such as air transportation, mining, and steel, which were extremely dependent on worldwide business cycles, registered massive deficits. Both the political uncertainty of the late 1970s and early 1980s, which translated into a lack of clear-cut managerial strategies, and the indiscriminate use of the public sector as a countercyclical instrument had further accelerated the deterioration of the INI's finances. To cushion the impact of the economic crisis during the democratic transition process, the center-to-the-right coalition socialized a large string of loss-making enterprises, mostly in the automotive, steel and shipbuilding sectors. As a whole, INI lost Pta 204 billion in 1983; Pta 131.7 billion of which were from losses incurred by companies nationalized from 1971 to 1981 (García Hermoso 1989). Meanwhile, the main railway company, Red Nacional de Ferrocarriles Españoles (RENFE), posted a deficit of Pta 221 billion. Consequently, even when one adds up strongly lucrative enterprises, such as Telefónica, by 1983 the Spanish public enterprise sector turned out to be highly unprofitable (see Fig. 5.2).

Closer to the Northern European social democratic tradition concerned with welfare policies and the overall goal of social equality than to the one embodied by its Greek and French counterparts in Southern Europe, who favored sweeping nationalizations, the PSOE government pledged not to expand the size of the public enterprise sector any further (Maravall 1992).[27] Instead, it directed its efforts toward rationalizing the public business sector.[28]

The government approved significant investment plans and set up generous programs for the 12,000 workers who were laid off in the steel, shipbuilding, and fertilizer industries. Similarly, it approved specific plans to rationalize particular companies in the areas of military and capital equipment, aluminum, air transportation, coal, and railways (García Hermoso 1989, Rus 1989). Throughout the public business sector, employment was cut over time – by more than a third in RENFE and INI. Apart from the expenses incurred through the adjustment programs, investment grew hardly at all. Total fixed capital formation in public firms went down or remained constant in real terms through 1986 (see Fig. 5.3). State transfers to public corporations were gradually reduced over time from 3 percent of GDP in 1983 to 1.1 percent of GDP in 1991.[29]

Turning public companies into profit-makers also involved trimming slightly the number of public firms through privatization. By 1987 thirty companies (out of almost five hundred) had been sold to the private sector. Those privatizations, however, resulted, not from a political strategy aimed at devolving responsibilities to the private sector, but, in the words of a former INI president, from "criteria of industrial and financial rationality linked to the main goal of INI: the maximization of its assets" (Aranzadi 1989, 258). The state sold either those businesses that were strongly internationalized but for which the public sector seemed to lack the material capacity to ensure their competitiveness in the medium run (such as SKF in the ball-bearing sector and SEAT in the automotive sector) or those that had no strategic interest for the public sector (such as textile industries or tourism operators) (Aranzadi 1989; García Hermoso 1989).[30] The

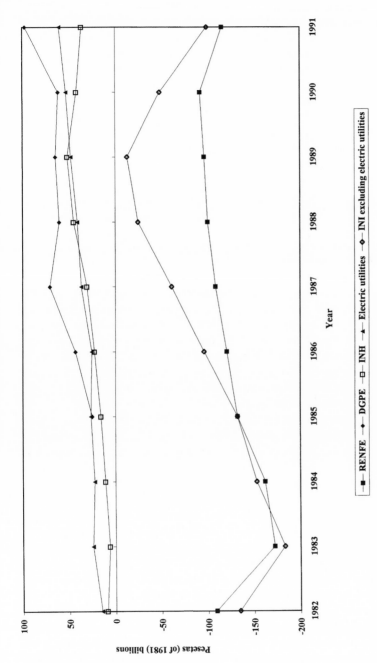

Figure 5.2. Financial results of public business groups in Spain, 1982–91

RENFE ■ DGPE ◆ INH □ Electric utilities ▲ INI excluding electric utilities ◇

Pesetas (of 1981) billions

Year

extent of the privatization process was relatively limited. Apart from SEAT, which employed almost 23,000 workers at the time of its sale, the privatized public companies had around 300 employees on average; a third of them employed fewer than 100 workers. Even after the privatization drive, the number of public companies kept on growing. According to IGAE, the Spanish government accounting office, in 1985 there were 479 state companies. Four years later, their number had increased to 553.[31]

Partly helped by the government strategy of cost containment and internal rationalization but mostly driven by the economic upturn of the second half of the 1980s, the financial balance of public companies improved greatly (see Fig. 5.2). The INI reported Pta 31 billion in profits by 1988. Similarly, from 1983 to 1988 the INH increased its profits sevenfold in real terms.

THE MID- AND LATE 1980S: THE SUPPLY OF CAPITAL AND THE STRATEGY OF INTERNATIONALIZATION

Once the economic pressures on the public budget eased substantially and many state businesses began to report profits in the mid-1980s, the government's strategy toward the public business sector was changed in favor of granting public companies a more active, albeit still selective, role in the economy. On the one hand, capital investment was raised in several sectors controlled by public companies in order to supplement the current fiscal strategy aimed at ensuring high levels of fixed capital formation in Spain. On the other hand, the government decided to turn some public corporations into strong national champions capable of competing abroad, opening new markets for other Spanish businesses, and supplying new technologies to Spain.

Figure 5.3 compares the annual change in real terms in the level of gross fixed capital formation by the general government, by all public enterprises, and by the private sector in the strict sense (i.e., once public enterprises are excluded). Capital formation in the public enterprise sector almost matched that of the private sector until 1986–87. This reflected a period in which public enterprises underwent a thorough process of rationalization in personnel and production systems. Yet from 1987 on, the rate of change in capital investment by public firms accelerated steadily. It first closely followed the pace of growth in capital formation by the general government, only to outstrip it by 1989. In 1988 and 1989, investment by public companies increased over 20 percent in real terms. From 1988 on, the rate of change (in real terms) in capital formation in the public business sector was twice the rate in the private sector.

Matching the general supply-side strategy of the government, the investment effort in the public business sector followed a distinctive pattern. Capital formation was directed toward the telecommunications sector (Telefónica tripled its investment in real terms from 1986 to 1990), internal transportation through railways (the state-owned railway company, RENFE, also tripled its investment in the same time period),[32] oil and gas (INH's investment in 1990

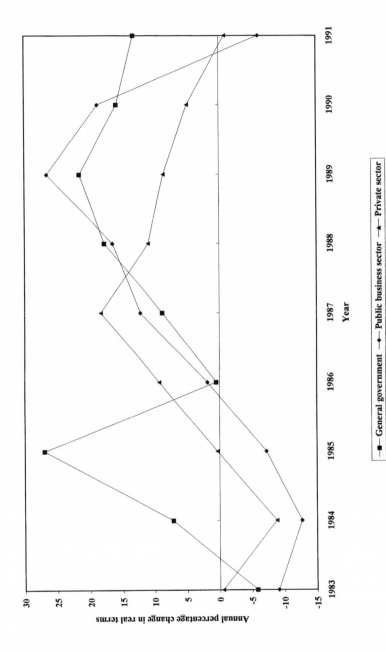

Figure 5.3. Annual change in gross fixed capital formation by sectors in Spain, 1983–91

was 2.5 times larger than in 1986 in real terms), and air and sea transport (investment grew eightfold from 1986 to 1990 in real terms). All other sectors, which included more traditional industries such as steel, mining, aluminum, and shipbuilding, had their rates of investment unchanged or even curtailed (always in real terms). Besides increasing fixed investment, public companies made an important effort in human capital formation: INI doubled its expenditure on research and development to 2 percent of its total sales in those years, putting it above the European average and at a level similar to other big European industrial concerns.

The investment buildup was related in several cases to the cabinet's attempt to launch certain companies into leading positions in the world market. Apart from those enterprises owned by the state, all the Spanish big exporting companies were in international hands. Believing that Spanish medium- and small-sized private companies were unable to reap the benefits of economies of scale, paid no attention to human and technological investment, and lacked comprehensive commercial strategies in foreign markets, the government found it only natural to employ the state to accomplish goals that private agents seemed unwilling or unable to achieve.[33]

To build something akin to a set of "national champions," the government pursued a strategy of rationalization and concentration of business lines around strong companies. After buying shares in several private companies, the electricity subholding company Endesa reinforced its predominant position in the domestic market and became one of the largest six electricity groups in Europe. The electronics sector was organized around Inisel through several mergers and share exchanges, becoming one of the biggest European subholding companies (Espina 1992).[34] In the area of potash production, INI bought Potasas del Llobregat and ended up controlling 88 percent of total national output in this sector. In the area of oil and gas production and distribution, the Spanish government successfully maintained INH in a solid position after the process of European integration injected competition into the sector. The persistent heavy investment and managerial rationalization within INH was completed with new acquisitions at the end of the decade in the gas sector (Gas Madrid and 50 percent of Catalana de Gas) and in the chemical industry (to reinforce REPSOL vertically). Similarly, in 1991 all state banks were merged into CBE (Corporación Bancaria de España – later Argentaria CBE) to form the third-largest banking group in the Spanish financial sector.

The government also promoted a direct strategy of internationalization – through the purchase of foreign firms. The process of internationalization was restricted, however, to a limited number of sectors, such as utilities, transportation, and telecommunications, which seemed to offer bright prospects and in which the Spanish public business sector had, by world standards, a set of medium-size companies. Excluded were declining sectors such as steel or aluminum that faced fierce competition from developing nations and where engaging in a long-term, aggressive industrial policy was out of the question. The public budget was constrained by the goals of deficit containment, direct capital formation, and new social programs. The EC laws on competition left little room for massive public aid.

In 1992 the electricity group Endesa agreed to exchange shares with RWE, a strong German electricity group, to open up new European markets. To become a strong international carrier, the airline company Iberia entered a joint venture with Lufthansa to develop an international charter company, participated in the international reservation system Amadeus, and launched an aggressive medium-term strategy to capture the Latin American market. A substantial investment was made to turn Miami into a vast air hub and Iberia bought stakes to control several South American companies – Viasa, Ladeco, and Aerolíneas Argentinas. Telefónica, the telecommunications company, made similar strenuous efforts to penetrate new countries, such as Argentina, Chile, and Venezuela in the late 1980s and Puerto Rico, Portugal, and Romania in the early 1990s.[35] All these acquisitions led to a significant expansion in the volume of business managed by Telefónica.[36]

As the world business cycle worsened, however, the financial recovery of the state business sector proved to be short-lived. After a period of promising results, INI again posted losses: Pta 86 billion in 1991 and Pta 79 billion in 1992.[37] Excluding the electrical sector, which had been profitable throughout the decade, the industrial group's deficit climbed to more than Pta 200 billion. Two thirds of the losses originated in steel, aluminum, mining, and air transport. As a result, the Socialist government again took a more subdued stance toward the public business sector. As in the previous economic downturn, the goals of containing the public deficit and maintaining welfare expenditure prevailed over channeling more public money into the state-owned business sector.

Following a political struggle within the governmental policymaking elite, the government favored a partial reduction in the role of the public business sector.[38] On the one hand, at the end of 1991 the government decided to split INI into two holding companies. The first group (Inisa, later renamed Téneo), gathering all companies in competitive sectors, was to operate as a commercial company, completely detached from the state budget – a goal that had been previously planned to affect the whole of INI. The second group, called Inise, would include unprofitable firms, such as steel and coal, which would undergo significant restructuring programs – in particular the steel sector, now under a specific subholding, Corporación de la Siderurgia Integral (Téneo 1992).

On the other hand, it was decided that selling parts of the public business sector could offer, from a political point of view, a less costly way of raising revenue to balance the budget.[39] A small part of REPSOL was sold in 1992; another sale, in 1993, reduced the public stake to less than 50 percent. In the spring of 1993, 25 percent of Argentaria (a recent merger of all financial public companies) was also sold to private agents.

CONCLUSIONS

Following its rapid transformation into a standard social democratic party in the late 1970s, and taking advantage of the collapse of the centrist coalition that had managed the democratic transition, the Spanish Socialist Party swept into power in 1982 with the support of a large coalition of middle- and working-class voters. The economic policies that the PSOE developed during the following eleven years broadly corroborate, with evidence of a more historical nature, the findings of the literature on the political management of the business cycle as well as the main theoretical propositions on supply-side economic strategies presented in this book. Governing in an era of highly integrated financial and goods markets, the González government emphasized the need to maintain a stable macroeconomic framework to attract investment and maximize long-term growth. Still, loyal to its social democratic aspirations, it planned to transform the supply side of the economy through increased public savings and massive spending on fixed and human capital to ease the set of structural problems that beset Spain: long-term unemployment and the substantial underdevelopment of vast areas of the country.

The analysis of the Spanish case also provides a first cut on the temporal sequencing and the political dimension underlying the statistical relationships unveiled in the previous two chapters. The combination of macroeconomic stability and the development of interventionist microeconomic strategies can be seen as a way of satisfying the main factions of the governing party. It pleased its moderate wing, which, convinced that the PSOE had to bring Spain back into Europe, championed opening its markets and anchoring its currency to the EC but granted that the state should play a major role in fostering national competitiveness through the state-run business sector and the public provision of productive factors. It appeased most of the radical wing of the party, which stressed the need for aggressive redistributive policies.

The implementation of the Socialist Party's economic strategy was partly contingent on the Spanish economic cycle and on the political support enjoyed by the government. Low levels of economic activity in the first parliamentary term hampered most of the government's investment plans. Taxation increased as planned, and spending on human capital formation was effectively raised. Yet, due to the economic downturn, the public deficit could not be easily contained. The government responded by freezing public fixed capital formation. The public business sector was rationalized, and some of its corporations were sold to private companies. Once the economy started to recover in the mid-1980s and the PSOE renewed its electoral majority in 1986, the government's economic program progressed, however, at a faster pace. Without having to rely on excessively tight policies, inflation eased and the trade deficit declined. The public deficit fell to half its 1982 level by 1987. Total public revenues rose 7.7 percentage points of GDP to 40.1 percent of GDP in 1991. The creation of a public stock of capital became a top priority. Fixed capital formation was doubled, reaching an annual rate of 5 percent of GDP. Human capital formation jumped from 3 to over 5 percent of GDP as well. More public investment was not just the by-product of a generalized pattern of higher spending. Public capital formation was increased by over 4 percentage points of GDP: as a result of the Spanish cabinet's emphasis on public investment, (fixed and human) capital spending went from representing a sixth of all public spending in 1982 to almost a fourth ten years later. Selected parts of the public business sector were also employed to build up a "public stock of capital." Moreover, the government now attempted to transform some key public corporations into "national champions" in foreign markets.

Beyond the impact that the business cycle had on the government's popularity, politics, nonetheless, played a much deeper role in the deployment of González's economic strategies. A divided and radicalized union movement made the reproduction of a corporatist pact impossible after 1986. In the context of a very rigid labor market, which the PSOE was unwilling to reform, González was forced to embrace extremely tight policies to quell inflation. Above all, the Spanish Socialist government faced a major political dilemma between increasing social spending (to meet the demands of workers and leftist voters) and stabilizing taxes (to keep the support of centrist voters). The combination of reluctant union support and some electoral losses would partially thwart the cabinet's investment policy and, above all, strain its supporting electoral coalition. The next chapter will examine in detail the institutional and electoral underpinnings of a social democratic strategy in the open and noncorporatist economy of Spain.

6

THE POLITICAL AND ELECTORAL DIMENSIONS OF THE PSOE'S ECONOMIC STRATEGY

The economic policies developed by the González government closely fit our theoretical expectations (and statistical results) about the policy choices made by social democratic cabinets in an era of highly interdependent economies. In Spain, macroeconomic discipline was given precedence over countercyclical demand management. Inflation was driven down from 14.4 percent in 1982 to 4.8 percent in 1988. The public deficit was cut by half between 1982 and 1987. Within a deflationary framework, the Socialist cabinet directed the public sector to raise the stock of fixed and human capital. Public revenues rose by over a fifth in a decade. Until the late 1980s almost all new revenues were spent on increasing public savings, building infrastructures, and financing education and training programs. Public businesses in key sectors stepped up investment and the government engaged in the formation of several internationally competitive "national champions."

Nevertheless, the PSOE's two-pronged economic strategy of macroeconomic stability and state interventionism was constrained by two factors: in the first place, Spain's industrial relations system and union movement; in the second place, the increasing difficulties González experienced in reconciling the demands of (anti-tax) moderate voters and (pro-spending) radical voters, who had jointly supported him in the first half of the 1980s.

The institutional organization of the Spanish economy, particularly the structure of its labor market, was only partially conducive to the PSOE's most preferred strategy. The construction of a social democratic corporatist regime, in the fashion of Northern European nations, based on ongoing negotiations between government and unions, might have substantially eased the political costs involved in achieving the two main goals of the González government: wage moderation, and hence macroeconomic stability; and a high rate of public investment. But, as shown in the first section of this chapter, the structure of the trade unions and the strategy they followed were not well suited to coordination with the PSOE. An income policy was possible only in 1985–86. As unemployment began to decline and unions urged the government to radicalize its policies, social concertation proved impossible after 1986 and Spain suffered notorious labor unrest and strong wage pressure. From mid-1989 to 1992, nominal wage increases consistently outpaced inflation and productivity gains. The combination of an overheated economy and union aggressiveness forced the cabinet to design restrictive policies to quell demand and inflation.

The conflictive relationship between trade unions and government only magnified the electoral dilemmas that the latter faced in developing its fiscal policy (which I have alluded to in a highly stylized fashion in Chapter 2). As examined in the second and third sections of this chapter, union pressure and the loss of voters to parties further to the left in 1989 forced the government to extend social transfers substantially. New tax increases to finance public transfers threatened to alienate moderate voters from the PSOE. Unwilling to sacrifice its ambitious investment plans to accommodate more social spending without raising taxes, the government gave way to an expansive fiscal policy. This deprived the Socialist cabinet from a key policy lever to quash inflation. González had to rely eventually on a tight monetary policy in order to stick to the European exchange-rate mechanism. Extremely high interest rates – to sustain an overvalued peseta – imposed strong costs on the private sector, making capital more expensive and affecting the export capacity of Spanish enterprises. They would only exacerbate the slowdown of the economy in the early 1990s.

Throughout the decade, the economic strategy of the PSOE was cast to sustain and extend the broad electoral coalition that voted for González in 1982. Accordingly, the commitment to follow prudent macroeconomic policies – to appeal to centrist voters – was combined, as shown in the fourth section, with progressive taxes, redistributive investment plans, and the extension of social spending to improve the material conditions and accelerate the social ascent of the lower and lower-middle classes. Yet, as the last section of this chapter shows, the set of competing demands – on taxes, investment, and social spending – that seized the government's attention beginning in the late 1980s partially strained the electoral standing of the Socialist Party: it eroded the centrist component of the Socialist electoral coalition and skewed its base of support toward the industrial working class, rural areas, and welfare-dependent social sectors.

INSTITUTIONAL BARRIERS TO MACROECONOMIC STABILITY: THE QUESTION OF UNION COOPERATION

Once the Spanish cabinet had chosen to embrace the process of European integration and to combat inflation in order to enhance national competitiveness, it was clear to top government officials that they were left with only two possible policy alternatives.[1] On the one hand, the government could attract unions into a social compact to ensure moderate wage increases and therefore lower inflation. On the other hand, if social concertation were not available, the cabinet would be forced to quell inflation "through either a more restrictive monetary policy, the exchange rate, appreciating the peseta, or a blunt reduction of public expenditure" (Solchaga 1988, 29).

The first alternative was clearly the preferred course of action for the Socialist cabinet. It responded to the traditional social democratic project that entailed the inclusion of the union movement in the policymaking process in order to build strong welfare policies. It avoided harsh monetary policies that could alienate an essential part of the Socialist electorate. And, finally, it had worked well during 1985–86 in reducing inflation and sustaining the economic recovery.[2]

For that purpose, the government made several attempts at social concertation during the decade. In order to control inflation, the government repeatedly asked economic agents to abide by the wage-bargaining system that had been employed since the first national accords were struck in 1978. In exchange for wage moderation, the government promised to negotiate a "social wage" around the "differences in taxation endured by wages and low incomes and by higher incomes; as well as the structure and volume of social expenditure" (Solchaga 1988, 30).

In the negotiating rounds for 1987, however, the Socialist trade union (UGT), which had been instrumental in securing the social agreement of 1985–86, disassociated itself from the governmental project of social concertation. As unionists tirelessly stressed, the social concertation of 1985–86 had resulted in a fall in real wages of almost 1 percentage point. The UGT leaders asked for a wage increase 2 percentage points above the official inflation target of 5 percent for 1987 and urged González to expand demand strongly to absorb unemployment. The clash over macroeconomic policies was compounded by growing disagreements on social policies and on the role of the state in the economy. The UGT pressed the government to comply with its promises concerning unemployment benefits in the 1984 national agreement (AES) and to accept the pension system UGT had drafted. Finally, the UGT called for an increasing public control of all investment through so-called investment funds.

The government was uncompromising. Veering away from what, to date, had been a pattern of wage moderation threatened the government's anti-inflationary policy. Furthermore, in the wake of a recovery in fiscal revenues, the reduction of the public deficit to increase the level of national savings and investment had priority over a boost of public consumption and social transfers. Negotiations quickly soured and a national collective agreement for 1987 turned out to be impossible.[3]

An optimal combination of accelerating growth and falling inflation during 1987 and the first semester of 1988 seemed to make any social compact unnecessary. But inflation, pushed by growing internal demand, bounced back to 5.7

percent at the end of the third quarter of 1988, therefore threatening to broaden the inflation differential with the EC and to upset González's macroeconomic strategy. New negotiations between the cabinet and the unions during the summer of 1988 stumbled over the same obstacles of previous years. Besides, a youth employment and training scheme to subsidize employers to take on school leavers on short-term contracts at the minimum wage was adamantly opposed by the unions. With negotiations in a stalemate, UGT and the Communist union, Comisiones Obreras (CCOO), joined in a one-day general strike in December 1988 to bring the government to its knees and to extract from it a set of social concessions whose cost was estimated to be at least $3.9 billion, or more than 1 percent of the 1988 GDP (Juliá 1988). Given the extraordinary success of the strike, González promptly conceded the cabinet's defeat in Parliament and agreed to both shelve the youth employment plan and adjust pensions and public-sector wages to inflation.

In spite of the increasingly confrontational nature of its relations with the union movement, the government attempted repeatedly to set up a new social agreement to cool down the economy in the following years. A setback in the General Election of October 1989, mostly to the benefit of a loose coalition to the left of the PSOE, which put the Socialist Party one seat below the absolute majority, pressed González to renew his efforts to achieve a grand social pact. Shortly after formal talks were revived at the beginning of 1990, the government made substantial concessions on social issues. In spite of them, all governmental expectations for wage moderation proved illusory. Disregarding calls from the minister of economy to limit wage raises to less than 7.3 percent, all wage settlements averaged 8.3 percent in the first quarter of 1990.

Government plans to unveil a global "competitiveness pact," aimed at stimulating Spanish productivity in the immediate future, were announced by the summer of 1990. The strict opposition of unions forced the cabinet to delay the negotiations on the pact. Pressed by the stringent conditions laid down in Maastricht for the European Union, yet willing to avoid restrictive fiscal and monetary policies, the government eventually presented a new competitiveness pact, called the Social Pact for Progress, in June 1991. The pact insisted that wage increases approximate the rates prevalent in low-inflationary European countries and asked for wage increases to be linked to productivity gains. Yet it now asked for salary reviews to be subject to a common clause in order to guarantee that wage earners would see some increase in real incomes. In a departure from a previous position within the government, it called for a set of controls on distributed profits, which could not grow at a pace higher than wages, and designed favorable tax incentives for those profits reinvested in the company. Although further away from a traditional income pact to control wages, the Social Pact for Progress failed again to attract the trade unions. Wage settlements for 1992 fluctuated around an increase of 7.2 percent, and after a renewed period of confrontations, the unions staged a second one-day general strike in the spring of 1992.

WHY DID COORDINATION PROVE TO
BE IMPOSSIBLE?

Why did a full, prolonged pattern of coordination between the Socialist cabinet and the union movement prove impossible to sustain?

As discussed by Scharpf (1987, 1991), the coordination of social democratic governments (pursuing expansionary policies) and unions (consenting to moderate wage settlements) works to the advantage of both groups. Expansionary policies and wage moderation should deliver full employment without inflation. This outcome is optimal for both groups involved in the deal because it satisfies the working class, does not endanger national economic performance, and does not alienate pivotal middle-class sectors (worried about inflation) away from the social democratic government. In short, it secures the reelection of social democrats and enough jobs for workers at the same time. This result is, however, far from easy to achieve. Although trade unions are well served by it, they always have an incentive, once expansionary demand policies are in place, to take advantage of them by making aggressive wage demands (in the tight labor market that results from the government's policy) in order to obtain both full employment and substantial pay raises.

The pattern of the interaction between unions and governments is made even clearer through its presentation in a more formal manner, employing a simple game structure – reproduced in Figure 6.1. Both social democrats and unions prefer expansionary policies to restrictive measures. Given an expansionary policy, social democratic governments prefer wage moderation to prevent inflation – and its electoral costs. Taking advantage of expansionary policies, unions are, instead, more likely to press for strong wage raises. (The exhaustive ordering of the preferences of both sides is reproduced below the matrix in Figure 6.1.)[4]

Given the way in which their preferences interact, the natural or automatic outcome will be one of expansion and wage aggressiveness (represented in the upper-left cell). In order to achieve the optimal outcome for the social democratic government (expansion and wage moderation), unions have to be drawn into wage moderation. This can only be achieved if the unions are characterized by two traits. First, they must be broad organizations encompassing most of the workforce: this makes them extremely likely to internalize the effects that wage aggressiveness may have on the overall levels of employment. If the opposite is true, that is, if they only organize part of the employed, they have strong incentives to bargain for higher pay, regardless of the consequences that this strategy will have on the number of jobs.[5] Second, unions must be well-organized institutions, with enough resources to keep sectors and firms in line (with the centrally negotiated wage rates) during the wage-bargaining rounds that follow after the negotiations at the national level are over. Without these institutional mechanisms in place, and foreseeing the inflationary costs of expansion, most social democratic governments are likely to shun expansionary policies in the long run.[6]

Neither of these two conditions is met by the Spanish trade unions. In the

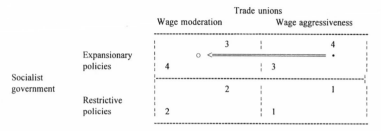

Underlying ordering of preferences according to Scharpf:

	Social Democratic Party	Trade Union
Expansive policy and wage moderation	4	3
Expansive policy and wage aggressiveness	3	4
Restrictive policy and wage moderation	2	2
Restrictive policy and wage aggressiveness	1	1

• Dominant equilibrium.

o Outcome optimal to social democratic government. Possible only under specific institutional conditions.

4 represents the most preferred outcome. 1 represents the least preferred outcome.

Figure 6.1. The interaction of Socialist governments and trade unions in the 1970s

first place, union membership in Spain is low – about 16 percent of all workers – and is mainly concentrated among skilled manual workers with permanent contracts in medium and large companies.[7] As a result, unions are hardly likely to embrace wage restraint in exchange for more employment among temporary and unskilled workers. During the economic expansion of the late 1980s, Spanish skilled workers, who were the first to benefit from supply bottlenecks in the labor market, soon gained political clout and became the main force behind wage aggressiveness (Bentolila and Dolado 1993). It is worth emphasizing that, even though the labor movement is small in size, the Spanish legal framework regulating the system of syndical elections and the collective bargaining process considerably amplifies the unions' power, and hence the interests of "insiders," in both the labor market and the political arena.[8] In the second place, the structure of the wage-setting system itself hinders the capacity of unions to reach and comply with any agreements on wage moderation. Negotiations for annual collective agreements are mostly conducted at the sectoral level (OECD 1992). Unlike wage bargaining at the company level, where any increase in the nominal wage would result in big job losses if no other companies approved the same rise, or at the national level, where the union internalizes the output effect of pay raises, bargainers at the sectoral level generally have few incentives to moderate wage agreements.[9]

The effects of the nature of the Spanish union movement (making social

		Trade unions		
		Wage moderation		Wage aggressiveness
			3		4
	Expansionary				
	policies	4		1	
PSOE					
government			2		1
	Restrictive				
	policies	3		2	

Underlying ordering of preferences in Spain:

	Spanish Socialist Party	Trade Union
Expansive policy and wage moderation	4	3
Expansive policy and wage aggressiveness	1	4
Restrictive policy and wage moderation	3	2
Restrictive policy and wage aggressiveness	2	1

4 represents the most preferred outcome. 1 represents the least preferred outcome.

Figure 6.2. The interaction of the Socialist government and trade unions in Spain

coordination highly unlikely) were reinforced by a change in the policy prefer-ences of the PSOE. The PSOE had been made particularly conscious of the po-litical costs of inflationary growth by the experiences of the British and French Socialist Parties since the oil shock. Although the Spanish Socialist Party still considered a social compact to be the optimal outcome, it now abhorred any wage aggressiveness that could endanger its commitment to balanced growth in the medium run. The organizational weakness of unions only increased the cabinet's skepticism about workers' ability to sustain centralized pacts. Suspecting that unions would be very unlikely to abide by a national income pact, it was rational for the Socialist cabinet to employ a restrictive macroeconomic policy to quell inflation.[10] As Figure 6.2 shows, the change in the policy preferences of the PSOE (i.e., in its preference ordering shown below the matrix) alters substantially the nature of the game between the PSOE and the unions.

In Figure 6.1 there was a stable equilibrium at the upper-right cell (i.e., an expansionary policy followed by aggressive union behavior), which could only be moved to the upper-left cell by having the proper institutional mechanisms. In Figure 6.2, a cycle game takes place. There is no natural and stable equilibrium. Instead, actors move around the cells. This indeed seems to respond well to the cyclical sequences in the history of Spanish income policy since 1982. A quasi-optimal outcome is a corporatist arrangement – the upper-left cell – such as the one in 1985–86. But as soon as unions threaten to ask for higher salaries, the government immediately responds by imposing a restrictive policy and moves the game to one of the worst scenarios for both groups. Given the weak institutional relations that tie the cabinet to the Spanish union movement, ensuring a social compact appears to be self-defeating in the long run.[11]

The confrontational relationship between the PSOE and the trade unions jeopardized the overall economic strategy of the government in two different ways. On the one hand, it deprived the government of an income policy instrument to reduce inflation. Without corporatist agreements, all wage agreements were settled well beyond the official inflation target and, except for 1989, pay increases largely exceeded annual inflation. Real wages grew 2.5 percent in 1990, 2.7 percent in 1991, and 3.4 percent in 1992.[12] With inflation peaking in 1989 and decelerating only slightly in the following years, even as the business cycle entered in its downturn, the government had no choice but to implement stabilization measures.[13]

On the other hand, the confrontation between unions and the PSOE was one of the factors threatening the governmental commitment to a balanced budget, and as the Ministry of Economy struggled to accommodate those social concessions with the planned budget, it altered in part its effort to foster public investment. I pursue this topic at length in the next section.

FISCAL DILEMMAS: SOCIAL SPENDING, TAX RATES, AND THE BUDGET DEFICIT

As discussed briefly in Chapter 5, from 1985–86 to 1989 the government was able to strike a "happy equilibrium" of strong public capital spending and fiscal consolidation. The general government deficit fell from 6.9 percent of GDP in 1985 to 2.8 percent of GDP four years later. The decline in overall net lending was driven more by the spectacular improvement experienced by the Spanish economy in the mid-1980s than by a disciplined fiscal policy. Adjusting for the economic cycle, it is clear that the government designed a restrictive fiscal policy only in 1986 and 1987 (see Table 6.1, last column). Fiscal restraint waned, however, from 1988 on. Even in the presence of a booming economy, the size of the "fiscal impulse" (i.e., the change in the budget balance adjusting for the business cycle) oscillated around 1 percent of GDP for four years in a row.

Up until 1988 all expenditure overruns were comfortably absorbed by unexpectedly high revenues. But from 1989 on, the governmental fiscal strategy underwent considerable strain. The intensifying pressure from unions to increase social spending could have been warded off had the PSOE kept its majority in Parliament. Yet the electoral losses suffered in 1989, which deprived the PSOE of an outright majority, persuaded the cabinet to increase social transfers to avoid losing more popular support. Minimum pensions were raised to the minimum wage level in 1990. Increases on pensions were scaled to favor the lowest income levels. The government established noncontributive pensions. Expenditure on unemployment benefits was sharply expanded from 2.7 percent to 3.8 percent of GDP in three years (Godé 1990; Jiménez Fernández 1990, 1991; Ruiz Alvarez

Table 6.1. *Fiscal policy in Spain, 1988-93*

	AS PERCENT OF GDP		
	GENERAL GOVERNMENT FINANCIAL BALANCE	CHANGE IN THE OVERALL GOVERNMENT BALANCE FROM PREVIOUS YEAR [b]	CHANGE IN THE STRUCTURAL GOVERNMENT BALANCE FROM PREVIOUS YEAR [a,b] (FISCAL IMPULSE)
1988	-3.2	+0.1	+1.5
1989	-2.8	-0.4	+1.2
1990	-3.9	+1.1	+1.0
1991	-4.9	+1.0	+1.0
1992	-4.6	-0.3	n.a.
1993	-7.5	+2.9	n.a.

[a] The change in the structural government balance corresponds to the change in the fiscal deficit that would have taken place if the GDP were to grow at its potential rate. The change in the structural balance therefore shows the net effect of governmental discretionary decisions concerning the budget.

[b] In figures on deficit change, a positive sign means expansionary change and a negative sign represents a restrictive change.

Sources: For the first two columns, IGAE (1993). For the last column, data from González-Páramo and Roldán (1992).

1992; García Perea and Gómez 1993). The expansion of social spending severely jeopardized the governmental budgetary plans. Reversing its slighly downward trend since 1985, total public expenditure rose from 41.1 percent of GDP in 1988 to 43.3 percent of GDP in 1990. Afterward, partly due to a sharp economic downturn, public spending increased quickly, at an annual average of 2 percentage points of GDP during the following three years. By 1993, it amounted to 49.6 percent of GDP.

Since the expansion of social expenditure was done without reducing capital spending, which still constituted the core of the PSOE's economic strategy, higher taxes would have been necessary to avoid a fiscal deficit. Taxes were raised, however, in a limited way. The PSOE reckoned that an increase in taxes could endanger its grip on key centrist voters. As a result, the general government deficit rose from 2.8 percent of GDP in 1989 to 4.9 percent of GDP in 1991 and then to 7.5 percent in 1993 (see Table 6.1). Public debt jumped from 45 percent of GDP in 1991 to 64 percent of GDP in 1994.

The government's incapacity to either restrain social transfers or increase taxes had two important effects. First, it partially thwarted the long-run strategy of sustaining public investment since most of the cuts carried out to compensate for increased social programs were implemented in the area of capital spending.[14] And, second, it forced the Socialist government to rely on a tight monetary policy to achieve its goals.

A TIGHT MONETARY POLICY

Until well into the economic recovery of the mid-1980s, monetary policy played a variable role in the overall economic policy of the González government: tight through 1984 and accommodating in 1985–86 under the Acuerdo Económico y Social with UGT and CEOE. After the summer of 1988, monetary policy came to play a stronger and more distinctive role. Economic and political conditions had clearly changed by that time. While inflation was experiencing an upturn, using social concertation to combat it looked increasingly unpromising. Public authorities eventually decided to raise intervention rates in early September. Further measures adopted in February 1989 to curb private credit and foreign capital inflows sent nominal short-term interest rates up to 15 percent. In real terms the latter were among the highest in Europe – about 5 percentage points above German interest rates (Figure 6.3).

In June 1989, the Spanish government decided to integrate the peseta into the European exchange rate system (ERM). To sustain the commitment to an (implicitly) coordinated monetary policy (with the EC), the integration into the ERM was followed by a package of fiscal measures to reduce the deficit and a temporary set of credit controls. Yet, since the public deficit could not be effectively controlled, monetary policy was left alone to sustain the disinflationary macroeconomic strategy of the Socialist government. Leading to a strong appre-

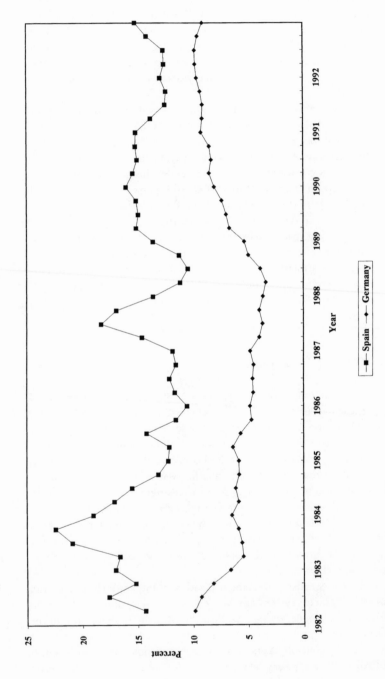

Figure 6.3. Evolution of nominal interest rates in Germany and Spain, 1982–93

ciation of the peseta (whose real exchange rate went up by 44 percent from mid-1983 to mid-1992),[15] the monetary policy necessarily damaged, at least in the short run, the competitiveness of Spanish small- and medium-sized firms abroad.[16]

Even in the face of a sharp downturn in economic activity, interest rates remained extremely high until 1993. Nominal short-term interest rates reached 16 percent at the end of 1989 and then fell to 15 percent throughout 1990. Although inflation and interest rates subsequently fell somewhat, that modest downward trend was reversed in 1992. In spite of declining domestic demand, wage increases and inflation remained high. Then, as the year progressed, a mounting climate of uncertainty over the Maastricht project turned against the ERM. In September 1992 the generalized financial turmoil of European markets put pressure on the peseta. With the government committed to sustaining a tight monetary policy, nominal short-term interest rates jumped to over 15 percent. As the European Monetary System crisis extended over time and the world-wide economic downturn hit Spain, it became apparent that the government was increasingly trapped into implementing a very costly economic strategy. Only a prolonged round of devaluations forced by the international financial markets and the clear loss of the Socialist majority in 1993 would finally compromise monetary discipline and therefore break up the strained equilibrium of political pressures and competing policies that had characterized the González government since the mid-1980s.

BUILDING A SOCIAL DEMOCRATIC COALITION: THE REDISTRIBUTIVE PROFILE OF THE PSOE'S POLICIES

As first explored in theoretical terms in Chapter 2, all governments design their economic strategy to serve two central goals: responding to the concerns of their main constituencies – the redistribution of wealth and the creation of employment in the case of the center-to-the-left Spanish electorate; and expanding their electoral base.

The PSOE government deliberately developed its economic and political strategy to consolidate the vast coalition stretching from the political center to the traditional left that supported González in 1982, in the way social democratic governments have managed to do in other European countries (Martin 1979; Esping-Andersen 1985; Pontusson 1988). In order to appeal to centrist and white-collar sectors, and in spite of the extensive degree of trade union opposition this generated, the González government committed itself to a strong market economy within Europe and prudent macroeconomic policies. At the same time, it pushed for substantial tax increases and approved strong investment plans with a highly redistributive bent to improve the lives of the less qualified workers and the most underdeveloped regions. Finally, the expansion of social benefits, in the form of universal health care and higher pensions, was aimed at welding both middle and lower classes to the government's social democratic project.

The significant increase in tax collection achieved under the PSOE was mostly implemented through a very progressive personal income tax. This had significant redistributive effects. In 1982 the Gini index of Spanish income distribution was 0.331 before taxes and 0.304 after taxes. In 1990, it was 0.416 before taxes and 0.367 after taxes. That is, even though the initial distribution of declared income had become more unequal, the redistributive effect of the income tax system had increased (Lasheras, Rabadán, and Salas 1993).

The aggressive buildup of fixed capital stock, mostly in the form of ambitious infrastructure projects, was unequally distributed across regions according to two factors: purely redistributive concerns in favor of the least-developed areas and the level of support for the party in government. For the period 1987–92, the central government spent Pta 106,000 per inhabitant in the whole country on nonmilitary investment (in 1990 pesetas). Whereas the central government spent less than Pta 30,000 per inhabitant in public investment in the Balearic Islands and the Basque Country, and around Pta 40,000 per inhabitant in Catalonia and Navarre, it allocated more than Pta 110,000 per capita in Andalusia, Castille–La Mancha, Extremadura, and Murcia.

Table 6.2 reproduces the statistical analysis of the factors that affected the territorial allocation of public capital formation. The dependent variable is the volume of nonmilitary investment by the central government from 1987 to 1992 per person (measured in 1990 pesetas) in each of the seventeen Spanish regions. Since the constitutional devolution of power to regional governments that took place in the 1980s was dissimilar and led to different levels of administrative and budgetary autonomy across regions, and since it is highly likely that the investment decisions by the central government were influenced by that varying degree of autonomy, I have introduced a dummy variable in all the calculations to control for the legal and constitutional rank of each region. This variable takes three values: 0 for regions with low autonomy, 1 for regions enjoying medium levels of autonomy, and 2 for highly autonomous regions.[17] As expected, the empirical analysis shows that the lower the level of autonomy, the larger the volume of investment assumed by the central government: with each step of higher autonomy, public investment by the central government decreases by around Pta 25,000 per capita.

Yet it is clear that the flow of public investment responded to the long-term goal of overcoming underdevelopment as well as to the structure of political support of the PSOE. The level of regional per capita income (in 1985) is negatively correlated to public capital formation.[18] According to the results reported for Model 1, for each Pta 100,000 of per capita income, the government decreased its investment by Pta 11,480. For example, Extremadura, whose per capita income in 1985 (Pta 496,202) was two-thirds the Spanish per capita income, re-

Table 6.2. *Political determinants of the regional distribution of public gross fixed capital formation in Spain, 1987-92*

NONMILITARY INVESTMENT PER CAPITA BY THE CENTRAL GOVERNMENT
IN 1987-92 (IN CONSTANT PESETAS OF 1990)

INDEPENDENT VARIABLES	MODEL 1	MODEL 2
Constant	99,742.0 (67,448.4)	108,977.0* (53,645.4)
Regional per capita income [a]	-114.8* (45.0)	-74.2 (51.9)
Socialist vote in 1982-86 [b]	1,778.7** (1,007.7)	
Socialist membership [c] per inhabitant		9,185.9* (4,265.2)
Level of autonomy [d]	-25,460.8* (10,079.1)	-25,261.4* (9,325.8)
R²	0.729	0.753
Corrected R²	0.667	0.695
Number of observations	17	17

[a] Regional per capita income in 1985 in current pesetas.

[b] Socialist vote in 1982-86: Average of the proportions of PSOE votes among total ballots cast in the 1982 and 1986 General Elections.

[c] Socialist membership: Members of PSOE per 1,000 inhabitants in April 1984. Own estimates based on data presented in Puhle (1986).

[d] 2= Basque Country. Navarre. 1=Andalusia, Canary Islands, Catalonia, Galicia, Valencia; 0= Rest of regions.

Estimation: OLS.
Standard errors in parentheses.
* Statistically significant at 0.05 or less.
** Statistically significant at 0.1 or less.

ceived around Pta 27,000 per capita (or around 25 percent of the average level of investment) more than regions with the national-average per capita income (but the same political characteristics as Extremadura), and Pta 64,000 per capita more than the richest Spanish region, the Balearic Islands (whose per capita income was Pta 1,045,445 in 1985).

The allocation of public capital was also partly driven by electoral and partisan concerns. The average proportion of the Socialist vote in 1982–86 alone explains 49.6 percent of all the variation in public capital formation in the following five years (this result is not shown in Table 6.2).[19] Controlling for per capita income, the statistical strength of the Socialist vote weakens (Model 1).[20] Nonetheless, a primarily internal factor such as the level of militancy and the weight that each territorial group has within the governing party played an even stronger role than the electoral success of the PSOE in the allocation of new public capital. The ratio of Socialist membership to population (which oscillates from 9 members per 1,000 inhabitants in Extremadura to 2 in Catalonia) alone explains 60 percent of all the variation in central government investment (the result is not reproduced here).[21] When regressed jointly with the level of autonomy and per capita income, it continues to play a strong role – to the extent that per capita income loses all statistical power (Model 2).

Straight redistributive goals dominated social spending as well. Social expenditure went up from 25.3 percent of the disposable household income in 1980 to 33.7 percent ten years later. Contributive pensions were upgraded and to some extent equalized, and new categories, such as noncontributive pensions, were created. Unemployment benefits were extended to cover more than half of the registered unemployed by 1991. Health coverage was improved and expenditure on public education increased more than any other item excluding fixed capital formation. The allocation of new expenditure was extremely progressive. Public expenditure as a proportion of the average consumption of the lowest income decile went from 119.2 percent in 1980 to 204.3 percent in 1990. For the fifth income decile, it went up from 48.4 percent to 75.1 percent. For the top income decile it hardly changed: public expenditure represented 31.0 percent of the average consumption in that income fraction in 1980 and 36.6 percent ten years later (Gimeno 1993).

The redistributive strategy of the PSOE government had an undeniable impact on how Spanish citizens judged the government's tax and expenditure policies – and, as shown in the following section, on their electoral realignment over the decade. In July 1991 56 percent of all surveyed thought they were paying more in taxes than what they were receiving in public services. That proportion reached 92 percent among businessmen and top managers and 69 percent among midmanagerial positions. Among industrial workers it was 56 percent – that is, the national average. Instead, only 40 percent of retired people and 33 percent of agricultural workers said that they were receiving less than what they had paid. A similar gap appeared in relation to income level. Whereas 72 percent of those earning more than Pta 200,000 every month said they were receiving less than they were paying, among those earning less than Pta 50,000, the percentage was only 36 percent.[22]

THE FORTUNES OF THE PSOE'S ELECTORAL COALITION

The redistributive policies of the González government and the mix of macro-economic imbalances of the early 1990s – derived from the conflict between strong demands for more social spending from the PSOE's leftist electors and the growing opposition to higher levels of taxation from the political center – clearly affected the character of the Socialist electoral coalition. Although the PSOE consistently led in the polls throughout the 1980s, its electoral base suffered a steady erosion over time. After receiving the vote of 37.7 percent of all the electorate in 1982, the aggregate electoral performance of the PSOE worsened quickly. Both the harsh period of adjustment through 1984, which drove un-employment from 17 percent in 1982 to 21.5 percent in 1985, and a flip-flopping policy toward NATO reduced the Socialist vote to 30.6 percent of all the electorate (or 44.4 percent of valid votes) in the elections of 1986, mostly ben-efiting the radical Left and increasing abstention again. The Socialist vote further declined to 27.6 percent of the electorate (or 39.5 percent of valid votes) three years later. In 1993, however, after an aggressive campaign that mobilized leftist sectors of the electorate that had tended to abandon the PSOE for the abstention camp (Arango and Díez 1993), support for the PSOE tilted slightly upward to 29.8 percent of the electorate. Still, its lead of 17 points over the second-placed party in 1982 had declined to 3 points.

Sources of support for the PSOE also underwent some change. Support for the PSOE remained relatively high among traditional blue-collar workers. But it fell sizably among urban middle classes. The PSOE instead grew more de-pendent on voters from rural, agricultural, underdeveloped areas and on state-dependent populations (such as the unemployed and pensioners).

To examine the evolution of electoral preferences and the impact of economic and social policies and outcomes of the González government, I employ two different procedures. First, I examine the evolution of the Socialist vote from 1982 to 1993 through an aggregate, ecological analysis. Second, I compare the proportion of Socialist vote across different social and economic categories ac-cording to the postelectoral surveys of 1982 and 1993.[23]

EVOLUTION AT THE PROVINCIAL LEVEL

The ecological analysis of the evolution of the Socialist vote from 1982 to 1993, carried out using data gathered at the provincial level, already points to a sig-nificant shift in its composition. Although the level of Socialist support declined in almost all Spanish provinces, the extent of the decline was rather divergent.

In a small number of provinces, support for González actually increased over time, in some cases by more than 5 percentage points (as a proportion of the whole electorate) in absolute terms. At the other end of the scale, in populous, heavily urbanized, and manufacturing or service-oriented districts, such as Barcelona, Madrid, and Valencia, the Socialist vote dropped more than 10 percentage points in absolute terms – or around a quarter of the 1982 vote in relative terms.

Figure 6.4 presents, for all 50 provinces, the percentage of the workforce employed in the primary sector (horizontal axis) and the change of the Socialist vote (as the difference between the percentage obtained in 1982 and the support won in 1993), and reveals that the PSOE fared especially well in the most rural areas. In all provinces where the primary sector employed (in 1989) more than 20 percent of the workforce, the reduction of support for the PSOE was lower than the loss suffered at the national level.

Figure 6.5 depicts in turn the effect of the volume of net public transfers on the Socialist vote. Public transfers are here estimated as the difference between the gross provincial product per capita (GPP) and the so-called disposable family income per capita (DFI).[24] Although the relationship between the evolution of the Socialist vote and the volume of public transfers is less sharp than the one between Socialist vote and agricultural employment, it stills points clearly to the structure of the Socialist vote in 1993.

More stringent results, obtained through regression analysis, are shown in Table 6.3. In Model 1 I show (mainly for purposes of comparison with Model 2) that the fall in Socialist support is related, although only partly, to the initial level of support in 1982. The result implies that for each percentage point of vote in 1982, the PSOE experienced a decline of a third of a point during the decade. In the second model, the evolution of the Socialist vote is explained by the initial level of support in 1982, the proportion of workers in the primary sector, the volume of public transfers, and the proportion of the provincial population living in towns with over 100,000 inhabitants. The total variance explained by these variables is a striking 82 percent. According to this result, within a general framework of decline, each percentage point employed in the primary sector resulted in an increase of the Socialist vote by 0.175 points. This means that in a province in which 30 percent of the active population is employed in the primary sector, the PSOE received 5 percentage points more than in a province with no primary sector. In contrast, neither service nor industrial employment, alone or in combination, has any explanatory power on the evolution of the Socialist electorate (the statistical results have not been included here). The volume of public transfers bolsters the vote for the PSOE as well. Each (standardized) point of net benefits increases the vote by 0.1 percentage points. According to this result, 2.34 percentage points in the increase in support for the PSOE in Zamora (from 1982 to 1993) derive from the extraordinary level of transfers poured into this province by the government. In turn, the PSOE lost 2.1 percentage points in Madrid due to the extent of disposable income sacrificed by this province – to finance other areas

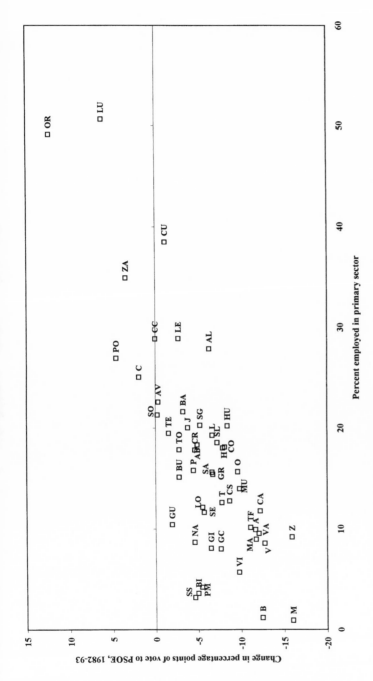

Figure 6.4. The ruralization of the PSOE, 1982–93

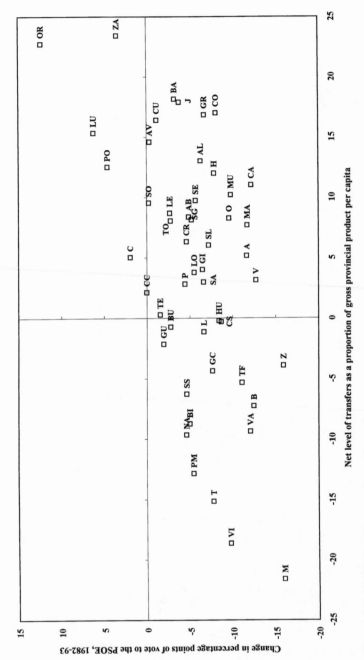

Figure 6.5. Level of public transfers and vote for the PSOE, 1982–93

Table 6.3. *Social and economic determinants of the evolution of the PSOE's vote from 1982 to 1993*

INDEPENDENT VARIABLES	VOTE LOST BY PSOE, 1982-93 [a]	
	MODEL 1	MODEL 2
Constant	7.876* (2.492)	-2.461 (2.461)
Percent vote for PSOE in 1982	-0.379* (0.068)	-0.301* (0.046)
Per cent employed in the primary sector (in 1989)		0.175* (0.055)
Volume of public transfers [b]		0.100* (0.043)
Percent population living in cities with over 100,000 inh.		-0.055* (0.018)
R^2	0.391	0.832
Corrected R^2	0.378	0.817
Number of observations	50	50

[a] Calculated as the difference in percentage of votes of total electorate between 1982 and 1993.

[b] Volume of public transfers: Difference between the gross provincial product per capita and disposable family income per capita. Both measures are standardized (in relation to the national mean) and for 1991.

Estimation: OLS.
Standard errors in parentheses.
* Statistically significant at .05 or less.

of Spain.[25] Finally, the proportion of urban population has an independent and statistically significant impact.

EVOLUTION ACROSS SOCIAL SECTORS

Table 6.4 presents a second analysis of the evolution of the Socialist vote during the 1980s. It reproduces the proportion of the electorate that voted for the PSOE and for the conservative party, Alianza Popular (AP; later Partido Popular, PP), in 1982 and 1993 according to different social categories. The balanced pattern of support for the PSOE in 1982 gave way to a more fragmented, polarized vote eleven years later. In 1982, the level of support for the PSOE across social sectors did not fall below four-fifths of 37.3 percent, the national average. The only exceptions were the oldest age cohort (where the Socialist vote was 30 percent, or three-fourths of the national vote for the PSOE), university-educated voters, nonsalaried employees (where the Socialist vote was less than two-thirds the average in other groups), and practicing Catholics.

In 1993, the disparity in electoral behavior had widened and the support for González had become fragmented and strongly divergent. The PSOE had clung successfully to its natural stronghold: 40 percent of the workers in the industry and service sectors voted for González in 1993, somewhat fewer than eleven years before but still well over the national average. Among agricultural workers, support for the PSOE increased from 41 percent in 1982 to 43 percent; within this group the PSOE obtained a huge lead among temporary workers. The PSOE secured significant support among welfare recipients, who had been directly favored by the expansion of resources for social policies in the late 1980s. The vote remained stable among retired people who had held a job before. Although the unemployed had abandoned González in huge numbers, those who had held a job previously (and hence were likely to receive unemployment benefits) were still trusting the Socialist government; 33 percent voted PSOE in 1993 (another 12 percent voted for the radical Left, Izquierda Unida). A very different pattern appears among those unemployed searching for jobs for the first time (and thus unable to get unemployment benefits); only 18 percent voted for the PSOE in 1993.

White-collar employees, however, deserted the Socialist Party. Among the highest educational levels, support for the PSOE was almost half the national average. Most notably, the Socialist vote was a third of the national average among professionals and a half among both top managers and white-collar employees. The erosion of Socialist support was also substantial among the blue-collar elite of foremen and supervisors; 55 percent voted for González in 1982, but only 25 percent did so in 1993.

In terms of the ideological self-location of the voter, the PSOE was able to maintain its support among those on the left. More significantly, among center-to-the-left voters (those in position 5 on the left–right scale from 1 to 10), who represent the largest segment in the Spanish electorate, support for the PSOE declined from 40 percent to 27 percent.

CONCLUSIONS

This chapter and Chapter 5 have put us in a position to understand the purely economic and the political dimensions of a social democratic strategy – especially in a period of increasing economic interdependence – to achieve growth, full employment, and equality. The Spanish experience corroborates the literature on social democratic corporatism. Unless they can count upon a highly organized labor movement, left-wing governments progressively abandon expansionary policies to fight unemployment. Moreover, the Spanish case shows that the social democratic road to macroeconomic discipline is a notoriously bumpy one. The British Labour Party endured several electoral defeats before it dumped Keynesian recipes in the late 1980s. The French Left suffered something akin to an identity crisis (as well as the electoral setback of 1986) as it embraced the doctrine of the *"franc fort"* in the mid-1980s. In Spain, the González government never discarded the possibility of striking a deal with the union movement to secure low wage increases in exchange for full employment measures. But the incentive structure of the small and radicalized Spanish trade unions was seldom aligned with the goals of the PSOE government. A corporatist pact was only possible in 1985–86 in response to a critical economic downturn. As the economy overheated and the labor market tightened up in the late 1980s, any chances of a social pact waned, and the Socialist government could only use interest rates to choke inflation and sustain the peseta.

Social democracy is then, above all, public investment. Public expenditure rose by a fourth under the González government. Two-thirds of the increase was allocated to raise public savings as well as fixed and human capital formation. Key public firms were asked to join the effort to revamp the supply side of the Spanish economy. Notice that some of the statistical results of Chapters 3 and 4 (particularly on public fixed capital formation) help us interpret the Spanish experience as a specific instance of a more general pattern. Social democratic governments that rule in noncorporatist countries are especially hard-pressed (relative to socialist cabinets in corporatist nations) to pursue public investment policies to compensate for their incapacity to expand the economy.

The economic strategy of high taxes and public investment (and generous social transfers) maintained González in power for sixteen years (the last three with the external support of centrist regionalist parties). Although the PSOE lost part of its massive support of 1982, it consistently polled close to two fifths of the vote through the mid-1990s. Among blue-collar workers and the rural "proletariat" of temporary workers, the PSOE received 60 percent of the votes cast (or over 40 percent of the total electorate). Support was almost as high among pensioners and the unemployed receiving state benefits. In 1993 the PSOE continued to lead the Spanish center-to-the-right party among lower-middle classes with a small advantage.

The Spanish case also highlights the tensions underlying the social democratic project of high taxes and high public investment rates – tensions that, as

Table 6.4. *Proportion of PSOE and AP/PP vote in 1982 and 1993 according to social conditions*

	IN 1982		IN 1993	
	PERCENT VOTING PSOE	PERCENT VOTING AP	PERCENT VOTING PSOE	PERCENT VOTING PP
ACTUAL TOTAL VOTE	38	20	30	27
TOTAL VOTE ACCORDING TO SURVEY	39	12	31	21
DIFFERENCE BETWEEN ACTUAL AND REPORTED VOTE	+1	-8	+1	-6
AGE				
18-24	50	13	23	20
25-34	44	13	28	18
35-44	40	12	33	21
45-54	34	11	30	25
55-64	33	12	37	24
65 or more	30	12	36	18
EDUCATION LEVEL				
Less than primary schooling	38	13	35	19
Primary schooling	40	12	31	20
High school	44	12	22	22
Less than university	31	12	19	34
University	30	12	18	32
LEVEL OF URBANIZATION				
Less than 2,000 inh.	39	16	35	24
2,001 to 10,000 inh.	32	12	29	25
10,001 to 50,000 inh.	39	10	35	15
50,001 to 100,000 inh.	41	18	35	16
100,001 to 400,000 inh.	39	14	28	23
400,001 to 1,000,000 inh.	37	11	23	25
More than 1,000,000 inh.	44	10	30	19

Table 6.4. *Proportion of PSOE and AP/PP vote in 1982 and 1993 according to social conditions (continuation)*

	IN 1982		IN 1993	
	PERCENT VOTING PSOE	PERCENT VOTING AP	PERCENT VOTING PSOE	PERCENT VOTING PP
WORKING STATUS				
Active Population	42	13	29	24
Not Active				
Students	39	6	18	25
Unemployed	55	11	30	15
* lost job	n.a.	n.a.	33	14
* searching for first time	n.a.	n.a.	18	18
Retired	39	12	37	18
*working before	n.a.	n.a.	41	17
*household occupation before	n.a.	n.a.	25	23
Household occupation	32	12	34	19
OCCUPATIONAL STATUS				
(1) Nonsalaried:				
Professionals	24	21	12	44
Business owners with employees	28	28	22	38
Business owners without employees				
* in industry and services	24	23	24	25
* in agriculture	26	17	29	28
(2) Salaried. White-collar				
Top managers	36	11	14	34
Mid-level managers	24	22	22	28
White-collar employees (clerks, etc.)	42	11	17	30
Salesmen	44	11	27	17
Low nonmanual employees	35	14	27	18

153

Table 6.4. *Proportion of PSOE and AP/PP vote in 1982 and 1993 according to social conditions (continuation)*

	IN 1982 PERCENT VOTING PSOE	IN 1982 PERCENT VOTING AP	IN 1993 PERCENT VOTING PSOE	IN 1993 PERCENT VOTING PP
OCCUPATIONAL STATUS (cont.)				
(3) Salaried. Blue-collar				
Foremen, supervisors	55	14	25	25
Workers in industry and services	n.a.	n.a.	40	12
* skilled	49	7	n.a.	n.a.
* unskilled	45	7	n.a.	n.a.
Workers in agriculture	41	6	43	12
* With fixed contracts	n.a.	n.a.	33	17
* With temporary contracts	n.a.	n.a.	46	11
RELIGIOSITY				
Practicing catholic	29	18	27	33
Nonpracticing catholic	50	8	37	15
Indifferent/nonbeliever	51	3	26	6
Other religions	50	0	24	16
LEFT-RIGHT SCALE [1]				
Far left 1	37	1	40	1
Left 2	44	0	38	2
3	60	0	54	1
Center-to-the-left 4	60	2	62	4
5	40	9	27	21
Center-to-the-right 6	13	37	13	47
7	4	51	3	64
Right 8	6	57	4	75
9	1	60	4	92
Far right 10	6	47	0	68

All data as proportions of all surveyed (no-responses included).

Sources: Own estimations based on CIS survey no. 1327 (postelectoral survey) for the 1982 General Election, and CIS survey no. 2062 (June 1993, monthly barometer) for the 1993 General Election.

[1] Data for 1982 taken from Gunther (1986), table 2.1, p. 46.

stressed in Chapter 2, may have increased as a result of the growth of middle-class voters in postindustrial economies and as a result of structural shocks that have eroded the relative position of the most unskilled workers. In a country with a relatively unskilled workforce (the levels of educational attainment in Spain are low relative to other European countries), it made economic sense to intensify all capital formation efforts to avoid the trap of an excessively high social wage. Yet the almost exclusive focus on public investment until 1989 (to the detriment of public transfers) had important political costs. A severe general strike in 1988 demanding more social spending threatened to ruin the macro-economic strategy pursued by the government and to alienate important parts of the industrial working class from the government. In the 1989 parliamentary elections the PSOE's share of the vote dropped from 43.4 to 40.3 percent. The radical Left more than doubled its vote, from 4.6 to 9.2 percent. González responded by increasing social spending along with public capital formation. Since taxes could not be substantially increased without losing centrist voters, the public deficit began to rise rapidly. The resulting expansionary fiscal policy only reinforced the need to tighten monetary policy.

A decade-long period of tough tax policies, generous investment projects and social programs, and high interest rates partly reshaped the electoral coalition supporting the government. González did keep the support of the traditional working class: the blue-collar workers in the industrial and service sectors. The expansion of the welfare state and the active role of the state in building infra-structures and providing services furthered the position of the PSOE in the most underdeveloped areas, in the less favored sectors, and among those individuals most dependent on public transfers (the unemployed and the retired). In exchange, high taxes, unfulfilled expectations about the level and quality of serv-ices, harsh macroeconomic policies, and a string of corruption scandals eroded the Socialist support in urban areas, among the most educated, and probably in the most competitive, export-oriented areas.

TURNING AROUND THE POSTWAR CONSENSUS: DEFINING A CONSERVATIVE ECONOMIC FRAMEWORK IN BRITAIN

The same economic shocks of the 1970s that propelled the spectacular electoral victories of Socialist parties in Southern Europe led to a generalized shift to the Right among Northern European and American voters. The American Democratic Party suffered an embarrassing defeat at the hands of a resurgent Republican Party in 1980. Socialists were displaced by a coalition of Christian Democrats and Liberals in Belgium in 1981 and in the Netherlands and Germany in 1982. In Scandinavia the traditional hegemony of social democracy in both ideas and votes started to unravel for the first time in decades. Yet the most severe defeat of the Left took place in Britain. In May 1979 the strongest turnaround of public opinion since 1945 returned the Conservative Party to office. Helped by an impressive lead over a split Labour Party, the Tory Party would enjoy a comfortable parliamentary majority for the following decade and a half.

The prolonged British Tory government makes it possible to examine the systematic implementation of a conservative economic strategy, providing therefore a pointed contrast with the Spanish Socialist experience. After a long period in search of "true Conservative solutions" (Behrens 1980) to the declining British economy, which included the failed reformist attempt under Heath in the early 1970s, by the late 1970s the Conservative leadership was definitely committed to effecting a clean break with the postwar consensus built around the active involvement of the state in the economy. The Tory Party attributed the steady rise in unemployment during the 1970s to the deterioration suffered by the supply conditions of the economy, where an oversized public sector and a petrified labor market had stifled individual initiative. The inflationary pressures of the period were thought to stem, in turn, from an undisciplined public sector that accommodated the wage claims and price rises of the private sector. Accordingly, the Thatcher government devised a two-pronged economic strategy. On the one hand, it decided to establish a set of stable policy rules to make credible its commitment to quell inflation. Moreover, abandoning any attempt to stimulate demand, it planned to make fiscal policy consistent with, and reinforce the credibility of, the new monetary strategy. On the other hand, the Conservative cabinet understood that monetary discipline alone could not restore economic growth. Even after achieving price stability, the economy would remain operating close to potential output and to (a rather high) natural rate of unemployment. A tight monetary policy only functioned as a necessary precondition for a medium-term strategy focused on the supply side of the economy. From a Conservative perspective, growth and more employment could come only after cutting government claims on private resources, reducing the disincentive effects of high marginal tax rates, and reforming the labor market.[1]

The analysis of the British case mirrors the purposes and the presentational strategy (and organization) of the two chapters devoted to the Spanish Socialist government. This chapter begins by examining the point of departure of the Tory Party, that is, the gradual radicalization of its program in response to the growing economic trade-offs that Britain faced in the 1970s. It then proceeds to describe both the demand-side and the supply-side strategies of the Tory cabinet. The second section examines the fiscal and monetary measures adopted by the Thatcher government to break down inflationary expectations in the early 1980s, and includes a brief survey of their development through the early 1990s. The rest of the chapter sheds light on the most innovative dimension of the Tory government: the transformation of the structural conditions of the British economy.

As in the case of Spain, this chapter fleshes out the quantitative evidence gathered in Chapters 3 and 4 by detailing how public investment and public subsidies were cut, public enterprises were privatized, and the tax system reformed. Moreover, it introduces new information that completes our understanding of a conservative economic strategy: it discusses the deregulation of the labor market, the transformation of the educational and vocational-training system, and the changes introduced in the legal framework of industrial relations. Set in comparison with the Spanish case, the evolution of the Tory Party and of the British economy provides further detailed evidence that there might be increasing divergence, rather than convergence, in the advanced world in the area of economic policymaking. Finally, this chapter offers the platform to explore the electoral dynamics of a conservative economic strategy, a task mainly performed in Chapter 8. As in Chapter 5 for the Spanish case, the present chapter highlights, however, how the fluctuations of the business cycle, by making the employment–equality trade-off more dramatic, convinced the government to postpone part of its package of reforms.

THE RENEWAL OF THE CONSERVATIVE PROGRAM: A RESPONSE TO ECONOMIC DECLINE AND ELECTORAL CHANGE

A general commitment to the principles of liberty and the system of free enterprise constitutes the backbone of modern Toryism (Beer 1969, 1982; Särlvik and Crewe 1983; Heath, Jowell, and Curtice 1985).[2] Nevertheless, within this broad consensus, the Conservative Party has traditionally encompassed several ideological currents, divided on the precise role the state should play in a market economy (Douglas 1989). Each of them has been dominant at different periods of time, depending on the Conservative Party's capacity to manage the economy successfully and to sustain an electoral majority.

The memory of the Depression and the war, and the need to overcome the reputation, earned in the 1930s, of being the party of unemployment, threw the Conservative Party into the arms of Keynesian demand management and limited public intervention during the first part of the postwar period (Beer 1969; Hall 1986). This consensual approach to economic management remained acceptable to the Conservative Party only as long as growth was robust and the unemployment–inflation trade-off was at most marginal. When productivity dwindled, inflation crept up, and the general performance of the British economy declined in the 1960s, the Conservative Party no longer had any incentive to pursue expansionary and interventionist policies (Begg 1987). Accordingly, the Tory Party leaned again toward those in favor of an unimpeded market economy and a small public sector. In 1970 it approved the Selsdon Park Program, which called for the reform of the industrial relations system, a change in the structure of taxation to reward private initiative, and a hand-offs approach to industrial policy (Keegan 1984). The initial tough stance adopted by Heath, after winning office that same year, proved to be too costly from an electoral point of view, and by 1972 the Conservative government embarked on an extraordinary policy U-turn. A sizable fiscal expansion was engineered. Rolls-Royce and Upper Clyde Shipbuilders were rescued by the government. And a statutory income policy was introduced to secure the cooperation of the private sector needed to sustain a Keynesian strategy.

The two resounding electoral defeats of February and October 1974 definitively turned the Tory Party toward a new party leadership as well as new ideas based on the rejection of the postwar consensus. Preceded by a raging attack of the Heath policies by Sir Keith Joseph in the countdown to the October 1974 General Election, Margaret Thatcher was elected new parliamentary leader in February 1975. During the following years, first in opposition, and then in government, Thatcher gradually led the Tory Party to adhere to a noninterventionist economic program (Behrens 1980; Keegan 1984).

The Conservative success in building a fresh policy alternative was based, above all, upon Thatcher's capacity to develop a general political discourse that, in addressing the causes of the long-term decline of Britain and the accelerating deterioration of the 1970s, provided an authoritative position regarding the role of the state in a modern democracy. Public intervention – in the form of high taxation, excessive public expenditure, vast subsidies, and countercyclical management – was judged to be responsible for the feeble condition of the economy, in the form of low growth rates relative to other advanced nations, accelerating inflation, and rising unemployment. Moreover, state interventionism was purported to suffocate individual liberty, leading to a society whose members had given up all their individual economic and social responsibilities.[3]

The development and reception of like-minded theories among economists reinforced the political ascendancy that laissez-faire approaches were gaining within Conservative ranks as a result of the political and economic turbulence of the period. Once the available Keynesian models seemed unable to solve the stagflation crisis gripping the British economy, the competing paradigm of monetarism spread among economists and financial journalists and was warmly embraced by Thatcher and her followers (Hall 1992, 1993). Predicting that expansionary policies only led to accelerating inflation and larger public deficits without any effect on the economy's real variables, monetarism provided a cogent theoretical explanation for the disappointing equilibrium of high inflation and high unemployment in which Britain was trapped in the mid-1970s. Accordingly, it justified abandoning demand-management policies and reinforced the outspoken rejection of any income policy among Conservative politicians. Since inflation was a purely monetary phenomenon, the state should simply secure a stable supply of money while deregulating the labor market to ease its operation.

The radical Conservative program came to life amid a shifting climate in public opinion. Since the mid-1960s, class voting had declined among the British electorate (Särlvik and Crewer 1983);[4] party identification had progressively dropped (Särlvik and Crewer 1983; Alt 1984; Miller et al. 1990); and electoral volatility had increased. Electoral dissatisfaction with governmental performance skyrocketed in the late 1960s and early 1970s. In 1970 only 15 percent of those polled were dissatisfied with the government's policies; two years later, the proportion had climbed to over 50 percent (King 1975, 14). By the late 1970s, this growing restlessness had translated into a generalized shift toward the Right in economic issues. A standard question on the nationalized sector nicely captures the changing mood. Consistently until the mid-1970s, a third of the population favored more nationalizations and almost half were satisfied with the status quo. By 1979, however, the number in favor of privatizations had doubled to 40 percent. Those preferring more nationalizations had dropped from a third to a sixth of the population.[5] Although the shift in favor of privatizations was somewhat more pronounced among the upper and middle classes, it took place across all social sectors.

Combined with an erosion of the traditional class cleavage, the tilt of the electorate toward market solutions favored the Conservative Party. Drawn toward the Conservative Party by their general agreement with the Tory program of economic management, one out of four of those who voted Liberal in October

1974 voted Conservative in 1979.[6] Similarly, almost 10 percent of the 1974 Labour voters defected to the Conservative Party in 1979 (Särlvik and Crewer 1983, chaps. 6, 8, 9, and 11; Heath, Jowell, and Curtice 1985, chaps. 9 and 10).

ENGINEERING THE BREAKDOWN OF THE POSTWAR CONSENSUS: A NEW MACROECONOMIC FRAMEWORK

Breaking down the long tradition of demand-management policies and periodic income pacts that characterized the postwar consensus, the Thatcher government wholeheartedly adopted a monetarist strategy to reduce inflation. The June Budget for 1979–80 targeted the monetary aggregate sterling M3 (£M3) to grow 7–11 percent through April 1980. Moreover, to strengthen the monetary strategy, a set of tax increases and budget cuts were announced to reduce the public-sector borrowing requirement (PSBR) to 4.5 percent of GDP.

The reduction of inflation proved harder to achieve than monetarist economists had predicted. In the summer and fall of 1979, £M3 grew by around 14 percent (at an annualized rate), significantly above the target rate. Due to a new oil shock, the Cleggs Commission pay settlement for public servants, and indirect tax increases, inflation shot up to 16 percent in the third quarter of 1979, twice its 1978 rate. The government responded by tightening monetary policy further in mid-November. And in March 1980 it reinforced its policy stance with the formal introduction of the four-year Medium Term Financial Strategy (MTFS), which provided for a gradual reduction in the annual growth rate of £M3 to a 4–8 percent band in 1983/84 and a declining path for the PSBR from 3.75 percent of GDP in 1980/81 to 1.50 percent in 1983/84 (see Fig. 7.1).

Due to the deregulation of the bank's operations and the abolition of capital controls in 1979, £M3 grew well above the government's targets throughout 1980 (OECD 1981) (see Fig. 7.1). Still, other monetary indicators, such as M0, unaffected by the credit boom, showed a strong tightening in policy: its growth rate halved in the first half of 1980 and then fell by half again in the next year (Minford 1988). Jointly with the deepening world recession, the severe squeeze imposed by the government had strong real effects on the economy. Private consumption and domestic output started to decline in real terms in the second half of 1979. In 1980 GDP at market prices shrank by 2.7 percent in real terms. Total unemployment went up from 1.4 million at the end of 1979 to 2.5 million by mid-1981.

From the summer of 1980 on, opposition to Thatcher's policies started to gather momentum both within and outside government (Keegan 1984, pt. 2; Hall 1986, chap. 5; Lawson 1992, chap. 9; Thatcher 1993, chap. 5). The "wet" wing of the Conservative Party, which controlled all the noneconomic posts in the cabinet, lobbied for more spending to counter the recession. At the same time, British industrialists argued for measures to ease the pressure put on them by an overly high exchange rate. The erratic behavior of £M3 and the deterio-

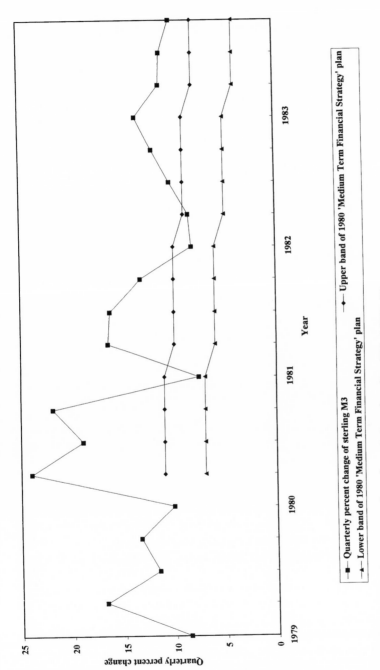

Figure 7.1. British monetary policy: the evolution of sterling M3, 1979–83

Table 7.1. *Fiscal policy in the United Kingdom, 1978-83*

| | AS PERCENT OF GDP | | | |
	PUBLIC SECTOR BORROWING REQUIREMENT (PSBR)	CHANGE IN PSBR [a]	STRUCTURAL BALANCE [b]	CHANGE IN THE STRUCTURAL BALANCE FROM PREVIOUS YEAR [a c]
1978	-4.9		-4.5	
1979	-4.4	-0.5	-4.4	-0.1
1980	-4.9	+0.5	-2.5	-1.9
1981	-3.6	-1.3	1.0	-3.5
1982	-2.8	-0.8	2.6	-1.6
1983	-3.6	+0.8	1.7	+0.9

All figures refer to general government.

[a] In figures on deficit change, a positive sign means expansionary change and a negative sign represents a restrictive change.

[b] Structural balance is the noncyclical part of PSBR, that is, if GDP had grown at its potential rate.

[c] The change in the structural government balance corresponds to the change in the fiscal deficit that would have taken place if the GDP had grown at its potential rate. The change in the structural balance therefore shows the net effect of governmental discretionary decisions concerning the budget.

Source: Miller (1985).

rating condition of the economy prompted Thatcher to loosen monetary policy to weaken the currency, to cut interests rates by several points, and to stabilize M0 at a growth rate of 5 percent (Walters 1986; Minford 1988).

The moderate relaxation of monetary policy did not imply abandoning the strict anti-inflationary strategy initially devised by the Conservative government. On the contrary, explicitly rejecting any policy U-turn, Thatcher engineered a significant tightening of the fiscal balance in the 1981/82 Budget. The Conservative government approved substantial tax increases – close to 4 percentage points of GDP – and, in spite of an extraordinary increase in cyclical spending, the PSBR fell from 4.9 percent of GDP in 1978 to 2.8 percent of GDP in 1982. Table 7.1 shows that, adjusting for the level of economic activity, fiscal policy was severely tight: the structural budget balance went from a deficit of 4.4 percent of GDP in 1979 to a surplus of 2.6 percent of GDP in 1982.

In the event, the harsh fiscal measures of the spring of 1981 represented a fundamental turning point in the conduct of British macroeconomic policy. Inflation peaked at 21.5 percent during the second quarter of 1980 and then fell to less than 4 percent by mid-1983 – the lowest value in fifteen years. Although purely technical errors in forecasting monetary conditions as well as notable political infighting within the Conservative Party over whether to join the EMS almost led to double-digit inflation in the late 1980s, the Conservative anti-inflationary framework was never questioned again. By the mid-1990s inflation was firmly stabilized around 3 percent.

REVAMPING THE SUPPLY SIDE OF THE BRITISH ECONOMY

Price stability within a predictable macroeconomic framework was a necessary yet insufficient condition to guide the economy onto a sustainable growth path. In the eyes of the Tory cabinet, the poor performance of Britain in the last decades had resulted mainly from the suffocating intervention of the state in all domains of economic life. Inflation had been one of its consequences and it accordingly had to be tamed. But tackling the underlying structural conditions of British economic decline required reducing the level of state intervention and injecting more private competition into the British economy.

To reduce the size of the state and thus liberate enough private resources to boost the economy, the Conservative Party championed, above all, a general reduction in the aggregate level of public expenditure. After a dramatic recession in the early 1980s had increased public spending to unprecedented levels, the Thatcher government eventually curbed social transfers and cut public spending on capital formation and industrial subsidies. By the end of the decade, total government expenditure declined to 38.6 percent of GDP (its lowest level in twenty-five years), the budget balance experienced a surplus, and total public debt fell to around 30 percent of GDP. The reduction in public expenditure was accompanied by a reform of the tax system to free private resources and boost incentives to work and save. Income and corporate tax rates were greatly reduced, and allowances and exemption limits were raised. By contrast, indirect taxes gained an unprecedented weight in the tax system.

The reduction of state interventionism was especially successful in the area of industrial policy. A thorough process of privatization, particularly in the mid- and late 1980s, reported revenues close to 1 percent of GDP every year, cut both employment and investment in the public business sector by two-thirds, and resulted in the near suppression of all industrial subsidies.

Finally, the reform of industrial relations played a key role in the Conservation program. Heath's defeat at the hands of the miners' union loomed large among Tories. Moreover, the reform of industrial relations was unavoidable for strictly economic reasons. Conservatives judged unions' institutional strength to be one of the main causes of British economic decline. The operation of the closed shop and workers' capacity to engage, particularly through secondary picketing, in extensive and unlimited strikes enabled unions to hamper any business plan to reduce overstaffing, increase capital investment, and boost productivity. As a result, labor costs were too high in relative terms, British businesses were increasingly uncompetitive, and the share of their exports in world markets shrank steadily. In short, only a reform in the industrial relations system, which was inordinately favorable to unions, could free the labor market to again sustain healthy rates of economic growth (Behrens 1980, chap. 6; Thatcher 1993, chap. 4).

THE REDUCTION OF PUBLIC EXPENDITURE AND BORROWING

Although the Thatcher government initially planned a gradual reduction of public expenditure in real terms, the harsh economic downturn of the early 1980s ruined its fiscal strategy. The corresponding (cyclically induced) jump in unemployment benefits and social expenditure made it electorally impossible to control public expenditure, which climbed to 46.6 percent of GDP (or 47.5 percent of GDP if we exclude the proceeds from selling land and council houses) by 1982/83, more than 4 percentage points above the last Labour budget.[7]

As the economy started to improve and the budgetary squeeze relaxed, the Conservative cabinet could put into effect its supply-side economic reforms. To reduce the size of the public budget, Nigel Lawson, named chancellor in July 1983, designed a fiscal policy based on budgeting "a slower rate of growth for public spending than the sustainable growth rate of the economy as a whole, with the result that public expenditure would steadily decline as a share of GDP" (Lawson 1992, 305–6) – roughly by 6 percentage points to around 40 percent of GDP by the late 1980s (see Table 7.2B).

Benefiting from a dramatic upward swing in the economy, which lowered welfare payments, and hence public spending, farther than expected, public spending stabilized at around £157 billion (in 1985 prices) in the mid-1980s and shrank temporarily (in 1988/89) below its level of 1984/85. In relative terms, this implied an extraordinary reduction from 46.6 percent of GDP in 1982/83 to 39.6 percent of GDP in 1989/90. The public spending ratio of the late 1980s, even excluding privatization proceeds, turned out to be the lowest since the mid-1960s.

In accordance with the political and economic priorities of the cabinet, the effort to reduce government spending was distributed unequally across the public budget. Table 7.3 presents, for the years 1978/79, 1982/83, and 1989/90, total general government expenditure (excluding privatization proceeds), as well as those spending areas that experienced more variation under the Thatcher government.[8] After a period, from 1978/79 to 1982/83, in which public spending increased substantially (3.4 percentage points), general government expenditure contracted 7.8 points of GDP. Cyclical spending played a fundamental role in the evolution of public expenditure. Spending on social security benefits, health, and personal services increased 2.7 percent of GDP through 1982/83 – that is,

Table 7.2. *Budgetary plans for general government expenditure and actual results in the United Kingdom, 1982/83-1989/90*

A. GENERAL GOVERNMENT EXPENDITURE (EXCLUDING PRIVATIZATION PROCEEDS) IN 1985 PRICES (IN £ BILLION)

	BUDGETED [a]	OUTTURN	DIFFERENCE
1982/83	145.8	152.6	+6.8
1983/84	158.2	155.1	-3.2
1984/85	161.2	159.1	-2.1
1985/86	164.5	159.1	-5.3
1986/87	166.8	161.5	-5.3
1987/88	166.5	161.3	-5.2
1988/89	160.0	157.3	-2.5
1989/90	159.4	163.0	+3.6

B. GENERAL GOVERNMENT EXPENDITURE (EXCLUDING PRIVATIZATION PROCEEDS) AS PERCENT Of GDP

	BUDGETED [a] [b]	OUTTURN [c]	DIFFERENCE
1982/83	44.5	46.6	+2.1
1983/84	47.0	45.7	-1.3
1984/85	46.2	46.0	-0.2
1985/86	46.2	44.3	-1.9
1986/87	45.0	43.2	-1.8
1987/88	43.7	41.1	-2.6
1988/89	40.7	38.6	-2.1
1989/90	38.7	39.2	+0.5

[a] As planned in the annual budget (e.g., March 1985 budget for year 1985/86).

[b] As percent of nominal GDP projected by government.

[c] As percent of actual nominal GDP.

Sources: Own estimates based on figures reported in *OECD Economic Surveys. United Kingdom* (several years).

around four-fifths of all the net increase in that period.[9] The economic downturn of the early 1980s similarly boosted public spending on debt interest payments (0.6 percent of GDP), industrial subsidies (0.2 percent of GDP), and vocational training (0.2 percent of GDP). Sizable cuts in public expenditures on housing (from 2.7 percent of GDP to 1.4 percent of GDP), the only area in which the Conservative strategy had any success, were absorbed by a strong rise in defense and police spending (1 percent of GDP).

Following the economic recovery, most of the increase in the cyclical part of the budget leveled off by the end of the decade. Social security and health spending fell 1.9 percentage points through 1989/90. In 1989/90, however, it still remained 0.8 percentage points of GDP above its level in 1978/79. The long-term reduction in public spending – of about 4.4 percentage points from 1978/79 to 1989/90 – achieved by the Thatcher government had two main sources. On the one hand, it derived from a fall in debt interest payments (0.8

Table 7. 3. Evolution of the composition of public expenditure in the United Kingdom, 1978/79-1989/90

	AS PERCENT OF GPD			CHANGE FROM		
	1978/79	1982/83	1989/90	1978/79 to 1982/83	1982/83 to1989/90	1978/79 to 1989/90
Total expenditure excluding privatization proceeds	43.2	46.6	38.8	+3.4	-7.8	-4.4
Interest debt payment	4.3	4.9	3.5	+0.6	-1.4	-0.8
Trade and industry	1.8	2.0	0.9	+0.2	-1.1	-0.9
Housing	2.7	1.4	0.9	-1.3	-0.5	-1.8
Police and defense	5.8	6.8	5.9	+1.0	-0.9	+0.1
Social security	9.7	11.7	10.1	+2.0	-1.6	+0.4
Health and personal services	5.3	6.0	5.7	+0.7	-0.3	+0.4
Education, science, and vocational training	6.1	6.3	5.4	+0.2	-0.9	-0.7

Sources: U.K. Parliament 1992, 12; and own estimations.

points of GDP since 1979) – in turn, a consequence of a steady reduction of the budget deficit.[10] On the other hand, it came from a systematic cutback of public responsibilities in the areas of economic management: direct public capital formation and industrial subsidies. The decision, taken already in 1979, to curtail public investment (in the housing market) was thoroughly carried out over the decade. By 1989/90 public expenditure on housing was a third of the amount spent in 1978/79. Given the rampant recession of the early 1980s, industrial subsidies could not be cut without incurring excessive political costs. From 1984/85 on, however, expenditure in trade and industry fell rapidly to half its level of 1978.

The strategy of restraining public spending to spur private saving and investment did not automatically lead to a sizable reduction of taxation. Eliminating the public deficit was instead given priority by the Thatcher government. After a slightly loose budget due to the impending General Election of 1983, the chancellor planned new reductions in the PSBR to cut it by half in the next two years. Mostly as a result of the effects of the prolonged miners' strike of 1984, all forecasts failed and the PSBR lingered around 3 percent of GDP until March 1985 (over 4 percent if all sales of public assets are excluded). Once the strike was defeated and economic growth accelerated, however, the PSBR was halved in just one year to 1.6 percent of GDP in 1985/86. From that point on, the cabinet followed a rather neutral fiscal policy intent on maintaining the PSBR at around 1 percent of GDP through 1991 (Bean and Symmons 1989; Lawson 1992). Nevertheless, a higher than expected buoyancy in non-oil revenues continued to reduce the PSBR during the following years. In March 1988 the PSBR turned negative and had to be christened "public sector debt repayment" (PSDR). In 1988/89 the PSDR peaked at 3 percent of GDP. Even if we exclude all public-assets sales (public corporations as well as public lands and houses), the budget ended 1988/89 in surplus (see Fig. 7.2).

A SLOW PATH TO TAX REFORM

Compared to its ability to curb public spending and the public deficit, the Conservative government was only mildly successful at achieving the twin goals, at the core of its program, of a smaller tax burden and a less distortionary tax system.

Making good on its electoral promises, the Conservative government immediately cut the basic income tax rate from 33 to 30 percent and the top tax rate on earned income from 83 to 60 percent and on unearned income from 98 to 75 percent in 1979. Tax rate bands for upper-income taxpayers were significantly widened and allowances were increased 18 points, twice the inflation rate during the previous year. Nonetheless, the reduction in the personal income tax burden was frustrated by the economic downturn. To cut a swelling PSBR, the 1981 Budget suspended the provision for the indexation of personal income tax

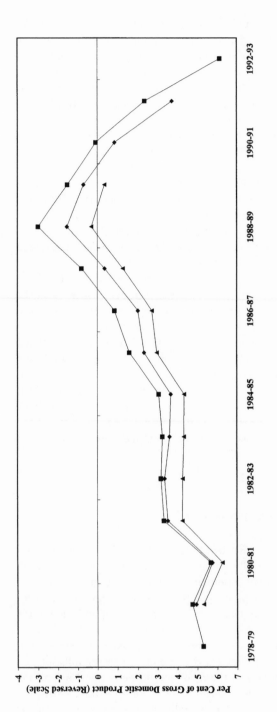

Fiscal Year

■— Public Sector Borrowing Requirements (PBSR)   ◆— PBSR Excluding Proceeds from Privatizations
▲— PBSR Excluding Proceeds from Privatizations and Home Sales

Figure 7.2. Financial needs of the British public sector, 1978/79–1992/93

allowances and band rates to inflation. This last measure, jointly with other tax increases, raised tax revenues from 34.3 percent of GDP in 1979 to 38.5 percent of GDP four years later.

Once the economy recovered, tax revenue (as a proportion of GDP) declined rather slowly due to the priority the Conservative government granted to the elimination of the structural budget. Tax revenues still represented 36 percent of GDP in 1991, almost 2 percentage points above the 1979 level. Total revenues, however, reached 38.5 percent of GDP in 1991, close to their level of 1979.

The Conservative government managed to make notable progress in reforming the internal structure of the tax system. In the first place, personal income taxation was moved closer to a linear tax system. Tax allowances were consistently increased above the annual inflation rate after 1982. The basic tax rate was cut 1 point to 29 percent in March 1986 and then to 27 percent a year later. In 1988 tax brackets were reduced from six to two; the top tax rate was set at 40 percent (down from 60 percent); and the basic rate was lowered to 25 percent.[11] Figure 7.3 compares the effective tax rates (i.e., the actual proportion of income paid in taxes) in 1978/79, 1979/80, 1988/89, and 1992/93 for incomes up to £50,000 in 1980 prices.[12] The reform of the personal income tax lessened the tax burden across all income segments, albeit in an unequal manner. Although the effective tax rate had declined at least a third by 1988/89 for all incomes, the effective tax rate for high income levels (over £30,000) had been almost halved. For an income of £5,000 (in 1980 prices), the proportion of income paid in personal income tax fell from over 24 percent to less than 17 percent. For ten times that income, the effective tax rate went from almost 64 percent to 35 percent.

A similar policy in favor of a simplified, broader tax was applied to the corporate income tax in 1984. The standard tax rate was lowered from 52 percent to 35 percent (later reduced to 33 percent); 100 percent first-year allowances for plant and machinery were abolished; and depreciation allowances for all kinds of investment were brought closer into line with true economic depreciation. In 1988 the capital gains tax rates were aligned with personal income tax rates, and the inheritance tax rate was unified at 40 percent (down from a top rate of 75 percent in 1978).

The system of social security contributions was rationalized to smooth out loopholes and eliminate the "poverty trap" problem. The National Insurance surcharge, in force since 1977, was eventually abolished in 1984. More significantly, two reforms, in 1985 and 1989, restructured the National Insurance system to eliminate the sharp steps in the rate structure and all potential disincentives affecting low-income earners.[13]

Although the main purpose of the reform was to simplify taxation, other economic objectives, as well as purely electoral motives, intervened to shape the government's tax policy and blocked, to some extent, the achievement of a completely neutral tax system (Leape 1993; Helm, Mayer, and Mayhew 1991). On the one hand, the Conservative government introduced several new schemes, such

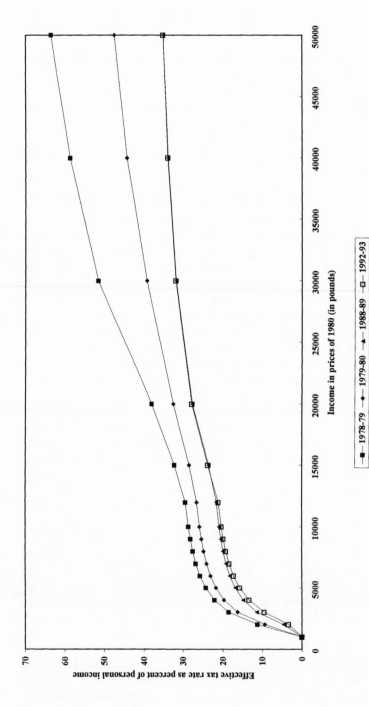

Figure 7.3. Effective tax rates on personal income in the United Kingdom, 1978/79–1992/93

Table 7.4. *Composition of British tax revenues, 1975-89*

	AS A PERCENT OF TOTAL TAX REVENUES			
	1975	1980	1985	1990
Personal income tax	37.9	29.8	26.5	26.6
Corporate income tax	6.7	8.3	12.6	12.3
Social security tax	17.4	16.6	17.6	17.6
Property taxes	12.7	12.0	11.9	12.6
Consumption taxes	23.6	27.5	29.5	39.3

Source: OECD (1991b).

as the Business Expansion Scheme, to boost the creation of small businesses, and Personal Equity Plans and tax-free savings accounts (TESSAs) to encourage personal savings (Leape 1993; Lawson 1992, chap. 27 and 66). On the other hand, strict political calculations partially dissuaded the Thatcher government from dealing with the electorally delicate issues of pensions and mortgage interest relief, particularly the latter (Lawson 1992, 362, 365, 819–21; Thatcher 1993, 671).

Given that the total tax burden hardly changed, the reduction of income tax rates was compensated by a stronger reliance on indirect taxation (see Table 7.4). In 1975 the personal income tax represented 37.9 percent of all tax revenues. In 1990 it had gone down to 26.6 percent. Meanwhile, consumption taxes had almost doubled, from 23.6 percent to 39.3 percent. A successful overhauling of the corporate tax also strengthened its role; its contribution to total taxation doubled from 1975 to 1990.

INDUSTRIAL POLICY AND THE PRIVATIZATION DRIVE

Plans to privatize the public business sector and dismantle the state's industrial policy played only a minor role in the 1979 Conservative manifesto. This squared well with the traditional stance taken by the Tory Party since the sweeping nationalizations of the Labour government of 1945–51. Mostly content with containing the Labour Party's nationalization drive, only occasionally did Conservative governments revert some businesses to the private sector. In the 1950s the Churchill government denationalized the steel and iron and the road haulage industries. A renewed call for further denationalizations in the Selsdon Park Program of 1970 broke down in the wake of the policy U-turn engineered by Heath two years later. Even after the sustained shift to laissez-faire positions among Conservatives in the mid-1970s, the strategy toward public corporations remained one of moderation. An internal Tory report on privatization policy, drafted in 1978, restricted the sale of public assets to those firms already in competitive sectors, and skeptical about the benefits of privatizing any public utility, it stressed instead the need for tighter financial controls (Ridley 1991, 15ff.; Riddell 1989).

The intensity of the economic recession further moderated the government's initial industrial policy. To stress the cabinet's commitment to a new economic approach, Thatcher appointed Sir Keith Joseph, who had strongly inspired the Conservative Party to change course to a more decidedly free-market strategy, as secretary of state for industry. Despite the fierce promarket rhetoric of the new minister, who circulated a reading list of laissez-faire authors to senior officials at the department (Wilks 1985), expenditure on industrial policy was only slightly reduced. The National Enterprise Board (NEB) and the National Economic Development Council (NEDC), the two institutions at the heart of all the planning attempts made in the last two decades, were barely altered. New programs, such as the Small Engineering Firms Investment Scheme and the Alvey initiative, to sustain high technology research, and the interest in fostering public purchasing as a means of promoting industrial efficiency represented a departure from the hands-off approach promised by the Thatcher government in the area of industrial policy.

Privatizations remained moderate during Thatcher's first years in office. Sales, modest in relative terms, never went above a meager 0.2 percent of the GDP in any given year and affected rather marginal corporations.[14] As for the core of the public business sector, the Conservative government believed that the tightening of the so-called external finance limits, the introduction of clearer financial targets for rates of return over the medium term, a set of measures to enhance market competitiveness (especially in the areas of telecommunications and transport), and the appointment of more-aggressive management boards could make public corporations efficient again.

The sudden explosion of total public expenditure in the early 1980s eventually pushed the Thatcher government to embrace a more radical industrial policy. The government initially covered the financial needs of several public firms because the economic crisis and the subsequent unemployment rate made it extremely difficult for the Conservative Party to let them go bankrupt (Thatcher 1993, 114–21, 139–43). Even after defeating a bitter strike of steelworkers which allowed the board of directors to impose a plan to halve the workforce of British Steel in five years, the Thatcher government acquiesced to channeling a formidable volume of capital to back the rationalization plan of British Steel: £1.5 billion in debt write-offs and new loans in June 1980 and another £4.4 billion the following year. Almost £1 billion in equity funding was channeled into British Leyland in 1981. A £200 million bank overdraft guarantee was approved for ICL. Finally, the Conservative government backed down in the face of a threatened miners' strike, relaxing the National Coal Board's external financial limit and postponing rationalization measures.

But the government shifted tracks shortly afterward. Its decision in March 1981 to stabilize the budget deficit made it impossible to accommodate the pressing capital needs that British Telecommunications (BT) was facing at that time. By late 1980 BT's modernization program, urgently needed to meet the challenges posed by an impending revolution in telecommunications, was estimated to require £1.2 billion. The government stubbornly refused to pay for an amount that equaled one-tenth of the PSBR. In order to get around the constraints imposed by Thatcher's budgetary plans, the British government and BT explored the possibility of issuing Telecom Bonds in the stock market. Because the sum that could be raised in this way was far below what was needed and because of doubts about the role of the government in the operation, both sides decided to discard that solution. This convinced Patrick Jenkin, then secretary of industry, to propose selling off BT. Although the idea was first met with resistance, it soon gained acceptance and was announced in the Budget speech of 1982 (Veljanovski 1988; Riddell 1989).[15]

The sale of BT proved to be a great political success, inaugurating a dramatic privatization drive in the following years. The first tranche of BT, offered for sale in November 1984, was several times oversubscribed, raised £3.9 billion, and was bought by approximately two million people – most of them buying stock for the first time ever. Encouraged by that response, the Thatcher government added to its privatization list the rest of Britoil (1985), British Gas (1986), British Airways (January 1987), Rolls-Royce (May 1987), British Petroleum (December 1987), the Rover Group (1988), the water industry (1989), and the electricity supply industry (1989).[16] Privatization proceeds rose from an annual average of 0.2 percent of GDP until 1983 to over 1 percent in 1986–87 and almost 1.5 percent in 1988–89.

The privatization strategy was gradually complemented by the subjection of most privatized firms to the discipline of a competitive market (Lawson 1992, 203ff.). Initially, the government had to postpone enhancing competitiveness for the sake of pushing the privatization package through swiftly. Without the co-operation of the top managerial cadres at both British Telecom and British Gas, who were adamantly opposed to breaking up these companies into smaller units, privatizations risked being delayed for several years. To avoid jeopardizing the governmental strategy, Thatcher had no other option than to sell them as whole entities – and to regulate them through independent agencies (Thatcher 1993, chap. 23; Lawson 1992, 213–16, 221–24). Nevertheless, as the privatization process gathered momentum in the next years and public worries and complaints about the quality of British Telecom's services increased, several privatizations of public utilities were carried out after they were broken up into smaller units. The electricity generating system was split into two companies and the twelve existing area boards were privatized as separate distribution companies. The water supply company was divided into ten regional companies. The Competition and

Service (Utilities) Act of 1992 was intended to reinforce the public regulation of utilities (OECD 1993b).

Such a thorough process of privatization had substantial effects on the size and role of the public business sector in the British economy. Employment in nationalized industries (including the Post Office) plummeted from 1,849,000 jobs in 1979 (7.3 percent of all the employed workforce) to 516,000 jobs in 1991 (2.0 percent of all the employed workforce). Whereas in 1979 public corporations provided 15.8 percent of gross domestic capital formation (or 2.9 percent of GDP), they supplied only 4.1 percent in 1991 (0.7 percent of GDP). Combined with the sharp reduction in public investment in housing, total gross domestic capital formation by the public sector dwindled from 29.9 percent of all domestic investment in 1979 to 16.9 percent in 1991 (see Fig. 7.4). Moreover, as public corporations were shifted to the private sector, loans and outright grants from the general government declined considerably, contributing to the reduction of public expenditure in the long run. In 1978–79, the total of government grants and loans to nationalized industries was 1.1 percent of GDP. After peaking at 1.7 percent of GDP in 1980–81, the total fell to slightly over 0.2 percent of GDP by 1988–89.[17]

REFORMING THE LABOR MARKET

The reform of labor market institutions occupied a fundamental role in the Conservative strategy to shift the British economy toward a more favorable equilibrium (i.e., one characterized by both low inflation and low unemployment). Given the cabinet's conviction that "other things being equal, the level of unemployment was related to the extent of trade union power" (Thatcher 1993, 272), Conservatives focused their attention mainly on curbing the unions' capacity to distort the workings of the market. This implied, on the one hand, legislative reforms to undo the privileges trade unions had gained throughout the postwar period. On the other hand, it required disciplining unions in the public sector, mostly in the nationalized industries. A tough stance by the cabinet was expected to set a clear example that would be followed by the demoralized private sector. Curbing the trade unions' power was complemented by measures to increase the flexibility of the labor market as well as to reduce the disincentives to work embedded in the tax and welfare system.

During the first parliamentary term, the Thatcher government for the most part abolished the amendments introduced by Labour in 1976 and returned the industrial relations legislation to the conditions set in the Employment Act of 1974. The gradual reduction of union privileges and the strict macroeconomic policies of the early 1980s provoked a long string of eventually unsuccessful strikes in the public sector. The steel strike of 1980, which accounted for nearly three-fourths of all working days lost through strikes in 1980, was eventually defeated (Thatcher 1993, 108–14; Hall 1986, chap. 5). The government was also

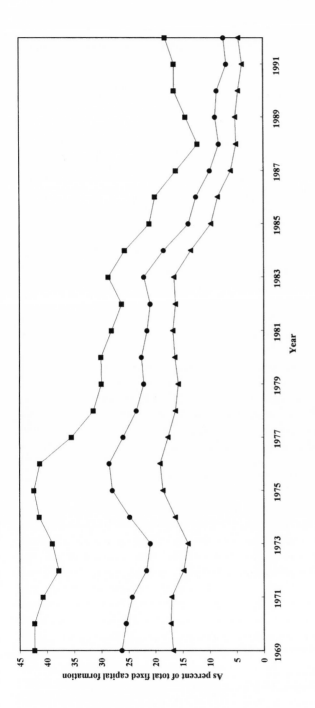

Figure 7.4. *Gross fixed capital formation by the British public sector, 1969–92*

As percent of total fixed capital formation

Year

■ Total public investment
● Sum of investment by public business sector and by general government on housing programs
▲ Investment by general government on housing programs

able to carry the day in the industrial disputes involving the civil service (1981), the national health service (1982), and the water supply system (1983). It was, however, the long and wearing confrontation between the Thatcher government and the National Union of Miners (NUM) in the course of 1984 that constituted the turning point of the government's strategy to reform the British labor market. In response to Thatcher's rationalization plans for the National Coal Board, which included cutting its workforce by a third, NUM began a nationwide strike in mid-March 1984 that lasted almost a whole year. In spite of widespread and at times violent picketing, the strikers could not bring the coal industry to a total standstill. As the winter progressed, NUM members began to return to work and the strike was officially called off at the beginning of March 1985.

With NUM defeated, the prospects for any centralized income policy were definitely buried. The government was completely free to implement a new legal framework for the British system of industrial relations that stressed the principle of democratic accountability and that expanded the sphere of individual rights for the rank-and-file members of the union. The Thatcher cabinet expected that, as the average union member gained in power vis-à-vis the union officer, the unions would become more moderate and mainstream in their objectives. Union leaders would have to abandon their traditionally politicized goals in favor of a cooperative stance towards pay and productivity issues. Moreover, by emphasizing the positive values of accountability, individual rights, and choice, the Conservative government calculated that the reforms could be introduced without provoking any serious resistance from unions (Dorey 1993). Accordingly, the Conservative cabinet required that strikes be approved in secret ballots, subjected union officers to periodic reelection, and mandated that the existence and use of political funds within labor unions had to be regularly put to the vote of the union members. The closed-shop system was first severely limited and eventually abolished in 1990. Finally, the government introduced a range of new rights for individual union members allowing them to take action against their own unions and backed them with a state-funded commissioner who would support such actions.

Government legislation on trade unions had important effects on wage bargaining and union membership (Metcalf 1991) – moving Britain toward a decentralized labor market system (Nickell 1990).[18] Union membership, which had peaked in 1979 at 55 percent of the employed workforce, fell to 37.5 percent a decade later (Purcell 1993). The proportion of industrial establishments that recognized trade unions declined steadily from around two-thirds in the early 1980s to slightly over half in 1990. The pattern of wage bargaining changed accordingly: the proportion of manual workers in manufacturing covered by collective bargaining diminished from 79 percent in 1984 to 70 percent in 1990; among nonmanual workers in manufacturing the figures were 59 and 50 percent respectively. For workers covered by collective agreements, there was a clear shift away from national bargaining to firm-level bargaining (Purcell 1993). Industrial conflict fell steadily. During the 1970s the number of working days lost in strikes (per thousand employed) averaged more than 500 – one of the highest rates of strike activity among OECD countries. In 1990 the number was 70 – an all-time low for the postwar period.

Along with the reform in union legislation, the Conservative government deregulated the labor market in other ways. In July 1982 the earning-related supplement was suspended and unemployment benefits were taxed. As a result, the average short-term income of the unemployed dropped from being close to 80 percent of the average income of all those employed in 1978 to 60 percent in 1983.[19] Moreover, the Fair Wages Resolution, which since 1975 had compelled firms to calculate their minimum wage rates according to those determined in the corresponding nationwide agreement, was repealed. In 1993 the last twenty-six Wage Councils, which set minimum wages for 2.5 million workers, were abolished. The qualifying period of employment for protection against unfair dismissal was extended from six to twelve months in 1980 and then to two years in 1985. The onus of proof on the employer in cases of unfair dismissal was reduced. The Conservative government resisted all attempts to extend social legislation adopted by the European Community to the United Kingdom. By the early 1990s, external observers could declare that the United Kingdom had "the most deregulated labor market of any EC country with respect to restrictions on lay-offs or hiring of temporary workers" and that "other institutional features such as the low proportion of non-wage labor costs, low unemployment insurance replacement ratios, and the absence of bans on weekend or shift work [indicated a] greatly enhanced labor market flexibility" (OECD 1991a, 83).

The transformation of British industrial relations and of hiring and firing legislation was accompanied by the gradual dismantling of public vocational training systems and their devolution to the private sector. The sharp deterioration of economic conditions initially thwarted the Conservative approach to vocational training. Upon arrival in office, the Conservative government engineered harsh cuts in training programs and approved the abolition of seventeen out of twenty-four Industrial Training Boards, which, organized on an industry-wide basis and including union, business, and government representatives, had the right to impose a levy on firms to finance vocational training. But soaring rates of unemployment forced the Tory government to dramatically reverse its laissez-faire approach to vocational training and to approve (mostly in a piecemeal, pragmatic manner) several new public programs, mainly for young people (D. S. King 1993). Public expenditure on employment training increased from £1.1 billion in 1978/79 to a peak of £3.4 billion in 1987/88, more than a 50 percent increase in real terms.

As soon as unemployment started to subside, however, the approach to vocational training that had prevailed through the mid-1980s shifted significantly. In 1987 the Conservative government was again reelected with a solid parliamentary majority under the banner of fundamental social reform – particularly in the field of education – to further the values of free enterprise, individual initiative, and productive work. Vocational training was progressively broadened and linked to parallel reforms in general education through the extension of technical subjects in secondary school, the creation of City Technical Colleges, and the granting of more status and autonomy to Polytechnic Universities (Finegold and Soskice 1988). The provision of training was gradually tied to the public system of social security and unemployment benefits. By the late 1980s, claimants for unemployment benefits had to provide proof of involuntary unemployment and show that they were actively seeking a new job. In 1988 the government decided to refuse social benefits to those not willing to participate in certain training programs (D. S. King 1993). Finally, trade unions were marginalized and businesses were given a larger say in the management of all training programs, which were dramatically decentralized. Support for publicly funded vocational training was progressively cut. From a peak of £3.4 billion in 1987/88 (£3.1 billion in 1985 prices) it went down to £3.2 billion in 1989/90 (£2.5 billion in 1985 prices). This was less than the amount the government had spent in real terms in 1982/83. As a proportion of GDP, it was below the level inherited by the Thatcher government in 1979.[20] Moreover, public expenditure represented a minuscule fraction of what private companies were investing in training programs by the late 1980s – over £20 billion (OECD 1991a).

CONCLUSIONS

In 1979 the Conservative Party was returned to office with a strong mandate to turn around what the public perceived to be a dismally performing economy. After several decades in which the Tory Party had been controlled by its centrist wing, the gradual slowdown of the British economy, a worsening unemployment–inflation trade-off, and two crushing electoral defeats in 1974 tipped the balance of power in favor of those supporting a clean break with the prevailing postwar economic consensus. Under the leadership of Margaret Thatcher, Conservatives now held that the political and economic renewal of Britain called for a return to the traditional values of individual responsibility and economic liberalism at the heart of Toryism. This translated into a two-pronged economic strategy that literally reversed the corporatist and interventionist policies in vogue up through the 1970s. In order to contain inflation, the government championed substituting a set of credible monetary rules for the traditional nationwide wage negotiations between unions, business, and the state. Expansionary fiscal policies had to be abandoned for the sake of financial discipline. The Conservative government acknowledged, however, that such a stable monetary framework would not by itself significantly raise the long-run growth rate of the British economy. What was needed was a thorough reform of the supply conditions of the British economy in order to liberate the energies of a private sector suffocated by the state. Accordingly, public spending had to be curtailed, taxes had to be reduced and geared toward the promotion of private initiative and saving, and the labor market had to be deregulated. When set against the social democratic policies of the González government in Spain, and in the light of some of the statistical evidence gathered in Chapters 3 and 4, the British conservative experience of the 1980s highlights how the structural shocks of the last two decades have generated a growing trend toward divergent policy solutions in OECD nations.

For more than a decade the Conservative Party strove to fulfill its program. As in the case of the Spanish Socialist government, this meant a long, strenuous process in which the British cabinet had to manage, at the same time, the constraints imposed by the fluctuations of the business cycle and the requirements of electoral competition. A sharp economic downturn in the early 1980s restricted the government's ability to effect substantial change. Confronted with falling popularity and serious squabbling within the party, Thatcher focused her strategy on the control of inflation and postponed any serious attempt to reform the supply side of the economy. High inflationary expectations were eventually broken down. Yet, contrary to her plans, the prime minister had to accommodate a sizable upsurge in social transfers that put total public spending close to the historical records reached in the mid-1970s. Moreover, under the pressure of swelling unemployment, industrial subsidies were cut only slightly, and new spending on vocational training had to be approved. The institutional reform of the labor market also proved hard to implement.

Nonetheless, as the economy improved in the mid-1980s and electoral support remained high, the government could make fundamental progress in revamping the supply side of the British economy. Public expenditure fell rapidly to 38.6 percent of GDP in 1988/89 – its lowest level since the mid-1960s. The budget balance experienced a surplus for the first time in almost two decades. The tax system was reformed thoroughly. The tax rate structure was flattened, and indirect taxes now accounted for more than half of tax revenue. After the systematic privatization of most public firms, employment in the public business sector fell from 7 percent to 2 percent of the total workforce. Public investment declined to half its 1979 level. Industrial subsidies were cut to a negligible 0.2 percent. The British case fits clearly into the standard conservative response, described in Chapter 2, to the structural trade-offs confronted by OECD countries. Notice, moreover, that it actually provides new evidence (not presented in Chapters 3 and 4) about the overall nature of a right-wing economic strategy. The reduction of the active involvement of the state in the supply of productive factors was accompanied by a deregulation of their provision and a lowering of the British "social wage": minimum wages were abolished; unemployment benefits were reduced and linked to participation in training schemes and an active search for work; unions and collective bargaining were weakened; and social expenditure was contained.

As in the Spanish case, Thatcher's conservative strategy implied building and sustaining a particular electoral coalition. Similarly, it had to confront a clearcut dilemma between the popularity of the welfare state and the need to bolster the competitiveness of the British economy. Accordingly, we will now turn to the examination of the political dimension of the Tory economic policies.

8

THE POLITICAL AND ELECTORAL DIMENSIONS OF THE CONSERVATIVE ECONOMIC STRATEGY

For a decade and a half, the British Conservative government engineered a radical break with the economic management practices in place during most of the postwar period. On the one hand, demand management policies coupled with a periodic resort to income pacts were replaced with tight monetary policies and fiscal discipline. The public budget was balanced by 1988 and public debt was cut in half from 1979 to 1990. Inflation went down from an average of 16 percent in 1974–79 to less than 4 percent in the early 1990s. On the other hand, the Tory cabinet engaged in a drastic overhauling of the structural conditions of the British economy. After overshooting in the early 1980s, public spending was contained and progressively reduced. Tax rates were cut to spur private savings and investment. The labor market was deregulated. Finally, the public business sector was thoroughly dismantled.

As in the case of the Spanish Socialist government, Thatcher's economic strategy must also be thought of as a political strategy – intent both on making Tory principles hegemonic and on building a stable social and electoral coalition that could maintain the Tory Party in power. In a period of increasing partisan and social dealignment, the Conservative government consciously deployed its economic strategies to secure high levels of electoral support. Stable prices, lower taxes, low interest rates, mortgage interest relief, and an expansion in private choice in the provision of social services and pensions allowed the Tory government to secure its traditional basis of support, that is, professionals, high- and intermediate-level managers, and nonmanual lower positions, whose overall weight was bolstered by a long-term shift of the British economy away from manufacturing and toward the service sector. The extension of home and share ownership (two key elements of Thatcher's economic reform) to working class voters and the decline of union membership (partly due to changes in industrial relations legislation) crippled traditional Labour strongholds and allowed Tories to make substantial inroads in historically non-Conservative sectors. Finally, the construction of such a broad electoral coalition through material benefits was strengthened by the development of a political discourse that legitimized the conservative values of entrepreneurship and individual responsibility.

The successful implementation of the two-pronged economic strategy of price stability and structural flexibility was partially constrained by the institutional structure of the British economy. As pointed out in Chapter 7, even though the government embraced tight monetary policies to cut inflation, price stability took longer to achieve than had been initially forecast. It was only when the structural reforms of the labor market were completed by the late 1980s that inflation declined to minimal levels and structural unemployment fell rapidly. Nevertheless, the most acute political dilemma that Conservatives had to face was, as in the case of the González government, electoral in nature. The reduction of public expenditure and taxes was constrained by a strong popular attachment to the welfare state. Heavy electoral support for the bulk of social spending made the implementation of measures to overhaul welfare programs virtually impossible. Similarly, an attempt to introduce a "community charge" to finance local government and therefore to curb local spending had to be substantially revised after a strong drop in public support for the Conservative Party. As a result, public expenditure could be lowered only by about 4 percent of GDP during the 1980s. Compared with the increasing trend of public expenditure in most OECD nations, that was a substantial achievement, but it was still far from the initial expectations held by the Tory Party in 1979.

This chapter is organized as follows. Partially inverting the order employed in Chapter 6 for the Spanish case, the first section examines the nature of the Conservative electoral coalition and the strategies the government employed to secure and extend it. The rest of the chapter deals with the key dilemma of center-to-the-right governments in an era marked by structural changes and higher foreign competition: making the tax cuts and supply-side reforms, demanded by conservative constituencies compatible with the maintenance of much of the welfare state, which receives overwhelming support from middle-class voters.

FORGING THE POLITICAL BASIS OF A NEW MODEL OF ECONOMIC MANAGEMENT

Conservatives went into office with the conviction that theirs was a program for the moral and political renewal of Britain. Accordingly, the Tory cabinet was particularly determined to use its economic policies to mold public opinion in favor of its program of social and political change. The transformation of the British citizenry implied, above all, a general change in its attitudes toward the role of the state in running the economy. Economic change could not come solely from specific policy changes or even from a thorough deregulatory strategy. It depended as well on the transformation of basic social values among all private agents. For the Conservative economic strategy to be successful and lead to rapid economic growth, a renewed entrepreneurial ethos had to replace the excessive economic interventionism practiced by the British government since 1945.

Such a change in social values was expected to have political consequences too. Once the new Conservative policies started to work and reinvigorate the British economy, the average British voter would have a vested interest in preserving them. The hegemony of social democratic ideas during the postwar period – the "socialist ratchet," as Sir Keith Joseph had called it in the mid-1970s (Behrens 1980) – that had previously thwarted all Conservative efforts to move Britain in the right direction would at last be broken. Labour would have to adapt to the new consequences and move to the center or otherwise face continuous electoral decline. Similarly, it was expected that under these new circumstances the Conservative Party would secure a major role and, most likely, considerable electoral advantage.

The forging of new social values and the construction of an ample electoral coalition by the Conservative government were attempted during a period of extensive partisan and social dealignment and increasing electoral volatility within British public opinion. After World War II and through the mid-1960s, parties drew most of their votes from their "natural" social class: Conservatives and Labour were consistently supported by over two-thirds of the middle and working class respectively (Butler and Stokes 1974; Heath, Jowell, and Curtice 1985). Yet by the mid-1970s only half of the electorate was voting according to a class-based model. Party identification had also declined substantially. In the mid-1960s close to half of the voters declared themselves to be very strong supporters of one of the main political parties. Ten years later, that proportion had diminished to one-fourth. As a result, the voters' opinions on both policies and parties' performances in office started to have more weight in explaining the vote than all structural socioeconomic characteristics taken together (Särlvik and Crewe 1983; Franklin 1985; Rose and McAllister 1986).

Confronted with an increasingly dealigned electorate, partisan strategies to capture it began to diverge. By the late 1970s, these strategies had been rewarded very unequally in electoral terms. The gradual erosion of class-based voting worked mostly to Labour's disadvantage. Support among its traditional electoral stronghold dwindled steadily. In 1983 fewer than half of all manual workers voted Labour, down from over two-thirds in the 1960s. Moreover, the proportion of the working class had itself declined over time. In 1964 manual workers were 72 percent of the electorate. Two decades later they were less than 50 percent. Labour, which had construed its support mostly in terms of class identity and class interests (Särlvik and Crewe 1983, chap. 5), was unable to move beyond its dominant class-based electoral strategy. As a result, the Labour vote declined from over 45 percent in the mid-1960s to the secular low of 27 percent in 1983.

The Conservative Party managed, instead, to maintain high and stable levels of popular support. Once it recovered from striking losses in the elections of 1974, the Conservative share of the vote barely moved from 42 percent in the

following decade. Moreover, the electoral support for the Conservative Party experienced little change in each social and economic group over time. In 1964,
over two thirds of professionals and managers and 58 percent of those in intermediate-level jobs voted Conservative. In 1979, support for the Tory Party had
eroded marginally among the former and increased slightly among the latter to
62 percent (see Table 8.1). By 1992, the Conservative share of the vote had
declined to around 50 percent among all nonmanual sectors, for the most part
in line with its general decline within the whole electorate. Support among
skilled and unskilled manual workers stood at 34 and 29 percent respectively in
1964. In 1992, it was 38 and 29 percent – a hardly significant change when
compared with Labour's loss of a fourth of the vote of skilled manual workers
and a fifth of that of unskilled manual workers in the same period of time.
Stability across social sectors resulting from housing tenure and union membership was especially marked: 56 percent of all homeowners voted Conservative in
1964, 56 percent in 1979, and then a slight decline to 51 percent in 1992.
Among council tenants and private tenants, the conservative share of the vote
remained the same in both 1964 and 1992.

The partial erosion of support among those sectors that traditionally lean
toward the Conservative Party (professionals, managers, intermediate cadres,
homeowners, and nonunionized members) was outweighed by their steady
growth as a proportion of the population. This partly reflected a process of long-
term structural change in the British economy which in turn affected the country's occupational structure. The decline of the manufacturing sector and the
emergence of a "service economy" doubled the share of nonmanual occupations
from the mid-1960s to the mid-1980s. This mechanically contributed to the
erosion of Labour support and the boosting of Conservative ranks. In 1964 only
40 percent of the Conservative voters belonged to the middle class. By the late
1980s, the relation had turned the other way around: fewer than 40 percent of
the Tory votes came from the working class.

The growth of an electorate more inclined to choose Conservative was also
the work of an explicit political strategy devised by the Thatcher government.
First, accelerating a historical trend toward extended home ownership, the Conservative government engineered a vast sale of council houses in the hope of
securing more votes to the cause of free markets and to the defense of property.
Similarly, home mortgages were granted a privileged tax treatment, and interest
rates were carefully managed to favor homeowners. Second, the sale of public
corporations was consciously designed to maximize its impact on the population.
As Lawson put it, "the widespread ownership of private property [would give]
the citizen a vital sense of identification with the society of which he is a part.
It gives him a stake in the future – and indeed, equally important, in the present.
It creates a society with an inbuilt resistance to revolutionary sense."[1] This would
electorally benefit the Conservative Party, "for the more widely the shares were
spread, the more people who had a personal stake in privatization, and were thus
unlikely to support a Labour Party committed to renationalization" (Lawson

Table 8.1. Conservative and Labour vote by social sector in the United Kingdom, 1964-92

	1964			1979			1992		
	SHARE OF POP.	CONS. VOTE	LABOUR VOTE	SHARE OF POP.	CONS. VOTE	LABOUR VOTE	SHARE OF POP.	CONS. VOTE	LABOUR VOTE
ALL VOTERS	100	42	47	100	47	38	100	44	36
SOCIAL CLASS									
Professional/managerial	14	69	17	20	62	21	29	51	19
Routine nonmanual	14	58	24	11	62	19	24	54	25
Skilled manual	45	34	55	46	41	44	21	38	44
Unskilled manual	27	29	60	23	34	47	24	29	52
HOUSING									
Owner	48	56	30	57	56	27	72	51	26
Private tenant	23	38	54	11	46	39	7	39	40
Council tenant	29	22	70	31	28	60	19	18	62
TRADE UNION									
Union household	35	24	66	45	34	49	n.a.	28	50
Nonunion household	65	52	35	55	58	29	n.a.	49	31

Sources: 1964-79: Crewe, Day and Fox (1991). For 1992: British Election Study of 1992, except data on unionization, taken from Sanders (1993).

1992, 208). Finally, part of the decline in union membership in the 1980s should be attributed to the changes introduced by the government in industrial relations legislation (Freeman and Pelletier 1990; Metcalf 1991).

Home ownership increased sharply from 57 to 72 percent of the population from 1979 to 1992.[2] Over a third of the increase was directly produced by the sale of over 1 million council houses to their tenants under very favorable conditions. The extension of home ownership was equally encouraged by a rather favorable tax treatment of mortgages and new legislation introduced to deregulate the private construction and renting of housing. In 1990 mortgage interest relief was two and half times larger in real terms than in 1978–79 (Hills 1991) and benefited over 8.6 million people (Forrest, Murie, and Williams 1990) – a rather sensitive number in political terms.[3] The expansion of home ownership, a variable which already had a bigger independent effect on vote than social class since the mid-1970s,[4] worked to the advantage of the Conservative Party; it won many voters to the principles of private property and scared them away from a Labour Party that, even in the late 1980s, pledged to reverse the privatization program.[5]

The effect of home ownership on the vote is shown through several measures of public opinion. Table 8.2 reproduces the data collected by Crewe comparing the evolution of the vote among council tenants who remained renters and those who bought their houses from 1979 to 1987 (Crewe 1991).[6] Those council tenants who subsequently bought their houses had already been more likely to vote Conservative than those who did not. In 1979, 46 percent of the former supported Thatcher, against 24 percent of the latter. In 1983 the proportions were 41 and 30 percent respectively. Still, the extension of home ownership changed the behavior of numerous voters. From 1979 to 1983 the support for the Tory Party actually increased 10 percentage points among new homeowners, from 46 to 56 percent. Even more important, support for Labour among new owners was cut in half, from 42 to 18 percent. As a result, the Conservative lead over Labour went up from 4 to 38 percentage points among buyers. Conversely, among non-buyers the Labour Party continued to lead by more than 30 points.[7] Although the sale of council houses from 1983 to 1987 had a weaker effect, it still carried some weight: new owners stayed loyal to the 1983 vote – among them, the Conservative Party kept a 10-point lead. Those who had not bought their houses voted Labour in increasing numbers; as a result, the traditional Labour lead over Tories broadened from 19 to 30 points.

In more general terms, home ownership stabilized an important part of the Conservative electorate. Throughout the 1980s, conservatives continued to lead Labour by around 25 points among homeowners (see Table 8.1). The effect of home ownership was remarkably stable across social classes. Table 8.3 breaks down the Conservative and Labour vote in 1992 according to class and home ownership. Support for the Conservative Party was 32 percentage points higher among those who owned their houses than among council tenants. The Conservative Party led Labour by around 40 points among nonmanual workers owning a house and drew the same level of support as Labour among propertied manual

Table 8.2. *Council house sales and vote in British General Elections, 1979-87*

| | VOTE [a] | | | | | | | | |
| | CONSERVATIVE | | | LABOUR | | | LIBERAL/SDP | | |
	1979[b]	1983	Change	1979[b]	1983	Change	1979[b]	1983	Change
Council tenants who bought house (1979-83)	46	56	+10	42	18	-24	12	25	+13
Council tenants who did not buy house (1979-83)	24	23	-1	63	55	-8	14	22	+8

| | CONSERVATIVE | | | LABOUR | | | LIBERAL/SDP | | |
	1983[c]	1987	Change	1983[c]	1987	Change	1983[c]	1987	Change
Council tenants who bought house (1983-87)	41	43	+2	31	32	+1	28	24	-4
Council tenants who did not buy house (1983-87)	30	26	-4	49	56	+7	21	19	-2

[a] Based on three-party vote.

[b] Based on 1983 recall of 1979 vote weighted by actual 1979 result.

[c] Based on 1987 recall of 1983 vote weighted by actual 1983 result.

Source: Crewe (1991), table 2.2, p. 34.

Table 8.3. *Party vote, class, and home ownership in the United Kingdom in 1992*

PERCENTAGE VOTING CONSERVATIVE

	Professional/ managerial	Routine nonmanual	Skilled manual	Partly skilled and unskilled manual	All
Homeowners	53	60	45	40	46
Council tenants	29	21	21	13	14
All	51	54	38	29	

PERCENTAGE VOTING LABOUR

	Professional/ managerial	Routine nonmanual	Skilled manual	Partly skilled and unskilled manual	All
Homeowners	17	20	38	42	23
Council tenants	53	56	57	69	50
All	19	25	44	52	

CONSERVATIVE LEAD OVER LABOUR IN VOTE

	Professional/ managerial	Routine nonmanual	Skilled manual	Partly skilled and unskilled manual	All
Homeowners	+44	+40	+7	-2	+23
Council tenants	-23	-35	-36	-46	-36
All	+32	+31	-6	-23	

Source: Own estimations based on British Election Study of 1992.

workers. A logit analysis of the 1992 vote shows that, controlling for class and income, home ownership increased the probability of voting for the Conservative Party by 21 percent.[8] Accordingly, if in 1992 the proportion of homeowners, private tenants, and council tenants had stayed the same as in 1979, all other things being equal, the Conservative Party would have received about 5 percentage points less than it did, which would most likely have kept it from winning an overall majority.[9]

In order to expand share ownership and build up a system of "popular capitalism," shares offered to the public were deliberately underpriced.[10] At the time Thatcher was elected, there were around 2 million shareholders, or 5 percent of the adult population. The sale of public utilities propped up the number of shareholders substantially: 2.3 million people bought shares of British Telecom in December 1984; British Gas was sold to over 4.4 million people in December 1986. Other big sales included British Airports Authority (BAA) (2.2 million buyers), Rolls-Royce (2.0 million buyers), and British Airways (1.1 million). Although many investors sold their shares rather quickly, overall a large number of buyers retained their stakes in the newly privatized companies. Several years after their privatization, between half and two-thirds of their original buyers still had their shares (Bishop and Kay 1988; Vickers and Yarrow 1988; Riddell 1989). As a result the proportion of people owning shares rose to almost 6 million in April 1986 (or 14 percent of the adult population) and then stabilized around 9 million people (over a fifth of the adult population) from 1987 on (Riddell 1989; Johnson 1993).[11]

Share ownership exercised an important effect on the direction of the vote. Table 8.4 shows the proportion of respondents who voted for either the Conservative or the Labour Party broken down according to social class and share ownership. Across all classes shareholders prefer the Conservatives by at least 15 points relative to nonshareholders.[12] Share ownership actually increases the likelihood of voting Conservative more than home ownership does.[13]

The extension of home and share ownership, the careful management of interest rates, and the shift toward consumption taxes, which provided the potential basis for creating and mobilizing a Conservative plurality, were matched by a clear realignment toward Conservative positions in the area of economic policymaking.

Since the mid-1970s there had been a sustained drift toward the Right among voters on issues concerning the management of the economy and the intervention of the state. As discussed in Chapter 7, that trend favored the Conservative Party in the polls (Särlvik and Crewe 1983, especially chap. 6–9). In 1974, 32 percent of those with an opinion supported further nationalizations. By 1979, the figure had declined to 17 percent and would remain at that level throughout the 1980s (see Table 8.5A). Similarly, in 1974, 56 percent of those with an opinion responded that the state should redistribute income and wealth to the poorer members of society. After Thatcher came into power, the figure dropped to 44 percent in 1987 – a majority was either opposed outright to any

Table 8.4. *Party vote, class, and share ownership in the United Kingdom in 1992*

PERCENTAGE VOTING CONSERVATIVE

	Professional/ managerial	Routine nonmanual	Skilled manual	Partly skilled and unskilled manual	All
Share owners	55	59	45	40	52
No share owners	38	40	28	21	31
All	51	54	38	29	

PERCENTAGE VOTING LABOUR

	Professional/ managerial	Routine nonmanual	Skilled manual	Partly skilled and unskilled manual	All
Share owners	5	9	19	25	17
No share owners	26	29	39	48	36
All	19	25	44	52	

CONSERVATIVE LEAD OVER LABOUR IN VOTE

	Professional/ managerial	Routine nonmanual	Skilled manual	Partly skilled and unskilled manual	All
Share owners	+50	+50	+26	+15	+35
No share owners	+12	+11	-11	-27	-36
All	+32	+31	-6	-23	

Source: Own estimations based on British Election Study of 1992.

Table 8.5. *Ideological change within the British electorate, 1974-87*

A. THE ROLE OF THE STATE IN ECONOMIC MANAGEMENT

	1974	1979	1983	1987	Change 1974-87
(a) Percentage favoring more nationalizations	32	17	18	17	-15
(b) Percentage saying that income and wealth should be redistributed	56	55	47	44	-12
(c) Percentage saying that laws regulating unions have gone too far	n.a.	n.a.	26	28	n.a.

B. SUPPORT FOR THE PUBLIC PROVISION OF WELFARE

	1974	1979	1983	1987	Change 1974-87
(a) Percentage saying that the state should spend more to end poverty	87	83	86	88	+1
(b) Percentage saying that welfare benefits are about right or should be increased	66	50	70	76	+10

Sources: Crewe, Day and Fox (1991) except Gallup Political Index for (1) (c).

income redistribution or judged it to be unimportant (Table 8.5A). Regarding
the issue of trade unions and the management of industrial relations, a strong
majority continued to support the Conservative approach. In 1987, around three-
quarters of those who had an opinion thought that the laws regulating trade
unions were right or still not strong enough (Table 8.5A). The Conservative Party
clearly benefited from the gradual increase in the numbers of those favoring less
state intervention in the economy. Voters overwhelmingly acknowledged the
Conservative Party to be more competent to govern the economy. In the 1992
General Election, still in the middle of an economic recession, the Conservative
lead over Labour fluctuated around 15 percentage points in the management of
inflation, strikes, and taxation. This was actually higher than the Conservative
lead in 1979 on the first two issues and only slightly lower in respect to taxation.
Labour was judged to be better only on unemployment (Newton 1993).[14] More
important, whereas 52 percent of those with an opinion thought that the Conservative Party was the best party to handle Britain's economic problems, only
31 percent favored Labour – a lead of 21 points, three times what the Conservative
Party had enjoyed in 1979. Similarly, the Major government enjoyed a 15-
percentage-point lead when respondents were asked to assess under which party
they would be better off (Sanders 1993).[15]

The shift of public opinion toward laissez-faire economic policies, however,
did not take place on the issue of social spending and the maintenance of the
welfare state. Support for the public provision of social benefits remained high
throughout the decade. As shown in the following section, this strong consensus
on the welfare state among British voters had fundamental repercussions on the
capacity of the Conservative government to further its supply-side strategy.

THE ELECTORAL DILEMMA OF THE CONSERVATIVE PARTY: TAX RATES VERSUS SOCIAL DEMANDS

By the fiscal year 1989/90, general government expenditure had declined to 38.8
percent of GDP, down almost 8 percentage points from the peak reached in 1982/
83. Most of the reduction was due to a strong economic recovery, which had
rapidly lessened social expenditure, but it was also due to significant cuts in
housing and industrial subsidies. Yet in spite of their generic commitment to a
smaller state, by the late 1980s Conservatives had hardly made a dent in the bulk
of structural public spending. The Tory government had been either reluctant
or openly opposed to challenging the public funding of any key welfare program,
although health, social security, and social services made up two-fifths of all
public expenditure. Moreover, a drastic attempt to curtail local spending, which
represented a fourth of all public spending, foundered in the wake of a strong
popular opposition and led to Thatcher's resignation. As a result, at the end of
the 1980s little progress had been made in reshaping substantial parts of the
government budget. Accordingly, in the wake of the deep recession experienced

by the economy in the early 1990s, in 1993/94 public expenditure rose 45 percent of GDP, not far from the level reached during the previous economic downturn.[16]

THE WELFARE STATE:
AN UNCHALLENGED CONSENSUS

In order to cut taxes further, which constitutes for Conservatives the key recipe for stronger growth, the British government should have reduced social spending (by moving the provision of services back to the private sector) as well as that of local governments – both accounting for three-quarters of all public expenditure. But, given the preferences of the British electorate (and, for that matter, the Tory Party itself), this could not have been done without jeopardizing both the unity of the party and its parliamentary majority.

As shown in Table 8.5, for the last two decades, close to 90 percent of those with an opinion had consistently supported public expenditure to end poverty. Moreover, the proportion that considered that welfare benefits should be maintained at the same level or increased went up from 66 percent in 1974 to 76 percent in 1987 (see Table 8.5B). Table 8.6 shows the degree of support among the electorate for particular welfare programs. Support for the public provision of health and retirement pensions runs high across all social sectors: four out of every five respondents attribute to the government the responsibility of securing such services (Table 8.6A). Differences across social sectors are marginal, particularly with respect to health care; 85 percent of all professionals and managers and 87 percent of manual workers believe the state should bear responsibility for health care. As a result, the transfer of the National Health Service to private hands or, for that matter, a slight reduction of public expenditure in that area could only be accomplished at high electoral costs. Even the introduction of a private system of provision alongside the public one – an option entertained by the Conservative leadership (see Thatcher 1993, 609; Lawson 1992, 616) – is strongly rejected by British voters. More than 70 percent of those with an opinion oppose a "two-tier" health service. By contrast, Table 8.6B shows that the level of support for so-called working-class benefits (the public provision of housing and unemployment benefits) is low and varies notably across social sectors.

Strict electoral calculations partially explain the Conservatives' conscious rejection of any substantial reduction in core welfare programs to achieve their overall goal of lower public expenditure. Popular support for the welfare state was just too strong. Reducing health spending, for example, would have induced a significant transfer of electoral support to Labour. But the Conservative commitment to social spending was also a matter of conviction for most party members. Conservative policymakers kept defending the basic fairness of having an extensive welfare system; Thatcher would always insist on "the NHS and its basic principles as a fixed point in our policies" (Thatcher 1993, 606). Tory leaders would at most quarrel with the internal management of welfare programs and with the disincentives inherent in the welfare system. Support for the public

Table 8.6. *British public opinion and the welfare state*

	SOCIAL SECTORS				
	Salariat	Routine nonmanual	Petty bourgeoisie	Manual foremen	Working class
A. SUPPORT FOR "MIDDLE-CLASS BENEFITS"					
Percentage saying it should definitely be the government's responsibility to...					
... provide health care for the sick	85	80	78	91	87
... provide a decent standard of living for the old	71	77	68	87	83
Percentage opposing a "two-tier" health service	77	72	79	75	70
B. SUPPORT FOR 'WORKING-CLASS BENEFITS'					
Percentage saying it should definitely be the government's responsibility to ...					
... provide decent housing for those who cannot afford it	38	39	36	52	56
... provide a decent standard of living for the unemployed	25	26	23	31	38
... provide a job for everyone who wants one	16	14	17	39	31

Definition of social sectors:
  Salariat: Managers, administrators, supervisors of nonmanual workers, professionals.
  Routine nonmanual: Clerks, salesmen, secretaries.
  Petty bourgeoisie: Farmers, small proprietors and own-account manual workers.
  Manual foremen: Supervisors of blue-collar workers.
  Working class: Rank-and-file manual employees in industry and agriculture.

Source: Jowell, Brook and Taylor 1991, 32-33.

provision of welfare was widespread within Conservative ranks as well. According to Rose and McAllister (1986, 124), in a range from 0 (no support) to 100 (complete support), in 1983 Conservative voters scored 80 in their support for the welfare state; Alliance and Labour voters scored 92 and 97 respectively.

The Conservative government adjusted well to public opinion. Whereas Thatcher denied in explicit terms any direct responsibility for the level of unemployment, withdrew the state from the housing market, and sold most public corporations, she maintained, and even reinforced, the government's commitment to a public system of health care and to most of the public expenditure on social security benefits. Conscious that the "NHS was seen by many as a touchstone for our commitment to the welfare state" (Thatcher 1993, 517), the government's approach to its reform was extremely prudent. Mostly prompted by Labour critiques and public worries about the deterioration in NHS services in the mid-1980s, the Conservative cabinet engaged in a thorough Health review during 1988. Concerned about its electoral consequences, Thatcher stressed the need to keep medical care universal and free and explicitly excluded charging for any service, which "would have discredited any other proposals for reform and ditched the review" (Thatcher 1993, 609; Lawson 1992, 616). The White Paper *Working for Patients*, published in January 1989, as well as the reforms that followed in the next years, rebuked privatization measures and limited change to the creation of an "internal market" in the NHS. Public expenditure on health went up under the Thatcher government from £14.5 billion (in 1985 prices) in 1978/79 to £19.6 billion (in 1985 prices) in 1989/90, an increase of 35 percent in real terms, higher than the total increase in real GDP. As a result, the Tory attachment to the basic tenets of the welfare state was never doubted by most voters. Although many thought that a Conservative government would introduce private competition in the provision of health service, by the early 1990s a rather small minority believed the NHS to be in danger under a Conservative government. Only 5 percent of all surveyed mentioned the possibility that a Tory government would abolish the NHS.[17]

Reforms in social security were also limited. An initial proposal to abolish the State Earning Related Pension Scheme (SERPS), a second state pension established by Labour in 1975 to complement the basic one, was watered down to a reduction in benefits (manly a reduction from 25 percent to 20 percent of one's own earnings) to encourage contracting private plans. Although private pension plans grew, public spending on pensions hardly changed, falling a meager 0.2 percent from 6.7 percent in 1979 to 6.5 percent of GDP in 1990 (OECD 1993c, table 21). The remainder of reforms produced some minor changes in the provisions of means-tested benefits. An attempt to reduce the Child Benefit program in the late 1980s triggered a strong opposition from the Department of Social Security that could only be overcome by allocating more money to the family credit (Lawson 1992, 725ff.). Overall, expenditure on social security benefits went from £31.4 billion in 1978/79 to £42.0 billion in 1989/90 (in 1985 prices), a 33.8 percent increase in real terms. Except for widows' pensions, all other benefits increased throughout the 1980s in real terms. In some cases, such as long-term disability benefits and family benefits, spending more than doubled.[18]

THE REFORM OF LOCAL GOVERNMENT

By the late 1970s local government spending amounted to around one-fourth of all public spending. Initially, local spending had been financed through domestic property taxes. As the demand for new services expanded, the central government had directed increasing resources to local authorities through a system of block grants that in the late 1970s funded half of all local expenditure.

To the Conservative government this prevailing financial arrangement was extremely unsatisfactory. Key Tory policymakers charged that local authorities, expecting to be cushioned by central government resources, could approve generous programs without having to pass their underlying costs fully to voters. There was no clear incentive for local councils to rein in spending: Conservative and Labour councillors alike would prefer to spend in the absence of any real local accountability. As a result, overspending by the local government directly threatened the key Conservative goal of reducing total public expenditure. During the first half of the 1980s, local expenditure was 9.5 percent higher every year than the financial plans laid down by the Thatcher government; in comparison, in the same period central government expenditure was on average 4.8 percent higher than forecasted.[19]

Although the relationship between local and central governments had begun to turn sour already under the Callaghan government, it was under the Thatcher government that it gave way to open conflict. Michael Heseltine, environment secretary through January 1983, first introduced "grant-related expenditure assessments," which measured the local authorities' spending needs, and a block grant system to punish overspenders. This was followed by a set of targets as well as specific limits on capital expenditure. A central Audit Commission was set up in 1982 to review local spending in England and Wales. Against the background of a tense confrontation with Labour Party local authorities, Thatcher decided to abolish the Greater London Council and the six metropolitan authorities. Still unable to control local spending satisfactorily, the government took steps in 1984 to directly limit the rates of those selected local authorities believed to spend in excess.

Although the 1974 Conservative manifesto already promised to abolish the system of domestic rates, it was not until the mid-1980s that the Conservative government attempted to overhaul the local finance system. Both a Green Paper drafted in 1981, *Alternatives to Domestic Rates*, and the White Paper *Rates* of 1983 explicitly advised against substituting the domestic rates framework. Some members of the government, however, became convinced that the incremental strategy that had been pursued had been operating at cross-purposes. In pursuit of more financial restraint the Conservative government had actually eroded the principle of local autonomy that it had cherished at the beginning as the solution to local overspending. Moreover, it was not clear either how effective rate capping would prove to be. In 1985 the cabinet had to face an unpopular revaluation of ratings in Scotland. Increases averaged around 20 percent for all households, and the Scottish Conservative Party, electorally in a rather weak position, urged the Thatcher government to abolish the prevailing system (Johnson 1993; Lawson 1992, chap. 45–46). After a long and tense review, the government voted for a new financial framework in the 1988 Local Government Finance Act. The central government's direct support, now allocated as a "lump-sum grant," was to fall to one-sixth of all local revenue. The law also provided for the nationalization of the commercial property tax through a uniform national business rate, whose proceeds would be allocated on a per capita basis. At the core of the new system, domestic property taxes were replaced by a flat-rate local tax, the "community charge," levied on each adult (Leape 1993).

The "community charge," or poll tax, was introduced in Scotland in 1989 and in England and Wales in the following year. By early 1990 it was clear that local authorities, far from limiting their expenditure, were increasing it and blaming the rise on London. Instead of the forecast of the Department of Environment in 1988 envisaging a poll tax of £200 a head, by 1990 the tax had gone up to £400. The community charge proved extremely unpopular. In March 1990, 72 percent of those with an opinion disapproved of the poll tax. Electoral support for the Conservative Party suffered a strong setback as the poll tax was being introduced. In April the Conservative Party was trailing Labour by well over 20 percentage points in the polls (A. King 1993; Norton 1993). Only a year before the Tory government had enjoyed a small lead. The collection of the poll tax proved to be extraordinarily slow during its first year (Barker 1992). Already in 1989 the government had to approve an increase of almost £3 billion in the central government grant to local authorities to lessen the impact of the poll tax. Another £3 billion was allocated in 1991 to fund the so-called Community Charge Reduction Scheme and drive the poll tax bill down to £140 per capita.

Compounded with high interest rates and a slowing economy, the extreme unpopularity of the poll tax led to Thatcher's resignation in November 1990. The Major government readily announced the abolition of the community charge to go into effect in the fiscal year 1993/94 and proposed a new "council tax": a banded property tax based on two-adult households. The government emphasized, however, its goal of capping spending above a certain level and of not accommodating higher-than-average expenditure through its grants. In its aftermath, however, the ill-designed poll tax episode boosted local expenditure. In 1979, total local expenditure was £40.7 billion (in 1985 prices). Despite not achieving its targets for local spending, the Conservative government was actually able to lower it in real terms by 1982 and, after a slight increase, to hold it below £43 billion throughout 1988. After the introduction of the poll tax, however, local spending shot up to almost £48 billion (in 1985 prices) – a sharp increase that put local expenditure close to its 1979 level as a proportion of GDP. Moreover, local autonomy had hardly gained ground. As of 1990/91, around a half of all local spending was paid by the central government; another fifth was raised through a commercial tax whose rates were determined in London.

PUBLIC SPENDING UNBRIDLED

After a whole decade in government, the Conservative Party had hardly dented the biggest expenditure programs, and thus the level of public expenditure continued to be extremely dependent on the business cycle. It was not long before the conservative success in lowering expenditure was revealed to be less striking than it had appeared at the peak of economic activity.

After experimenting with different money supply targets to curb inflation, by 1985 the Thatcher government had turned to the exchange rate. Two years later, the chancellor adopted an implicit policy to shadow the German mark at the DM3 rate that, even though initially aimed at reinforcing the anti-inflation credibility of the government, required substantial cuts in interest rates. As a result, monetary policy turned out to be too loose. Combined with a strong upsurge in domestic demand, partly generated by the deregulation of financial markets, and high wage settlements, it put inflation at 9.5 percent in 1990. Base interest rates were doubled to 15 percent between June 1988 and October 1989. As the tight stance of monetary policy percolated into the economy, inflation declined to 4 percent. Output contracted in real terms in 1990. Affected as well by a downturn in the world business cycle, unemployment almost doubled to about 3 million people by mid-1992. As in the early 1980s, public spending escalated rapidly. After bottoming at 38.5 percent of GDP (excluding privatization proceeds) in 1988/89, general government expenditure rose close to 41 percent of GDP in 1990/91. Two years later, it was almost 45 percent of GDP (see Table 8.7).

Whereas in the early 1980s the Conservative government had relied on a harsh fiscal policy to sustain its Medium Term Financial Strategy and quell inflation, the Major government resisted any tax increase to balance the budget. With general elections to be held in April 1992, the new chancellor, Kenneth Clarke, instead decided to lower the income tax rate on the first £2,000 of taxable income to 20 percent, halve the car tax, and introduce transitional relief for business tax rates. Public spending on health, social security, and local government was slightly increased as well. As a result, the public sector debt repayment of 0.9 percent of GDP (excluding privatization proceeds) in 1990/91 swung to a public sector borrowing requirement of 8.5 percent of GDP three years later. However, around 70 percent of the deterioration in the budget balance since 1990 was due to purely cyclical factors (OECD 1993b).

The dilemmas posed by the economic recession and the response engineered by the Major government shed light on the overall question of controlling public spending. Although the reduction of the state in the economy was a pervasive goal of the Conservative government, the success of its policies was mixed. As shown in Figure 8.1, the Conservative government was willing and able to sta-

Table 8.7. *Fiscal policy in the United Kingdom in the early 1990s*

GENERAL GOVERNMENT EXPENDITURE AS A PERCENTAGE OF GDP

	EXCLUDING PRIVATIZATION PROCEEDS			INCLUDING PRIVATIZATION PROCEEDS		
	Forecast	Actual Outcome	Difference	Forecast	Actual Outcome	Difference
1990/91	39.6	40.6	+1.0	38.7	39.6	+0.9
1991/92	40.4	42.5	+2.1	39.5	41.2	+1.7
1992/93	43.9	44.7	+0.8	43.0	43.4	+0.4
1993/94	45.0	45.0	0.0	44.2	44.2	0.0

PUBLIC SECTOR BORROWING REQUIREMENT AS A PERCENTAGE OF GDP

	EXCLUDING PRIVATIZATION PROCEEDS			INCLUDING PRIVATIZATION PROCEEDS		
	Forecast	Actual Outcome	Difference	Forecast	Actual Outcome	Difference
1990/91	-0.3	0.9	+1.2	-1.2	-0.1	+1.1
1991/92	2.5	3.7	+1.2	1.4	2.4	+1.0
1992/93	5.6	7.4	+1.8	4.7	6.1	+1.4
1993/94	8.8	8.6	-0.2	8.0	7.9	-0.1

Sources. *OECD Economic Surveys. United Kingdom*, several years; U.K. Parliament 1992; EIU 1994, first quarter.

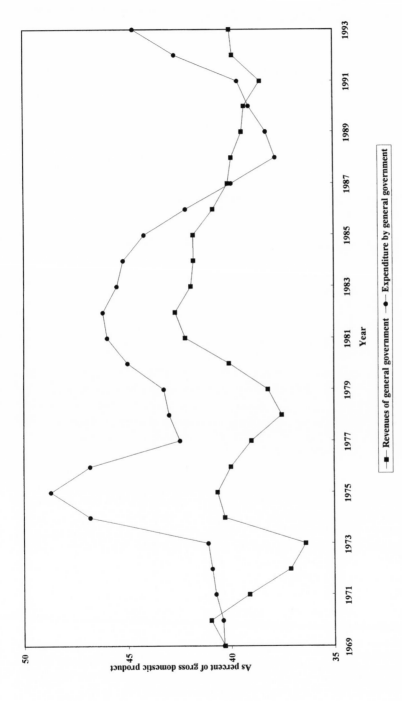

Figure 8.1. Evolution of general government revenue and expenditure in the United Kingdom, 1969–93

bilize the level of tax revenues in spite of strong pressures to increase expenditure. Moreover, it reduced the level of public spending under similar economic conditions: in the peak year of 1988 general government expenditure was around 4 percentage points lower than in 1979, the last year in which a similar economic upturn was registered. Yet the gains that had been made were still moderate and mostly at the mercy of economic conditions. If the Conservative government wished to cut the equilibrium level of public spending even further, it had no other option, once industrial subsidies and capital investment had been fairly pruned, than to limit the public provision of welfare benefits. This solution seemed politically unfeasible. Social and political support for the welfare state remained remarkably high among the electorate. Only if the Tory Party convinced voters that the private provision of most social programs, such as health care and pensions, would benefit most of the electorate, as it had done in disposing of council houses and public corporations, could such a strong level of social consensus be broken and the welfare state dismantled. Yet such a radical approach had at that time marginal support within the Tory Party itself. Accordingly, although overall successful in reshaping the supply side of the economy, the Conservative economic strategy had reached its limits in terms of further reducing the weight of the state.

CONCLUSIONS

This chapter and Chapter 7 jointly provide a detailed account of the economic and political dimensions of a conservative strategy developed to respond to the economic slowdown and the worsening trade-off between employment and the redistributive policies in most advanced countries in the last two decades. In the light of the previous analysis of the Spanish case, macroeconomic discipline appears as an increasingly common objective across all (noncorporatist) economies since the oil shocks of the 1970s, regardless of the party in power. Still, there are some noticeable differences in the extent of their progress toward price stability, which have to do with the underlying political coalitions and institutional conditions of each partisan government. In Spain, the Socialist government, heavily relying on the support of working-class voters, did not couple tight monetary policies with a thorough reform of the labor market. The González government optimistically hoped to secure an income pact in order to avoid implementing restrictive measures. At the end, however, the result was suffocatingly high interest rates. By contrast, in the United Kingdom, the conservative government, politically free from unions, turned the labor market into a decentralized and flexible arena. Although it took time, deregulation brought about a happy combination of less inflation and declining unemployment by the early 1990s.

As shown in Chapters 3 and 4 and fleshed out in detail in Chapter 7, conservatism amounts to lower taxes and private investment. This also involves a specific (and, at least in Britain, a relatively successful) political strategy. As has been the case in many social democratic governments, the success of the British Conservative program lay in the government's ability both to create long-term electoral attachments to the Conservative Party and to reshape the British political culture in favor of their cherished values of liberty, entrepreneurship, and property. The Conservative electoral hegemony of the 1980s was bolstered in part by the gradual transformation of British society: the number of nonmanual workers, among whom the Conservative vote hovers around 60 percent or more, increased from being one-third of the electorate in 1979 to over one-half in 1992. But the Conservative electoral coalition was equally the outcome of a conscious political strategy. The tax reform was structured to benefit middle-class voters. Interest rates and mortgage credit were carefully managed to favor property owners. "Middle-class" social benefits such as health care and pensions were carefully protected. Moreover, the extension of home and share ownership eroded support for Labour and, due to the British electoral system, bolstered the Conservative parliamentary majority.

Even under improving economic conditions, there were inherent electoral limits to the Conservative capacity to reform the British political economy. In the Spanish case, the PSOE's supply-side economic strategy was effectively constrained, apart from the role of unions, by the competing electoral demands for more social services (particularly from the Left) and the stabilization of taxes (mostly from the Center) encountered by the González government. In Britain, the strong public support for the welfare state had a strikingly similar impact on the Conservative economic strategy. "Working-class" benefits, which do not have a universal character, were clearly affected by Conservative cuts. By contrast, "middle-class" benefits, that is, benefits that covered the whole population, survived mostly untouched. Since the latter represented the bulk of public spending, they automatically hindered the Conservatives' long-term commitment to reducing the weight of the public sector. If the Thatcher government had broken down their universal nature – by creating, for example, a two-tier health system – it might have been able to press forward with more reforms. But even within the Conservative Party, supporters of a radical change in social policy were a small minority. The generalized revolt against the poll tax indicated as well how strong the social consensus was for a rather progressive tax system. Unable to convince most of the electorate of the advantages to be found in the private provision of welfare benefits, the Conservative government could not drive government spending down any further. The reduction of government expenditure remained partly contingent on the business cycle. When a new economic downturn began in the early 1990s, the public budget shot up again to levels only marginally lower than those reached ten years earlier. To sum up, the British case shows that reforming the economy is possible. But it also makes apparent how difficult lowering the social wage may be.

9

PARTISAN STRATEGIES AND
ELECTORAL COALITIONS

Our inquiry into the sources of economic policymaking in the advanced world has pinpointed a tight relationship between the governing partisan coalition and the selection of particular structural economic strategies. As shown by both the statistical evidence of Chapters 3 and 4 and the historical examination of Britain and Spain in the 1980s, conservative governments cut taxes, slash public investment programs, sell most public businesses, and revamp the labor market to increase the profitability of capital and to induce the unemployed to actively search for jobs. Socialist cabinets, instead, raise tax rates on high-income brackets and boost public spending on infrastructure and human capital in order to ease the transition from an unskilled population profile to a well-educated workforce without having to lower the social wage.

Such a powerful link between economic policies and partisan politics has led us inevitably to explore the electoral motives that guide the behavior of parties and the electoral dynamics behind the development of each economic strategy. Accordingly, the book has moved beyond its initial assumption that parties adopt different economic policies due to the redistributive consequences they have on clear-cut electoral constituencies. This has been done in a theoretical manner in Chapter 2 and then, mostly in empirical terms, through an analysis of the Spanish and British experiences. As discussed in this chapter, the result has been a more elaborate and complex set of arguments about the electoral dimensions of economic policymaking, and hence about the actual interaction of politics and economics.

Broadly confirming the initial redistributive assumptions of the book, both cases show that economic policies respond to the material interests of each party's main electoral constituencies. In Spain, taxes were structured and investment was allocated in a sharply redistributive manner to buttress the initial Socialist coalition of blue-collar workers and lower-middle classes. In

the United Kingdom, instead, taxes and interest rates were managed to sat-
isfy the middle class and homeowners. The two cases also suggest a more
complex relationship between the development of economic policies and the
electoral strategies of the parties in power. With a varying degree of success,
all governments attempt to craft particular economic policies to expand their
political support beyond their initial coalition. In Spain, the González government consciously deployed heavy public spending programs to reproduce the
Scandinavian pattern of broad cross-class social democratic coalitions. Public
investment plans, generous unemployment benefits, higher pensions, and extended health care were designed to obtain the assent of the least skilled
workers to both a market economy and stable macroeconomic policies. But
the beneficial effects of more capital formation and the universal character of
social expenditure were also expected to weld parts of the middle classes to
the Socialist project. In Britain, the reform of the labor market and of the delivery of public services and the sale of public firms and council houses were
carried out to enlarge the size of the middle class and to attract working-class
voters into the Tory coalition.

The development of a supply-side economic strategy and the corresponding
formation of a stable electoral coalition are beset, however, by substantial political
tensions. The employment–equality dilemma that characterizes advanced economies requires economic reforms that, even if they imply long-run economic gains
for all the government's electoral constituencies, may impose short-term economic losses on parts or some of those constituencies. As a result, all governments
are confronted with policy trade-offs – between financing the social wage, minimizing the tax burden, and adding value to the factors of production – that may
jeopardize different segments of their electoral basis and hence the success of their
economic strategies.

Conservative cabinets, such as the Thatcher government, see their strategy
of lowering taxes and freeing private resources constrained by massive public
support for a substantial part of the welfare state (or, employing the terms of
Chapter 2, the social wage) in all OECD countries. Social democratic governments are affected by similar electoral dilemmas. To boost public capital spending
while maintaining the existing social wage, a left-wing government must raise
taxes. But, as the Spanish history of the early 1990s shows, this solution threatens
to slow down the economy and erodes the level of Socialist support among middle
classes (or highly educated or skilled workers). To finance its capital formation
projects without approving higher taxes, the Left has to either reduce or postpone
social spending – the strategy followed by the PSOE until 1989. But by the late
1980s, a substantial number of working-class voters had abstained or shifted to
the Spanish extreme Left. In other countries, such as Austria and France, they
have instead turned toward radical right-wing parties that promise to stop the
current fall of wages and the destruction of jobs through protectionist policies
and tough anti-immigration laws. As discussed in detail later, cutting across the
choice between higher taxes or lower wages, these new parties threaten to break

down the established party system and the dominant menu of policy alternatives in the advanced world.

The severity of the dilemma between restructuring the economy and sustaining the social wage mainly depends on the distribution of preferences (so that the lower the skills of voters and the stronger the intensity of redistributive demands, the harder it will be to cut the social wage) and institutional factors (such as the structure of party competition) that allow governments to retain the loyalty of voters who are hurt in the short run. But it also varies in part with the evolution of the business cycle. As the economy enters a recession, the need for higher social transfers and the fall in revenues make it politically harder to either increase public investment or approve a permanent reduction in taxes. Governments are then pushed to delay their supply-side economic reforms. To protect the unemployed without raising taxes excessively, the Spanish cabinet froze most public capital spending in the early 1980s and, to some degree, under the economic crisis of the early 1990s. Similarly, to avoid losing key electoral sectors, the British cabinet softened most structural reforms until the mid-1980s. As cyclical unemployment fell and subsidies to public firms declined, however, both governments started to gain enough political autonomy to revamp the economy.

This chapter, which weaves together the evidence gathered in the previous four chapters on the effects of electoral politics on the development of structural economic strategies, is organized as follows. The first section summarizes the ways in which economic policies represent (and attempt to enlarge) the corresponding electoral coalitions that sustain both conservative and socialist governments. The rest of the chapter examines the electoral dilemmas that underlie the growing employment–equality trade-off suffered by advanced countries. The second section explores, in the light of the evidence presented for the British and the Spanish cases, the policy choices and political trade-offs faced by both conservatives and socialists. The third section examines how the evolution of the business cycle temporarily shifts the social wage in a way that affects the electoral dilemmas of the governing coalition and distorts the pace of structural reforms. The last section rounds off the analysis of the electoral dimensions of the employment–equality trade-off by discussing how growing protectionist demands are altering the party systems and policy debates of several advanced democracies.

PARTIES, ECONOMIC STRATEGIES, AND ELECTORAL SUPPORT: BUILDING POLITICAL COALITIONS

The analysis of Britain and Spain shows that economics and politics are tightly interconnected – in two basic dimensions. In the first place, and as implied in the assumptions of this book's initial model, partisan governments construct their supply-side policies to please (and therefore secure) their supporting electoral coalition: low taxes and low interest rates fitted the demands of the mostly middle-class, homeowner British Conservative voters; heavy capital spending and a high social wage responded to the needs and expectations of the unskilled, working-class, and low-middle-class sectors supporting the PSOE. In the second place, the two cases make clear that it would be too simplistic to interpret economic policies as the mere reflection of voter preferences. As emphasized in the literature on the electoral basis of social democracy developed by Esping-Andersen (1985) and Przeworski and Sprague (1986), politicians carefully tailor economic and social policies to shape the political and policy preferences of voters and to expand, if possible, their initial electoral coalition.

BUILDING A SOCIAL DEMOCRATIC COALITION

Socialist parties believe that an economic strategy focused on maximizing the investment rate in a way that combines growth and more equality will sustain a broad cross-class coalition including the traditional working class and segments of the middle class in the following way. Higher tax revenues directed to finance public capital formation will increase the productivity of regions, economic sectors, and the workforce in general. A higher productivity rate will increase the competitiveness of the economy. It will attract private capital – always in search of high rates of return. And it will allow for higher wages across the board without threatening the performance of the economy. Higher wages directly reduce inequality – the primary goal of social democracy – and bolster the support of blue-collar workers. But they also imply an improvement among white-collar employees, who, at least initially, have had to put up with relatively higher taxes. More important, with higher average productivity, taxes can be even higher without scaring away private investors – that is, as long as the latter's net returns (after-tax profits) continue to be higher than in other countries.

With increasing tax revenues, social transfers can be generous and not affect economic performance. A universalistic welfare state can then strengthen the cross-class coalition that initially elected the socialist party: it can "manufacture broad class (even cross-class) solidarity and social democratic consensus," for by establishing the principle of universal solidarity and by marginalizing the market as the principal instrument of distribution, "the entire population must become wedded to the fate of the social citizenship state and must have an incentive to promote its cause actively" (Esping-Andersen 1985, 245). In other words, with the right investment policies in place, it will be possible to sustain growth and high wages and to generate tax revenues in a "virtuous circle" that will lure extensive middle-class sectors (necessary to win power) into the social democratic camp.

Full employment policies (in exchange for wage restraint), high levels of spending on education and manpower policies, and a universalist welfare state successfully welded a broad cross-class coalition around Scandinavian social democracy at least until the mid-1980s (Esping-Andersen 1985). In Sweden, usually seen as the most accomplished case of social democratic electoral hegemony, the social democratic party, the SAP, polled an average of 45.5 percent of the electorate from 1944 to 1988. In the mid-1980s, it still received the votes of two-thirds of the working class and two-fifths of white-collar employees. In countries in which socialists were less successful in managing the economy, such as Denmark and Britain, the mobilization of the electorate was less satisfactory. The level of support, which in the 1950s was similar to Swedish levels, dropped to around a half among blue-collar workers and a third among white-collar workers in the 1980s. Moreover, laissez-faire options in economic policy gained substantial ground in all classes in those countries.[1]

A similar strategy was pursued by the Spanish Socialist Party. Spending on infrastructure was mainly allocated to poor regions and left-wing strongholds. Expenditure on education and manpower policies, which was almost doubled, was aimed at improving the life chances of the core of the PSOE's supporting coalition, that is, agricultural laborers and the industrial working class. The González government also calculated that, in accelerating the competitiveness of the Spanish economy, the active involvement of the state in the process of capital formation would be seen as advantageous by substantial parts of the middle classes. Similarly, the expansion of unemployment benefits and, in particular, the deployment of universalistic pension and health care systems were expected to consolidate the vast coalition stretching from the moderate middle class to the traditional Left that had voted for the PSOE in 1982.

The dominant position of the PSOE was undoubtedly helped by the lack of electoral appeal of a too conservative opposition party. Organized by former ministers of Franco, the Popular Party (PP) was consistently seen as a right-wing party by Spanish voters, who are clustered around center-to-the-left positions, and consequently trailed the Spanish Socialist Party by more than 10 percentage points in the polls until 1993. However, González's policies themselves played a decisive role in securing a strong following for the Socialist political project. After losing a fifth of its 1982 electorate in the following four years, the PSOE consistenty polled two-fifths of the valid votes from 1986 on. In 1993, in the middle of a painful economic crisis, with unemployment over 22 percent and a fall of real GDP of 1 percent, the sharpest decline in the last thirty years, it still received 38.5 percent of the votes and, albeit in a minority position, was able to form a government again.

FASHIONING A CONSERVATIVE PUBLIC OPINION

As is vividly revealed by the British case, conservative parties structure their noninterventionist economic strategy of lower taxation and strong private investment in order to build a broad electoral coalition – in this case formed by middle-class voters and propertied citizens. According to conservatives, low taxes and a deregulated economy should maximize the rate of investment and accelerate economic growth. The ensuing expansion of income should enlarge the size of the middle class, that is, the natural constituency of nonsocialist parties, and therefore raise the probability of a conservative electoral majority in the future. This natural transformation, fostered by economic growth, toward an affluent and "classless" society should be helped by the explicit transfer of economic and political resources from the state to individuals and by the creation of conditions that expand citizens' choices. Like social democrats, conservatives also aspire to create a society where classes do not matter. But, for them, the central principles to achieve it should be merit and individual effort with the market as the main allocative mechanism.

To please its electoral constituencies, the Thatcher government reshaped the tax system by lowering tax rates, increasing its reliance on indirect taxation, and approving extensive plans to favor private savings. Mortgage interest tax relief, particularly important for homeowners, rose 2.5 times, affecting 8.6 million people by the end of the decade. Moreover, private choice was expanded through the introduction of private pension plans and the creation of an internal market in the National Health Service.

The Thatcher cabinet actively attempted to transform all voters into propertied citizens, so that they would then have a stake in the free-market policies of the Tory Party. Over one million council houses were sold to their tenants. After the privatization of the British public business sector, the proportion of shareholders jumped from 5 percent in 1979 to 20 percent of the adult population in the late 1980s. Mostly as a result of specific legal reforms, union membership, which constituted one of the strongholds of the Labour Party, declined by a third. Thus, although Tory support among the Conservative Party's traditional voters – professionals, managers, intermediate cadres, and homeowners – declined marginally, the decline was compensated for by their increasing importance as a proportion of the population over the decade.

As in the Spanish case, the electoral success of the Conservative cabinet was partly a consequence of a too radical and politically weak opposition party. A split in the Labour Party in the early 1980s amplified the Thatcher victory of 1983. Moreover, Labour was increasingly perceived as too extreme by the British electorate. Whereas in 1970 only 33 percent of those surveyed thought that the parties differed a great deal, 47 percent did in 1979 and over 80 percent did in the 1980s. Nonetheless, the political hegemony of the Conservative Party was also the outcome of well-orchestrated policies and a convincing political discourse. Throughout the 1980s, the British electorate increasingly turned against redistributing income and in favor of privatizing public firms and reducing the power of unions. Moreover, the Conservative Party was consistently, and increasingly over time, rated the best party to handle the economy. By 1993 it led Labour by 21 points in public opinion, three times the advantage it had in 1979. As a result, the Conservative Party could maintain an average lead of 10.4 percentage points over Labour (7.6 points in 1992). Success was so great that Labour had no other choice than to embark on a painful, long process of internal transformation.

ELECTORAL DILEMMAS: PUBLIC OPINION, THE SOCIAL WAGE, AND TAXES

PUBLIC INVESTMENT AND THE SOCIAL WAGE: THE SOCIAL DEMOCRATIC TRADE-OFF

Even if a public investment strategy works (mostly in the medium run) to reduce unemployment without hurting the main constituencies of social democratic parties, in its deployment a left-wing cabinet faces two main electoral dilemmas that threaten its popularity and the nature of its policies. On the one hand, since raising the rate of public capital formation implies rising incomes in the future at the cost of less present consumption, substantial parts of the (least skilled) electorate may turn toward parties that promise an immediate increase in public transfers. On the other hand, insofar as intense public investment requires higher taxes (especially if social spending has not been contained or reduced), middle-class voters may decide to shift to nonsocialist parties.

As discussed mostly in Chapter 5, the González government steadily developed an active supply-side policy, to restructure the economy of a country ill-prepared to resist the pressures of external competition. The public deficit was halved. Public spending on human and fixed capital was raised by a third to almost 10 percent of GDP. In order to expand public savings and investment, tax revenues were increased substantially – by a fourth – while social expenditure was frozen and subsidies to public firms cut in real terms.

The PSOE could not avoid, however, the electoral costs and corresponding policy dilemmas that come attached to a public investment strategy. By a large majority, Spaniards expected the state to build up a complete, universalistic welfare system in a short period of time. In the mid-1980s, 70 percent of those surveyed thought that the state should ensure the welfare of all citizens.[2] Still, the PSOE's extraordinary electoral lead over a too radical conservative opposition and an embattled Communist Party gave the González government enough autonomy to commit most tax revenues to public capital formation plans. As the opposition moved to the center, however, the PSOE's hegemonic position weakened. Moreover, the PSOE lacked the organizational capacity to prioritize its investment policies over prowelfare demands in a sustained way. González could not count on the wholehearted support from trade unions available to Northern European social democratic governments. The PSOE's machine was weak: party members were just 2.5 percent of the party vote, a ratio almost twenty times lower than the member/vote ratio of the Swedish and Austrian Socialist Parties in the 1960s.

After a period of economic adjustment in the early 1980s, trade unionists broke from their previous cooperative stance toward González and staged a landmark general strike in December 1988 to force the government to boost social spending. In the General Election of 1989, the PSOE lost 3 percentage points of the total electorate, mostly to Izquierda Unida, a radical-left coalition. Calculating that he could not stop further electoral losses unless most of the popular demands for a broader welfare state were met, González increased unemployment benefits and pensions substantially.

To finance the corresponding jump in social spending, the government should have had to raise taxes. Nonetheless, the PSOE was now confronted with the second electoral dilemma of social democratic governments. In 1982 taxes were still 10 percentage points below the OECD average and far from the policy preferences of the Spanish median voter. By 1990, Spanish tax revenues were very close to the OECD mean. Excessively high taxes would have eroded the PSOE's level of support among middle-class voters to the point of losing the government. Accordingly, the income tax, the value-added tax, and employer social security contributions were only marginally increased in the early 1990s. The González government decided instead to curtail its investment plans and to allow the public deficit to grow again. Unable to draw unions into a social compact, the government then resorted to a policy of high interest rates to curb the inflationary effects of a growing public deficit (and to sustain the peseta within the ERM), which only magnified the economic downturn of the early 1990s.

The electoral dilemmas suffered by the PSOE and its policy responses contributed to the reshaping of its supporting coalition away from the quasi-catchall character it had back in 1982. The combination of high marginal tax rates, an overvalued peseta, and several corruption scandals eroded the Socialist vote in urban areas and halved the PSOE's support among white-collar employees and highly qualified blue-collar workers.[3] Meanwhile, the aggressive capital buildup pursued in the least developed regions and the expansion of the welfare state added, to a still solid working-class base, the vote of rural areas and the endorsement of welfare benefit recipients. Around 40 percent of the industrial working class and the agricultural "proletariat" (or close to 60 percent as a proportion of those who voted) supported the PSOE throughout the decade (against 12 percent for the conservative opposition, the PP). Over 30 percent of the unemployed (who had lost a job) and the pensioners (40 percent as a proportion of actual voters) voted Socialist in 1992, twice the rate of the Spanish conservative party.

The Spanish experience may be thought of as a particular instance of a pattern common to most socialist governments. In Scandinavian countries, public sector employment creation has played the role performed by the extension of welfare benefits in Spain. To combine earnings equality and a good employment performance, in order not to lose the support of increasingly impatient working and lower-middle classes, social democratic cabinets added, to their education and vocational-training policies, an extraordinary expansion of public-sector jobs. With the state turned into an employer of last resort, Northern European social democracy developed into a compromise between working-class groups, white-collar employees, and (instead of recipients of welfare benefits, as in Spain) civil servants.[4] An increasingly severe trade-off between equality and employment is threatening, however, to unravel that electoral coalition. Moreover, an excessive rise in public spending (and taxes) – driven by rising expenditure on health care and pensions – has compromised the rate of economic growth of Scandinavia and seems to alienate segments of the middle class that are essential to gain a parliamentary majority. But any movement away from policies to sustain a bloated public sector risks strengthening New Left parties at the expense of social democracy.[5]

THE SOCIAL WAGE AND TAXES: THE CONSERVATIVE DILEMMA

The employment–equality trade-off imposes, as well, important electoral constraints on a conservative economic strategy. On the one hand, since the reduction in the social wage may imply a substantial fall in income equality, semiskilled or low-middle-class sectors that traditionally vote conservative may shift to the Left in response to too radical measures. On the other hand, excessively slow reforms may jeopardize the support of high-income voters. As in the Spanish case (and the other social democratic cases mentioned above), the intensity of the conservative policy trade-offs and the extension of economic reforms hinge on the structure of party competition (in turn derived from the set of electoral norms and the competitive strategies of other political forces) and, above all, on the structure of skills and distributive demands in society.

Partly benefiting from the British first-past-the-post electoral system and the split of the Labour Party (which magnified all Conservative victories), but mostly helped by a changing public opinion in favor of less public intervention, the Thatcher government was able to reduce inflation and to turn around most postwar interventionist economic policies. Public investment was halved to a sixth of total investment. The core of the public business sector was sold. The income tax was reduced and its progressivity minimized. Unemployment benefits were cut and the labor market was thoroughly deregulated.

The promarket policies of the Tory Party were, however, constrained by a sizable degree of popular support for welfare-state benefits. Once public investment and subsidies to state-owned firms had been minimized, any further reduction in the level of total government spending could only come from trimming the welfare state. Yet this could only be done at the risk of suffering great political damage. In Britain nine out of ten persons attribute to the state a certain responsibility for ending poverty. Universal programs such as health and pensions are consistently supported by at least three-fourths of public opinion, with hardly any variation across social classes. The same results are obtained in surveys in the welfare state par excellence – Sweden (Rothstein 1993).[6] As a matter of fact, a systematic tax reform and the deregulation of the labor market – jointly with the exogenously determined demand shift for unskilled workers – had increased inequality to politically sensitive levels by the early 1990s. In 1979 the top quintile of the British population received 37 percent of all post-tax income. The two bottom quintiles received 22.5 percent of all post-tax income.

In 1990, the figures had diverged considerably to 45 and 16.3 percent in each case (HM Central Statistical Office 1993). Probably in response to widening inequality, in 1992 the percentage of British voters in favor of redistributing income had slightly risen to 48 percent, similar to the 1983 level. Moreover, the percentage saying that spending on welfare benefits was about right or should be increased went up from 50 percent in 1979 to 83 percent in 1992 (Crewe, Fox, and Day 1995).

The Thatcher government adjusted rather well to public opinion. Social expenditure was cut very little. Although some incremental changes were introduced in some areas, such as the pension system, the Tory cabinet actually oversaw a spending spree in some of the biggest welfare programs. Expenditure on social security benefits and on health actually grew in real terms and as a proportion of GDP under the Thatcher government. The only bold attempt to reduce public expenditure, by restructuring the local tax system, translated into a two-digit lead for the Labour Party in the polls and led to Thatcher's resignation in 1990.

Progress in reducing taxes and the overall level of public spending was rather limited. The level of taxes as a proportion of the British economy was only stabilized. Total public spending declined marginally by around 4 percentage points, once we control for the effects of the business cycle.[7] Although this was a substantial achievement (the European average increased by around 4 points of GDP in the same period), it was much less than what the Conservatives had hoped to accomplish back in 1979.

This does not mean that public opinion cannot be changed. As income levels rise across the board, and the risks the welfare state covers diminish, more citizens may stop thinking of the welfare state in a Rawlsian way, that is, as some sort of collective insurance to protect them from falling down the social ladder at some point. As a result, they will be less willing to bear its tax costs. Governments may also be capable of actively reducing the level of popular attachment to the welfare state by emphasizing the virtues of the private provision of social services, in the same way the Thatcher government did for housing and the nationalized business sector. Nonetheless, as the British case makes apparent, nonsocialist parties end up defending the core principles of social protection embedded in the welfare state: popular pressure for social expenditure is too strong to allow for excessive spending cuts.

ELECTORAL DILEMMAS IN THE SHORT RUN: THE IMPACT OF BUSINESS CYCLE FLUCTUATIONS

The evolution of the British and Spanish economic policies shows that, in the execution of their preferred economic strategies, governments are constrained, regardless of their political ideology, by the fluctuations of the business cycle. By exacerbating the employment–equality trade-off, an economic downturn severely limits the capacity of goverments to restructure the economy. The significant fall in tax revenues and the higher social spending that result from an economic crisis make it extremely difficult to increase public capital spending. Similarly, with rising unemployment, any downward shift in the social wage becomes politically explosive. Moreover, an economic recession implies a substantial fall in the government's popularity and therefore a loss of political resources needed to advance its agenda. The Thatcher government's popularity fell to 18 percent in the depth of the economic crisis in 1981 – only to recover to 40 percent by the second half of 1982. Under these circumstances, the party in office may postpone or soften its supply-side economic program depending on two conditions: its electoral strength and, above all, the capacity of the government to align macroeconomic aggregates according to its preferences.

The economic downturn of the early 1980s in Spain provides a good example of the policy trade-offs faced by social democratic policymakers. Following an economic shock, a leftist government is likely to delay the implementation of its medium-term public capital formation strategy, especially if it cannot count on the appropriate conditions (i.e., an encompassing union movement and a favorable international environment) to generate expansionary policies. With less revenue and growing unemployment, the options of a Socialist government are limited. Developing its investment plans (its long-term choice) would require raising taxes, running a larger public deficit, or cutting social spending. Approving new taxes to pay for investment risks aggravating the recession. Running a larger public deficit, which is tantamount to generating an expansionary policy, depends on the calculations the cabinet makes about its inflationary consequences and the support it can garner from the union movement. Only if unions commit themselves to a policy of wage moderation will a social democratic government expand the economy and spend on capital formation at the same time. It was only after securing the social pact of 1985–86 that the González government engaged in countercyclical policies. Many of these policy measures came in the form of fixed capital spending: the government increased capital spending by 27 percent in real terms in 1985, whereas in 1984 capital spending had been frozen. If raising taxes and engineering an expansion are discarded, a left-wing government can still embrace the third option: cutting social spending to expand investment expenditure. But cutting social spending (lowering the social wage) goes directly against the egalitarian, redistributive goals of social democratic parties. The initial response of the González government corroborates this analysis. Until 1985, before the Acuerdo Económico y Social with the Socialist trade union, UGT, was signed, public capital spending was actually reduced. Tax revenues were slowly increased. But they were mostly directed to accommodate higher social spending and to neutralize the effects of the economic downturn on the public deficit. In short, lacking the support of unions, the crisis clearly deterred the Spanish Socialist Party from fully embracing its long-term supply-side economic strategy for several years. The Spanish episode of 1983–84 fits quite smoothly (and therefore provides a good example of) the results and the simulations (on fixed capital formation) conducted in Chapter 3: in most cases social democrats prefer to wait until the economic crisis is over, and the public deficit under control, to develop new capital formation programs.

The historical experience of the Thatcher government shows how a worsening economic climate chokes off the initiatives of a conservative government as well. Unless conservatives are not concerned about inflating the public deficit, all tax reforms will be postponed. In Britain tax rates were immediately reduced after the General Election of 1979, and some spending cuts were approved in the following two years. Nonetheless, as the crisis worsened, tax allowances to compensate for inflation were suspended – in fact reversing the cuts of 1979 – to pay for a dramatic overshooting in social expenditure (and debt interests). The government decided to spend all its political capital on changing the British macroeconomic framework and on breaking down a long history of high inflationary expectations. As a result, most structural reforms, such as extensive layoffs in public corporations and the transformation of the labor market, which might have increased the pain of the crisis and threatened the electoral standing of the government, were slowed down. As a matter of fact, expenditure on industrial subsidies and vocational training went up, in contradiction to the initial cabinet plans.

Once the economy picked up, both parties experienced rising popularity and new electoral victories and enjoyed growing tax revenues. At that time, after 1982–83 in the United Kingdom and from 1986 on in Spain, both governments proceeded to act according to their political preferences and to "deepen" the economic strategies they had started to implement when they gained office.

THE EMPLOYMENT–EQUALITY TRADE-OFF AND THE RESURGENCE OF PROTECTIONIST DEMANDS

As emphasized above, the fall in either employment or wages experienced in industrial nations has exacerbated the search for and the extent of political conflict over the two available supply-side economic strategies: low taxes and private investment or high taxes and public investment. Moreover, it has made it harder for all governments to reconcile increasingly disparate social demands, to the point of slowing down or even disrupting "optimal" economic strategies. Conservatives have had to balance the pro-social-spending inclinations of the middle classes and the anti-tax attitudes of high-income employees in private service sectors. Social democrats have had to cope with the social-wage demands of the unskilled and the unemployed and the antistatist reactions of the well-paid skilled workers.

A sharpening employment–equality trade-off also threatens to transform the political discourse and reshape the party system in a more fundamental manner. The ultimate causes of the (downward) shift in the demand (and relative prices) for unskilled workers that has intensified the political trade-offs of all advanced countries are still the object of heated debate. The hysteretical unemployment that followed the stagflation crisis of the 1970s and a dramatic technological shock (the introduction of computers) seem to account for much of the obsolescence of low-skilled workers in the production processes of the industrialized world. Part of this demand shift, however, derives from increasing competition from unskilled workers in developing countries.[8] If increasing free trade with developing nations (or higher mobility of labor) accounts, or is thought to account, for that fall, policymakers will be tempted to adopt protectionist measures and erect trade barriers to return to the conditions of full employment and high wages of previous eras. By blocking the purported causes of the decline of demand for unskilled workers, protectionism would theoretically offer a way out from the electorally painful dilemma between higher taxes and lower social spending.

What clearly amounts to a third economic road (different from both the high public investment or low taxes solutions) has been systematically avoided by all of the OECD nations, both before and after the oil shocks of the 1970s, for several reasons. In the industrialized world, the economic sectors that benefit from free trade have consistently outweighed those harmed by foreign competition – at least until recently. Adequate side-payments, in the form of huge subsidies, have been made to neutralize the protectionist slant of the only economic actors that appeared to be damaged by liberalization – farmers. Finally, the extent of economic interdependence and the relatively small size of European countries probably make protectionism an implausible solution: the inefficiency costs of trade barriers would be noticed too quickly and voters would punish politicians almost immediately.

Nevertheless, as economic conditions have deteriorated, protectionist demands have intensified among the electorate in OECD countries. And although they have not been translated into actual economic policies, they have created a new cleavage (around the issue of free trade) that, in cutting across the traditional political divide between state interventionism (the Left) and free-market solutions (the Right), may erode the electoral strength of conservatives and social democrats alike.

As shown in Table 9.1, the attitudes of the French toward the process of European integration – which can be taken as an imperfect way of measuring the presence of protectionist demands – correlate strikingly well with the economic position and level of skill of voters. Among those holding university degrees, those who say that France will gain from the European project command a 17-percentage-point lead over those who say France will lose. Among voters with no primary education, anti-European integration opinions lead by 9 percentage points. A similar pattern takes place by social position. Business executives and liberal professionals favor European integration and voted yes in the 1992 referendum on the Maastricht treaty. Farmers, blue-collar workers, and white-collar employees are aligned against further dismantling of the nation-state. A free-trade cleavage similar in virulence to the French one has also appeared in the Scandinavian countries: low-paid unskilled workers and public employees opposed rather strongly joining the European Union.

Table 9.1. *French attitudes toward European integration in the early 1990s*

	Difference between those who say that France will gain and those who say that France will lose from the European project (in percentage points)	Percentage voting no in the 1992 referendum on the Maastricht Treaty
By level of education		
University degree	+17	n.a.
Secondary education completed	+2	n.a.
Primary education completed	-2	n.a.
No primary education	-9	n.a.
By economic sector		
Business executives, liberal professions	n.a.	20
Shopkeepers, small business	+27	52
White-collar employees	-6	57
Blue-collar workers	-20	60
Farmers	n.a.	62

Sources. For first column: Grunberg (1994). For second column: Boussard (1992).

The emergence of protectionist demands among the unskilled, low-paid white-collar employees and blue-collar workers mostly jeopardizes the position of social democracy. Historically, social democrats have governed around the principles of free trade and domestic adjustment through public capital formation.[9] But if the economic dislocation associated with free trade is too harsh or social democrats do not compensate losers adequately (due, for example, to the resistance of middle-class voters), the socialist electoral coalition could start to unravel. This has occurred to some extent in France, where the issue of protectionism has developed as a full-fledged electoral cleavage that has restructured the party system and eroded the unity and strength of the traditional Left. As shown in Table 9.2, in the last decade, French right-wing parties hardly experienced any change in their level of total and class-based support. By contrast, the share of the vote of left-wing parties has declined by 15 percentage points from 1981 to 1993. Most of the loss has been concentrated among anti–European Union white-collar and blue-collar workers. Meanwhile, Le Pen's National Front has clearly benefited from locating the sources of French economic strains in economic openness, that is, in the European Union and the entry of immigrants.

Again in line with our findings on the formation and maintenance of electoral coalitions by policy elites, the decline in material conditions among the least qualified workers does not mechanically translate into the breakdown of the current party system. Intense investment policies, a universal welfare state, and tightly organized parties and unions have been able to hold together blue-collar workers, lower-middle-class voters, and public employees behind the Scandinavian social democracy. Although in 1991 the Swedish SAP lost many blue-collar

Table 9.2. *Evolution of French vote by social groups, 1981-93*

| | GAIN (LOSS) BETWEEN 1981 PRESIDENTIAL ELECTION (FIRST ROUND) AND 1993 PARLIAMENTARY ELECTION (FIRST ROUND) (IN PERCENTAGE POINTS) | | |
	RIGHT [a]	LEFT [b]	NF [c]
Business executives, liberal professions	-16	-1	+8
Shopkeepers, small business	-5	-6	+15
White-collar employees	-4	-14	+17
Blue-collar workers	+2	-26	+15
Farmers	-2	-12	+3
Total vote	-6	-15	+13

[a] For 1981: Chirac and Giscard d'Estaing. For 1993: UDF and RPR.
[b] For 1981: Marchais and Mitterrand. For 1993: PCF and PSF.
[c] Le Pen did not run in 1981.
Sources: Own estimations based on data reported in Machin and Wright (1982) and Guyomarch (1993).

workers to the anti–European Union New Democracy Party and the radical Left, by 1994 it had recovered most of the vote and had returned to its average share of the vote in the postwar period. Whereas the French Socialist Party lost most of its anti–European Union voters (only one-fourth voted no on the 1992 Maastricht referendum) to other parties, the SAP managed to appeal to both camps (Swedish social democratic voters were split almost equally on the issue of European integration) and hence to survive as the largest Swedish party, with 45.2 percent of the vote in 1994. Similarly, because of its ability to sustain a broad cross-class coalition throughout the 1980s, the PSOE provides a stark contrast to the fortunes of the French Socialist Party.

Christian Democratic coalitions, which include an important contingent of blue-collar workers and lower-middle-class voters, have also been threatened by the growth of protectionist demands, with different effects depending on the country and party system. Table 9.3 compares the support of Austrian Christian Democrats and Liberals in 1986 and 1994 with their German counterparts in 1994. Although the social composition of both parties was very similar in the two countries through the mid-1980s, by 1994 they were strikingly divergent. The Austrian liberal party (FPÖ), which had embraced a strongly anti-immigration platform since the mid-1980s and opposed entry to the European Union, surpassed the Austrian Popular Party (ÖVP) in popularity among blue-collar workers and closed the gap among most social sectors. German Christian Democrats, by contrast, continued to hold together a truly broad-based coalition – undisturbed by the competition of both social democrats and right-wing Republicans.

Table 9.3. *Support for Austrian and German Christian Democrats and Liberals by social sector in 1986 and 1994*

	Austria 1986			Austria 1994			Germany 1994		
	ÖVP	FPÖ	ÖVP minus FPÖ	ÖVP	FPÖ	ÖVP minus FPÖ	CDU/CSU	FDP	CDU minus FDP
Farmers	93	5	+88	74	16	+58	64	9	+55
Business, liberal professions	60	15	+45	40	30	+20	52	15	+37
Civil servants	33	9	+24	23	14	+9	43	8	+35
White-collar workers	36	13	+23	25	22	+3	38	7	+31
Blue-collar workers	27	10	+17	15	26	-11	37	3	+34

Source: Plasser and Ulram (1995).

CONCLUSIONS

Chapter 2 presented a very stylized model for understanding the ultimate sources of supply-side economic policies. In the context of (and in response to) a particular distribution of skills (and assets) among voters and a specific level of social protection, parties develop different policies because the redistributive consequences of the policies vary across voters. The following chapters showed that such a simple set of assumptions carries considerable empirical weight in accounting for the evolution of structural policies in the advanced world.

The book then moved on to explore in detail the electoral assumptions that motivate the behavior of parties – employing the cases of Britain and Spain as well as references to other advanced democracies. Most of this new evidence has been reviewed and systematized in this chapter. The result has been a more elaborate set of arguments about the electoral dimensions of economic policy-making. Economic policies respond to the ultimate preferences of electors. In other words, political parties are carriers of rather fixed interests (the industrial working class has traditionally constituted the core of social democracy; professionals, managers, and the old middle classes have aligned themselves with non-socialist parties) that shape the set of economic policies. But economic policies shape voter preferences as well – or, at least, party elites employ policies to organize electoral coalitions out of initially very heterogeneous interests. As discussed in the following chapter, these results point to a particular understanding of political parties: although they are in part "transmission belts" for interests, they are also organizations that structure interests around broad ideological principles and specific economic strategies.

10

CONCLUSIONS

One of the most striking developments in the discipline of political science today is the extent to which the research on democratic politics and performance and the literature on political economy are at odds with each other. On the one hand, political scientists have managed to accumulate an impressive array of knowledge and models on political participation, the formation of voter attitudes, electoral behavior, and partisan competitive strategies that provides very powerful insights on the workings of modern mass democracies. On the other hand, however, political economists have downplayed the significance of voter preferences and partisan programs to explain policies and economic outcomes. Until the early 1980s, corporatism, that is, the continuous bargaining among organized economic interests, was offered as the paradigm of how politics was (or ought to be) conducted in most parts of the advanced industrial world. Several scholars then turned to the analysis of the state and its political institutions to account for the notoriously different levels of inflation and budget deficits that the OECD countries experienced in the aftermath of several consecutive oil shocks. Today many have decided that globalization and economic interdependence are finally washing out any differences that may remain among nations. What all these research agendas have in common, however, is the rather tangential role they have ascribed to electoral politics and the impact of partisanship.

This study does not try to overturn all these explanations. Domestic institutions and the various constraints imposed by the international economy are clearly needed to understand the different political–economic equilibria that characterize advanced countries. But it shows that politics, in its raw sense, does play a more fundamental role than has been traditionally granted. Redistributive conflict and electoral coalitions of interests and ideas are behind a substantial portion of the policy decisions, economic strategies, and economic outcomes of today's democratic regimes.

To examine how electoral politics, partisan forces, and governments affect the economy, this book has attempted to weave together several dimensions or layers of variables: a model of the political economy of advanced countries that attempts to capture the constant tension between the requirements of growth and the demands for redistribution; the ultimate preferences of parties and their economic constituencies; the ideas or instrumental models (about how the economy works and how it can be manipulated) that policymakers employ; and the institutional settings (mostly of an economic sort but also of a political–constitutional nature) within which governments operate. This concluding chapter restates these variables and shows the ways in they can be employed (separately and in interaction), rather fruitfully, to understand the contemporary condition and dilemmas of the advanced world.

ECONOMIC PERFORMANCE AND REDISTRIBUTION

INITIAL CONDITIONS: CAPITAL MOBILITY, THE PRODUCTIVITY OF FACTORS, AND STATE RESPONSES

A very simple set of factors lies at the core of the political and economic decisions every state has to make to generate sustained growth and higher levels of social welfare. Economic growth depends on investment. Investment in turn depends on profits. As a result, states and politicians are ultimately constrained by the rational calculations of the holders of capital, who are always in search of the highest rate of return for their assets. Since capital moves to the most profitable countries, all states are pushed to maximize the rate of return of private investors. Otherwise, they face decreasing investment rates and economic stagnation.[1] In other words, states are structurally dependent on capital.[2]

For the proponents of the thesis of the structural dependence of the state on capital, reformism and redistributive policies are severely curtailed by the threat of exit of capital. In order to lure private investors, states will outbid each other through low taxes and by offering significant incentives. Accordingly, to escape from the "systemic" advantage that capital enjoys over states by virtue of its mobility, and to maintain high taxes, countries have only two solutions. They can nationalize capital, as did the former communist regimes of Eastern Europe and the former Soviet Union. Or they can minimize its mobility by closing their borders, a strategy adopted in most developing countries under political regimes of a populist bent.

In fact, however, low taxes do not automatically attract private investors. Although many Third World countries have low taxes, capital inflows from the industrialized, high-tax nations have been modest. This is because, in order to maximize profits, capital holders invest in those countries (or economic sectors) that offer the highest *net* rate of return, that is, the widest wedge between the gross rate of return to capital and taxes. By lowering taxes and holding wages down, it might be possible to boost profits and therefore encourage private investment. But the rate of return of capital is equally dependent on the productivity of the input factors that enter the production process (Lucas 1990). In fact, since what mainly determines gross profitability is the productivity of the input factors, taxes can be high as long as productivity remains high enough to deliver the highest net profits (compared to other places) to capital. Capital will always prefer a country where taxes are high, as long as productivity is very high, to a country where both taxation and productivity are low.

Two fundamental points derive from this discussion. In the first place, taxes and redistributive spending are not automatically rendered impossible by the mobility of capital and the investment decisions of its holders. The capacity to redistribute, or, in the terms of this book, the level of the social wage, is a function of the productivity of capital and labor. A country endowed with a highly qualified workforce can sustain high levels of social spending without jeopardizing its economy. Europe has enjoyed a highly developed welfare state as a consequence, among other things, of its high productivity relative to other low-labor cost economies. Capital flight takes place only when the owners of capital have a better place to go. But, again, the underlying logic of private investment makes apparent the limits or trade-off that states face in their pursuit of redistributive policies. In a country where labor is very unskilled, pure redistribution will only lead to unemployment and economic decline.

In the second place, it is true that states are constrained by the mobility of capital. But, given the determinants of net profitability and therefore investment, policymakers have room to embrace different policy alternatives to attract private investors.[3] First, they can simply minimize taxes (actually driving them below what would be possible without endangering net profits) to encourage private savings and therefore boost private investment. Naturally, this solution, which is based on giving absolute priority to the private accumulation of capital, has substantial redistributive consequences. Low taxes imply skimpy public transfers and, probably, extended inequality, at least in the short run. In the long run, however, rapid growth is likely to improve the absolute condition of all sectors (including the least advantaged), although not necessarily their relative position in the economic ladder. Second, governments may decide to keep the social wage at the level permitted by the productivity of capital and labor in the marketplace. The price to be paid is the lack of change in the given or initial level of inequality. Moreover, if the productivity of the input factors declines (in either absolute terms or in relative terms – in this case, as a result of an increase in the productivity of other nations), this strategy requires lowering the social wage and accepting higher levels of inequality for the sake of economic efficiency. Finally, those policymakers who want to increase economic equality (yet reject closing their nation's borders or nationalizing capital) are left with only one possible solution: increasing the productivity rate of the domestic input factors in order to keep their highly taxed country attractive to private capital. In this case, they employ the state to speed up the rate of investment and to raise the productivity rate of labor and capital to a level that, even in the face of high taxation (needed to pay for social transfers and more public investment programs), still lures private investment. Nevertheless, this strategy has its price: basically more taxes as well as the uncertainty of not knowing whether public investment will be efficiently allocated.

ECONOMIC SHOCKS

The policy strategies designed by states take place in an economic structure affected by two factors that modify the relative value of the input factors and their productivity: economic shocks and, in part, the institutional organization of the economy.

The demand for and income of labor and capital inputs vary as a result of several sorts of economic shocks: technological transformations, the emergence of foreign competitors (employing a similar mix of inputs to produce at lower costs), and the fall of transportation and communication costs (which intensify the appearance of new competitors abroad). As the productivity of the production factors changes, so does the redistributive capacity of each country – that is, the level at which the social wage can be set without distorting the economy.

 The case of the advanced countries in the last decades has provided the most relevant example in this book of the changing relationship between productivity and the social wage: a relative decline of productivity of certain sectors has, in turn, eroded the redistributive capacity of the whole country.[4] In the 1960s, the productivity of capital and labor was relatively high. The skills of all the workforce matched the technological requirements of mass production. Competition from developing countries was weak and the transportation and communication costs between countries exceeded any savings that investors could gain from producing goods in underdeveloped nations for their sale in the advanced world. As a result, all advanced countries were able to finance extensive social policies at little economic cost. The background conditions under which governments made policy in the postwar period were modified by the slowdown of economic growth in the 1970s, technological breakthroughs raising the relative demand for highly qualified workers, and the emergence of new competitors abroad. The resulting fall in the demand for unskilled workers made apparent once more the natural tension that exists between the allocation mechanisms of markets and economic redistribution. In the terms employed in the book, as part of the labor force became more unskilled in relative terms, the social wage grew too high and the trade-off between equality and employment became more acute. Naturally, within the common trend toward a harsher employment–equality trade-off in all OECD countries, there has been a substantial degree of variation across advanced nations. Such variation, which results from the initial conditions of the labor force in interaction with the level of the social wage, conforms to the parameters of the model of this book. Already highly educated nations, such as Northern European nations, have experienced only relative increases in unemployment.[5] Nations that had a meager social wage to begin with, such as the United States, have kept their long-run unemployment rate low. By contrast, countries (or regions within countries) with highly unskilled populations, such as Spain, have suffered the most from these exogenous shocks.

INSTITUTIONS AND THE PROCESS OF ADJUSTMENT

If the literature on institutional coordination is right, the productivity of the input factors, and thus the harshness of the trade-off, will depend as well on the institutional mechanisms each country has to adjust to economic and technological shocks.

Highly coordinated economies, that is, economies in which business, labor, and financial institutions have developed strong linkages, such as Germany, were able to retrain their workers to prepare them for the new production requirements of the 1980s.[6] German unemployment hovered around 7 percent in the mid- and late 1980s – a rate similar to the American one in spite of having a substantially more regulated economy than the United States.[7] By contrast, decentralized economies, like the United Kingdom, lacking the institutional conditions required to overcome the fall in the relative price of (unskilled and semiskilled) labor, are confronted with a rather dramatic employment–equality trade-off.

The nature of politics (and policy) is thus likely to be different in different institutional structures. In decentralized economies, policymakers face in very stark terms the choice between lowering the social wage to avoid the trap of high unemployment or intensifying the effort in public capital formation, since they know that lowering the social wage will result in great inequality. Coordinated economies – always assuming that they adjust to exogenous shocks in the smooth way claimed by the proponents of this literature – alleviate, instead, the harshness of the employment–equality trade-offs that governments face. In that case, policy would change very incrementally, if at all.[8]

PARTISAN POLITICS

Jointly with the initial conditions of the production factors and probably the institutional structures of each country, the nature of the supply-side economic policies determines the economic performance and level of economic equality in each nation. As the evidence accumulated in this book suggests, in the context of the tension between redistribution and economic performance that grips all nations, the determination of those structural economic policies mainly depends on the partisan coalition in power.

Because they are concerned about equality, yet committed to the market economy and free trade, social democratic governments raise taxes substantially to achieve two – interconnected – goals: a balanced budget, which, by generating public savings, boosts the domestic rate of total savings; and a high rate of public investment to increase the productivity of all economic sectors and, in particular, the productivity of the worst-off workers and regions. This higher productivity should in turn translate into better wages. But it will also give more room to levy higher taxes that will then be employed (without threatening the growth rate) to finance comprehensive social policies. Consider the Spanish case, which offers, jointly with the historical evidence we have on the social democratic governments in Scandinavian countries, the British Labour Party, and Mitterrand's France, an eloquent proof that the Left generally designs a set of coherent supply-side economic policies to maximize the domestic rate of fixed and human capital formation. Under the González government, public revenues rose 7.7 percent of GDP in ten years. Another 2 percentage points were saved by cutting down state subsidies. Both the new revenues and the internal savings were first meticulously allocated to raise public savings by cutting the public deficit. As observed in Chapter 3 with the aid of statistical techniques, most social democratic governments follow this pattern. Whenever they are faced with an increasing deficit, they prefer to avoid expansionary policies (as well as higher levels of capital spending) for the sake of a balanced budget. Social democrats see savings as a precondition for further growth. But increasing savings does not suffice to maximize growth. Since socialist governments fear that savings will not be automatically directed by the private sector into profitable forms of investment, they plan to (partially) control investment to maximize growth. A whole decade under a socialist government implies around 2 percentage points of GDP more in public fixed capital formation – or two-thirds of the OECD average in public investment. Similarly, in regard to human capital formation, countries under left-wing governments generally end up with public spending on education and vocational training well above the OECD average.[9]

Conservative governments favor, instead, minimizing the intervention of the public sector. They expect private businesses and workers to make the proper consumption and investment decisions to maximize their individual incomes. That should in turn maximize the country's global economic performance. Governments refrain from distorting private decisions since their intervention can only reduce the optimal level of savings and investment. Accordingly, taxes are kept low. In the late 1970s, the effective tax rates on high incomes were around 30 percent if a conservative party had controlled the government since the early 1960s, and they would stay unchanged in the 1980s under the same party. A conservative cabinet inheriting high effective tax rates in 1980 would cut them by almost half, to around 40 percent, by 1990. This contrasts sharply with the evolution of taxes under a left-wing cabinet: in the late 1970s high-income earners were paying over two-thirds of their personal income in taxes whenever a socialist party had been governing for the previous fifteen years, and they continued to bear similar tax rates in the late 1980s if social democracy remained in power until then. Mirroring their tax policy, nonsocialist governments have always kept public fixed investment and public spending on education and vocational training below the OECD average.

In the way predicted by this book's model, the pervasive economic transformations and the changing relationship between economic performance and the social wage that has characterized the advanced world in the last decades have only exacerbated the extent of political conflict around the selection of supply-side strategies to be implemented. In the 1960s, partisan governments deployed their preferred economic strategies free, to a great extent, from the inefficiencies and employment losses that became associated with a high social wage as the demand for certain sectors of labor fell in the following decades. Social democrats (mostly governing in very open economies) pursued a high-tax–high-investment strategy mainly to speed up the process of economic equalization. Conservative governments favored deregulated markets and lowered public capital formation programs instead. But, because growth was so fast, they only mildly resisted the pace of expansion of social spending. In short, political disagreement was often muffled by the rapid pace of productivity increases.

The changing prices of the factors of production (or, more accurately, of specific economic sectors) altered the political scenario after the 1970s. Burdened by the effects of having more unproductive workers, conservative parties adopted a more radical agenda, particularly in those countries affected by a severe employment–equality trade-off. Privatizations, led by right-wing parties, have boomed in the last fifteen years. In Britain, the public sector accounted for 40 percent of total investment until the early 1970s. In 1990 it controlled only 15 percent. By contrast, socialist governments have blocked all proposals to privatize state holdings. Only a long period of declining economic performance in the 1960s and 1970s, like the one experienced by New Zealand, forced a leftist government to dismantle the public business sector. Tax reforms have become the staple of conservative programs. Finally, the conservative strategy of dismantling public investment programs has been complemented by the thorough deregulation of the labor market and, if necessary, a reduction of the social wage: the Thatcher government abolished the minimum wage, cut unemployment benefits, contained social spending, and weakened unions and the system of collective bargaining. Instead, social democratic parties have reasserted their commitment to spending on education, manpower policies, and infrastructures. In short, divergent policies rather than convergence is what seems to result from the growing interdependence of all domestic economies.

POLITICAL PARTIES AND DEMAND POLICIES

Compare these results with what we know about the political control of the economic cycle. Left-wing parties are tempted to follow a Keynesian strategy – to counter the natural variability of the economy and protect the weakest social sectors. By contrast, right-wing parties are more likely to follow policies that stress macroeconomic discipline and price stability. But even if partisan governments have distinctive preferences in regard to macroeconomic policy, they are heavily constrained by the domestic institutional settings in which they operate. When facing labor markets with powerful built-in mechanisms that make any anti-inflationary policy very costly to implement, conservatives tend to give up their stabilization plans. Conversely, social democratic governments only succeed in expanding the economy if they can secure wage restraint from workers. Moreover, even when institutions are compatible with governments' macroeconomic plans, high (and nowadays) increasing levels of trade and financial integration are depriving policymakers of any autonomy they still have to determine fiscal and monetary policy.

ELECTORAL COALITIONS AND ECONOMIC POLICIES

To facilitate the construction of a model that, with few assumptions, could be fruitfully used to interpret reality, social democrats and conservatives were initially hypothesized to develop policies in response to the preferences of clear-cut electoral constituencies: the least skilled voters and the more qualified workers respectively. In spelling out the model in Chapter 2 and throughout the rest of the book, a more complex image, however, has emerged. Parties shape preferences as much as they represent them.

There is no doubt that Socialist parties receive much of their support from working-class voters and that nonsocialist parties poll most of their votes from middle-class sectors. As a consequence, their electoral chances partly depend on the relative size of each class – or, in the terms of the model of Chapter 2, on the distribution of skills and incomes in each country. There is thus some truth to the claim that, because the traditional blue-collar working class has declined, the heyday of social democracy is over. Yet one temptation that should be avoided is to assimilate political parties to raw interests or, even, to specific economic factors or sectors. Voters come to the electoral arena with multiple interests. Candidates and parties run on projects that mobilize certain kinds of interests but not others. And partisan governments employ bundles of policies to organize winning electoral coalitions. Social democratic parties attempt to attract both unskilled and relatively skilled workers around their commitment to economic growth, public investment policies, and redistribution through universal social programs. Relatively uneducated workers accept the workings of a market economy – to which they might be in principle ferociously opposed – in exchange for redistributive policies. To employ Katzenstein's terms, they support a social democratic project that promises domestic compensation in return for adjusting to the consequences of free trade. The beneficial results of strong public capital formation and a universal welfare state should co-opt at the same time a significant portion of high-wage, relatively skilled workers. By contrast, conservative governments appeal to middle-class sectors, offer growth as a way to climb the social ladder, and structure the provision of social services to reward individual merit.

A rather qualified understanding of parties arises then from the evidence of this book. A definition of political parties equating them to rather specific interests or classes is only true in part. Since parties structure interests around ideological principles, parties are also defined by their programmatic appeals and their economic strategy. For example, social democracy can only be partially labeled as the party of the working class. More precisely, social democracy is the programmatic commitment to free markets and economic equality, which has been implemented mostly, but not exclusively, with the support of blue-collar workers. In the comparative political economy literature, an influential strand of thought derives policy outcomes from the relative size and power of social classes or sectors. But this line of argument forgets the role that parties and political elites play: they forge interests and coalitions in ways that do not always follow a linear relationship between economic interests, political struggles, and policy outcomes.

Because policies are tools to build coalitions out of initially divergent economic interests, they can always spur conflict within the electoral coalitions they mobilize and serve. The Spanish Socialist government had to face very strong demands for social spending from left-wing voters that jeopardized its public investment strategy as well as the support of key parts of the middle class. The Thatcher government could not please the "dry" wing of the Tory Party as systematically as it had wished: revamping the welfare state in a thorough way would have only led to the loss of moderate voters and to certain electoral defeat. The recent changes in the relative demand for unskilled and qualified workers have intensified the policy dilemmas confronted by both social democrats and conservatives. With unskilled workers suffering a decline in their wages, left-wing parties are forced to step up investment and social transfers to avoid losing their votes. But key middle-class sectors resist the higher taxes required to buy the consent of unskilled workers. Among conservatives, pressures to cut a swelling budget to pay for more unemployment benefits are growing. But parts of the lower-middle class that support nonsocialist parties feel threatened by excessive cuts in welfare spending. If the tensions cannot be resolved, each political camp will fracture into smaller units. Moreover, politicians may be more tempted to resort to a solution that cuts across both the low-taxes and the high-public-investment strategies: the introduction of new controls over capital and protectionist measures. The emergence of extreme-right and radical-left parties in OECD countries, with their support for tariff barriers and, in many cases, tough anti-immigration laws, in the last years results partially from the incapacity of several social democrat and conservative parties to convince parts of their traditional constituencies that free trade and markets are beneficial to all.

THE WESTERN HEMISPHERE AND THE WORLD POLITICAL ECONOMY

As one examines the possible electoral coalitions that emerge in response to economic conditions, it becomes apparent that the evolution of the economic structure and the alternative political responses in the advanced nations can be understood as a particular instance of a pattern common to all political economies. Although it exceeds the scope of this book, it should be possible to extend this logic to developed and developing countries alike. As stressed before, all countries are subject to the same structural logic: capital moves to maximize its (net) rate of return. And, again, given the determinants of profitability, all policymakers have three alternative courses of action available to them. These three alternatives encompass the different political–economic regimes that have been adopted throughout the world.

In the first place, policymakers can keep taxes, labor costs, and regulations as minimal as possible to raise the profitability of capital and therefore induce investment. Economic agents are literally forced to adapt to new circumstances and to find, as fast as possible, the sectors in which they enjoy a comparative advantage. This strategy naturally entails considerable social costs. During the transition period that follows any economic shock, there is substantial dislocation and probably increasing inequality, a result of unskilled workers having to either lower their wages to match cheaper labor abroad or adapt to new technological conditions.[10] This situation is thought to be transitional: medium-term costs are paid for what will become, in a Ricardian world of free trade, a more efficient economy in the long run. The United States and the United Kingdom have partly trodden this path in the last two decades. Among developing countries, the Chilean adjustment strategy followed since 1973 also fits into this category.

The dislocation that comes from economic change, however, may be politically unbearable. Even if free trade and the mobility of factors pay off in the long run and nations are well served by exploiting their comparative advantage, states are tempted to overcome the discipline that capital requires and, instead, decide to control it at its source. They may nationalize capital: this is the case of peasant revolutions that, in response to the strains of modernization, led to communist regimes. States can also respond by erecting trade and financial barriers and blocking international competition. Higher tariffs and public subsidies allow the country to sustain strongly redistributive policies in the medium run, that is, to keep the social compact alive and ensure social peace. As with the nationalization of capital, the price to be paid, however, is economic stagnation. This is the case of countries where there are large uncompetitive economic sectors or where competitiveness is declining: the Latin American populist regimes (Haggard 1990) and, to some extent, the urban-based coalitions governing most of sub-Saharan Africa (Bates 1984). With more foreign competition and internal technological changes eroding the economic advantages of the least skilled American and European workers, and demands for protectionism increasing in the advanced world, protectionism may become a possible alternative in the Northern Hemisphere as well.

Finally, policymakers may accept the logic of capital mobility while attempting to increase the productivity of domestic labor and of home industries. The expansion of the high school system pushed by the American progressive coalition at the turn of the century to respond to the challenges of massive industrialization, most of the policies that sustained the European postwar consensus, and the programs of trade liberalization and intensive human capital formation embraced by several East Asian economies fall into this economic strategy.

As emphasized in some of the literature, which solution a country adopts partly depends on the political strength of the beneficiaries of each policy. The larger the high-skilled tradable sectors, for example, the greater the incentive a country has to embrace free trade (Rogowski 1989; Frieden and Rogowski 1996). But one lesson of this book is that, since policies come in bundles, political coalitions can be structured in ways that defy the logic that should derive from the most immediate interests of the particular social sectors that integrate those coalitions. We cannot think of "free trade versus protectionism" and "low taxes versus high taxes" as separate policy debates and decisions. They combine in different ways. As a result, even losers from trade will join an antiprotectionist coalition if they are amply compensated with extensive public intervention. It is up to politicians to craft particular coalitions of interests in one way or the other. Economics is the domain of necessity, of mechanics: as we have seen, there are few alternative strategies available to policymakers. Politics instead lies closer to the realm of possibility. Politicians craft coalitions in several different ways – precisely by employing different combinations of policies to glue together heterogeneous demands. And we should look at parties, and in nondemocratic regimes at political elites more broadly understood, to account for the sources of economic policymaking.

CONCLUDING WORDS

Let me conclude by turning again to the purely political dimensions of the economic choices that political parties and governments have to make, and by speculating on the future evolution of supply-side economic strategies in OECD nations along two, somewhat opposite, lines.

We should expect that the processes of growing economic interdependence and technological change that are altering the demand for and relative prices of both unskilled and skilled workers will only intensify in the future. By magnifying the employment–equality trade-off in most industrial democracies, they will probably increase political conflict. The harshness of the policy dilemmas, and their political consequences, are especially visible in those countries that are trapped in particularly suboptimal situations, that is, in those countries where the quality of the productive inputs is low, the social wage is higher than what can be sustained in an open economy, and unemployment is very high – probably the case of Spain. But the magnitude of the employment–equality trade-off is an undeniable phenomenon throughout the advanced world. It is hard to tell which sort of economic policies will prevail in the future. Social and economic outcomes vary extraordinarily among advanced countries. They do so in good measure as a result of the structure of their production sectors, the institutional frameworks within which industries are embedded, and past policy strategies. Accordingly, the intensity and direction of social and electoral pressures to resolve the issues of unemployment, equality and growth will vary greatly among countries. What is clear is that politics will be even more important than before. It is also impossible to predict which electoral coalitions will crystallize in the future. With some exceptions – perhaps the United States – in all advanced countries there is substantial opposition to inequality and to lowering the social wage. Therefore, strictly conservative solutions may be impossible to implement. Pressures for public spending might be too high for major cutbacks to be made. As a result, social democratic forces might be able to regain a hegemonic position in the future – to a greater extent than it is fashionable to say today. The question that remains is whether, once they are in power, they will be able to abide by a pure public investment strategy or whether they will have to acquiesce to strong welfare demands (that would be unbearable without a corresponding increase in the rate of productivity). Again, which solution will be adopted will depend on purely electoral and political factors. The only possible way to reconcile more social protection without significant increases in productivity will be to embrace protectionism, a solution that is increasingly fashionable among both the most extreme right-wing and left-wing parties. But that choice would have the most catastrophic effects, as the populist regimes of Latin America show.

This book has emphasized how different policymakers engineer distinct policies to respond to different redistributive concerns and distributional coalitions. Still, it would be mistaken to conclude from it that politics is merely a clash of material interests. By defying the clear-cut definitions of Left and Right that prevailed in the interwar period, the emergence of Christian Democratic parties allowed Europeans to create a broad social compact around the institutions of a market economy and a generous welfare state after World War II. Similarly, I have referred briefly to the growing consensus that has emerged among policymakers concerning the most appropriate policies to manage the economic cycle. This has taken place in part as a result of learning from previous experiences and publicly discussing their effects. In other words, over time, redistributive conflicts have given way, to some extent, to rational argumentation. We may expect that a similar process will happen in regard to the development of the most appropriate competitive strategies. The wide experimentation that goes on, across all countries, to achieve healthier and more competitive economies may slowly result in most countries adopting those solutions that prove to be both more efficient and equitable. That learning process would also pertain to the sphere of politics – politics here understood in its noblest sense: as an ongoing reasoned discussion about how to better our lives in common.

NOTES

CHAPTER 1. INTRODUCTION

1 M. Thatcher, interview in the *Times* (London), 9 February 1984, quoted in Heath et al. 1989.

2 For the use of this initial assumption to model partisan politics, see Hibbs 1977, 1987; Lipset 1983; Alvarez, Garrett, and Lange 1991; Alesina and Rosenthal 1995. For recent empirical research done at both mass and elite levels showing that this classic divide between Left and Right on the extent of government management of the economy, the degree of public ownership of industry, and the reduction of income inequality constitutes the key political dimension in most Western party systems, at least since World War II, see Budge, Robertson, and Hearl 1987; Inglehart 1984; Laver and Hunt 1992.

3 Notice that, for the purposes of this model and its empirical validation, I assume a very narrow set of preferences among nonsocialist parties. See, however, the broad variation of conservative ideologies in Britain in Beer 1982 or the role of Christian Democratic ideas in continental Europe in building the welfare state in Flora and Alber 1981; Wilensky 1981; Esping-Andersen 1990.

4 In other words, if no costs were attached to achieving equality, conservatives would pursue it as much as social democrats. But once certain trade-offs, such as lower growth rates or more taxes, are thought to come with policies specifically designed to equalize conditions, conservatives will be more likely to avoid them than social democrats.

5 There are as well political limits to the extent to which conservative governments may tolerate or neglect the consequences of economic inequality. Conservatives will have to fight extreme inequality whenever it threatens the electoral majority sustaining them in office, regardless of their first-order preferences about the economic strategy to pursue. A similar point applies to social democratic cabinets: they can hardly pursue policies that, in attempting to reduce poverty, are too onerous for the majority of the electorate. I come back to this point in the final section of Chapter 2.

6 This does not mean that substantial public transfers and high taxes to finance them automatically force capital to exit and hence threaten economic growth. Firms will not stop investing if the net rate of return to capital is positive and higher than in countries where taxes are, in fact, lower. Welfare policies are always possible if domestic productivity is high enough to compensate for generous public spending. This explains the capacity all advanced nations had to finance the welfare state to date. Nevertheless, socialist policymakers need to be concerned about the basis that makes possible the combination of both welfare transfers and capital profitability.

7 For the effect of dominant neoclassical theories on socialist policymakers in the 1930s, see Weir 1989; Lee 1989.

8 Even though expansionary policies may lead to higher inflation, the Keynesian paradigm, which dominated mainstream economics in the 1950s and 1960s, took the unemployment–inflation trade-off, represented through the so-called Phillips curve, to be rather stable and predictable.

9 For analysis showing that full employment policies have redistributive consequences particularly favorable to the lowest socioeconomic strata in the United States, see Hibbs 1987.

10 For an analysis of the reception of Keynesianism among social democratic parties, see Hall 1989. Besides Keynesianism, theories of public goods and market failures equally strengthened the social democratic case for government intervention.

11 See also Skidelsky 1979; Ruggie 1982; and, more generally, Hall 1989.

12 The anti-inflationary bias of nonsocialist parties has been attributed to the redistributive costs that inflation imposes on the core constituencies of conservative parties (Hibbs 1987). Since, however, the potential redistributive costs of inflation seem to be less than clear-cut (see Alesina and Rosenthal 1995, pages 169–70), nonaccommodating economic policies must be thought of as deriving from the conservative parties' concern with growth and from their search for policies that secure the stability that private agents require to invest – even if those anti-inflation policies do not safeguard some sectors from the hardship that comes from a temporary fall in economic activity.

13 It is worth stressing, as the specialized literature has repeatedly done, that partisan preferences should always be understood in relative terms. Conservatives may dislike unemployment as much as social democrats, but they dislike inflation even more.

14 A different strand of research has emphasized, instead, that parties behave solely as vote maximizers. Accordingly, they pursue the same kind of policies – with no regard for their ideological commitments or positions. Immediately before elections they engage in expansionary policies to stimulate the economy, which, in turn, feeds higher levels of inflation. After the election, inflation is checked through restrictive policies. See Nordhaus 1975, 1989. For variations on this "political business cycle model," that incorporate rational expectations and rational voters, see a review in Alesina 1993. For its empirical examination, which rejects this literature, see Alesina and Roubini 1992; Alesina, Cohen, and Roubini 1992.

15 For a critique of the underlying assumptions on rational expectations and on the model adopted for wage contracts, see Hibbs 1992. See a response, however, in Alesina 1993.

16 Inflation, however, is likely to remain above its preelection level under a left-wing government since the latter's natural preference for expansionary policies erodes its anti-inflationary credibility.

17 Although temporary, the differences seem to be substantial. After a year and a half in office, a leftist government delivers a growth rate 2.5 percentage points higher than a rightist cabinet, and 1.5 percentage points less of unemployment.

18 The breakdown of encompassing union movements and corporatist arrangements is in fact a growing phenomenon in OECD countries since the early 1970s. See Pontusson 1991a; Iversen 1995.

19 See, for example, Frieden and Rogowski 1996.

20 See Bruno and Sachs 1985 for a technical, stylized account of how the nature and interaction of production factors affect the performance of any economy. The importance of structural factors does not exclude that macroeconomic policies might determine the rate of growth since, for example, by reducing the equilibrium rate of unemployment, they may favor a more efficient use of labor, or, by reducing the public deficit, they are likely to avoid crowding private investment out. For an empirical exploration of the effect of macroeconomic policies on the long-run output rate within the context of the new growth theory, see Fischer 1991.

21 Both expressions will be used equally in the book to refer to the same kind of policies.

22 Using more formal tools, Alesina and Rodrik (1991) have also underlined the range of choices that, in regard to the tax rate and the share of public investment, governments have to maximize growth.

23 In the empirical domain, see also the discussion in Quinn and Shapiro 1991 on corporate tax policies in the United States, and the analysis of tax policies in Swank 1992.

24 Since supply-side policies were already important before the 1970s, the lack of scholarly attention to them has probably been due to the theoretical hegemony that Keynesian ideas and the management of the business cycle have had among economists and the policy elites, especially in large economies such as the United States.

25 On new growth theories, see Romer 1986; Lucas 1988; Barro 1991; among others. On the relationship between unemployment and skills, see OECD 1994b.

26 For the most recent analysis of the strengths of quantitative and qualitative research and their commonalities and dissimilarities, see King, Keohane, and Verba 1994.

27 This excludes Iceland and Luxembourg. For lack of reliable data, Turkey is also excluded.

28 The historical period varies somewhat, however, depending on the availability of data. For the strategies toward the public business sector, the analysis is restricted to the post-OPEC period.

29 For an excellent defense of the value that case studies add to statistical research, see Simmons 1994, 13–19.

CHAPTER 2. POLITICAL PARTIES AND THE STRUCTURAL
CONDITIONS OF THE ECONOMY

1 For current economic theories on the causes of unemployment, see a survey in
   Lindbeck and Snower 1985. See also Katz 1986; Blanchard and Summers 1987;
   Layard, Nickell, and Jackman 1994.
2 The effects of the social wage can be also looked at from a different point of view,
   which, although not considered in the main text for the sake of simplicity, should
   be regarded as equally important. Imagine that the cost of SW is borne by firms
   instead of workers. In this case, the cost of each worker for any firm is the sum
   of the wage paid to the worker and the tax paid to the state to finance SW. As a
   result, firms will only hire workers whose productivity, once netted from the
   wage, is higher than nonwage labor costs, that is, taxes. Accordingly, in Figure
   2.1 SW can be interpreted as the level at which taxes are set to still make it
   profitable for any firm to hire the least skilled worker.
3 Except for the least skilled worker, whose wage was already equal to SW.
4 To use terms recently crafted in economic theory, long-term unemployment has
   hysteretic effects. It sustains itself over time since the long-term unemployed are
   unable to find jobs given their declining qualifications. See Blanchard 1991 for
   a formulation and analysis of the hysteretic effects of long-term unemployment.
5 Or, again, firms will not hire workers to the left of U^*.
6 Better physical capital, in the form, say, of more infrastructures that reduce transportation costs, boosts as well the productivity of firms and, like skills, adds to
   the efficiency of the economy and eventually to the disposable income of workers.
7 This is true if one controls for the bargaining power of companies and workers
   and the resulting wage-bargaining patterns.
8 For a skeptical analysis of the negative effects of a higher social wage on employment creation, see Blank and Freeman 1994; and, more generally, all the contributions in Blank 1994. The conclusions of these papers suffer, however, from
   two limitations. First, they only examine the employment effects derived from
   marginal changes in existing social programs. Second, they do not control for the
   level of skills and the quality of fixed capital: whenever workers are highly qualified, extremely high levels of social protection and labor regulations should have
   marginal effects on employment.
9 Again, as the evidence presented in the book shows later, the selection of a specific
   supply-side economic strategy was politically relevant before and after the 1970s,
   particularly in small- and medium-sized economies (most OECD nations). In
   nearly closed economies (basically the United States), where demand-management
   policies seemed adequate to ensure full employment, the political debate was
   mostly dominated by Keynesianism in the 1960s. Only after the shocks of the
   1970s did supply-side debates and solutions intensify in the American political
   realm.
10 The precise impact of each variable (technological change and trade openness) is
   still the subject of considerable debate. In an already vast literature, see Freeman
   and Katz 1994 for an analysis of the effects of new technologies on the demand
   and supply of labor, and Wood 1994 for the impact of growing competitiveness
   from new industrialized countries. See also OECD 1994b.

11 The data are taken from OECD 1994b, table 8.2.

12 The organizational power of labor is measured, following Cameron 1984, as the average of the average proportion of the unionized labor force and the sum of the measures of organizational unity and labor confederation power in collective bargaining. It has been modified for the 1980s to take into account recent changes in the organization of the labor movement across OECD countries, following the data presented in Golden and Wallerstein 1994; Lange, Wallerstein, and Golden 1995; Traxler 1994. The index, which is standardized to homogenize results before and after 1980, goes from 0 to 1.

13 For a similar analysis that emphasizes the difference between cyclical and sticky unemployment but that considers another set of explanations, see Bertola and Ichino 1995.

14 The ratio of wage dispersion is taken from OECD 1993d. The evolution of private-sector employment is taken from OECD 1994b, table 1.1.

15 The correlation coefficient is 0.63 (0.75 if we exclude the United Kingdom). Some countries, particularly in Scandinavia, have attempted to overcome the employment–equality trade-off by expanding public-sector employment. As a result, the correlation coefficient between annual change in total employment (private and public sectors) and a broadening wage dispersion falls from (0.63 when we only consider the private sector) to 0.50. Since those countries that have chosen to expand public employment appear to be paying state employees above their market-determined wage rate (otherwise, the mere creation of public jobs would not have the intended result of miminizing wage dispersion), the recourse to this strategy can be equated with the maintenance of the social wage unless these new public jobs operate as a means to train and upgrade initially unskilled workers. For a more extended discussion of this strategy – and particularly of its electoral dimension – see Chapter 9.

16 Notice that throughout the book I assume that conservative and social democratic parties differ in the policy space, that is, that there is no convergence around the median voter. For a very strong theoretical and empirical justification of this position, see Alesina and Rosenthal 1995, chap. 2.

17 For accounts in which capital (instead of labor) plays an equally important role in enforcing wage coordination, see Katzenstein 1985 and especially Soskice 1990 and Swenson 1991.

18 See Garrett and Lange 1991 for the view that fully interventionist policies cannot be implemented in decentralized economies.

19 See Martin 1979. For an exploration of the Norwegian model, see Esping-Andersen 1985, chap. 7.

20 For arguments that, under different labels ("flexible specialization," "diversified quality production," "institutional coordination") and with somewhat different causal logics, stress the importance of "coordination" in the economy, see Katzenstein 1985; Soskice 1991; Streeck 1991. See a review in Hall 1995.

21 The effects that different institutional regimes may have on the initial conditions (and on the employment–equality trade-off) faced by any government are taken up again in Chapter 10.

22 It is true, however, that a country rich in generic skills and a country rich in company-specific skills may end up having different production profiles. With abundant company-specific skills, capital would be prone to invest in German-

style machine-tools industries. With generic skills, service industries may be more likely to flourish.

23 A good review of the growing internationalization of capital markets can be found in Frieden 1991a. For an analysis of the forces behind the dismantling of domestic controls over capital flows in the last two decades, see as well Goodman and Pauly 1993.

24 Notice that the fact that most capital is highly asset-specific gives social democratic governments enough leverage (i.e., time) to implement a high-tax–public-investment strategy, whose productivity effects generally take place in the medium and long run. If the opposite were true, that is, if most capital were instantaneously mobile, private investors would rapidly flee the country in the wake of new tax increases, therefore defeating any attempt at building a public investment strategy.

25 I am grateful to David Rowe for suggesting to me the broader notion of "assets" (which includes skills and other resources such as property, inherited income, etc.) to examine the political–electoral foundations of different economic strategies.

26 The division of the electoral space into two partisan camps is appropriate only if one makes rather strict assumptions about the institutional setting in which parties develop their strategies. See Shepsle 1991 and Cox 1997 for an analysis of the conditions that lead to stable two-party systems.

27 This model abstracts from other potential cleavages, such as religious practice or ethnic identity, that also influence the vote. By the end of the section, I briefly consider how they affect the construction of social democratic and conservative electoral coalitions and the development of their policies.

28 This paragraph simply follows the logic developed by Meltzer and Richards 1981 in applying the median voter theorem to account for different levels of public spending across nations and time periods.

29 That would be the case only if all policy decisions just involved redistributing or transferring income. Taxes and spending would be set at the level preferred by the median voter. Left-wing parties would appeal to those with incomes equal to or below the median voter. Right-wing parties would appeal to those with incomes equal to or above the median voter.

30 See a thorough critique of Przeworski and Sprague's argument in Kitschelt 1994, chap. 2.

31 To employ the terms of the spatial theory of politics, policies are used to change the preferences of the median voter.

32 I assume that the budget is balanced and that therefore government spending equals taxation.

33 This only holds true, however, if public capital formation is at least as productive as private capital formation.

34 Other factors – to some extent related to the slowdown of economic growth – have also aggravated the dilemma of choosing between social spending and public investment: the rise of health expenditure and pensions (due to a change in the ratio of working and retired people) and the growing servicing costs of public debt have reduced even more the room for raising capital spending without increasing taxes.

35 It is true, however, that most of this literature explains this increasing sectoral

electoral and partisan fragmentation as a result of a decline in redistributive conflict rather than as a consequence of more intense economic conflict. See Inglehart 1984 and, in general, the volume edited by Dalton, Flanagan, and Beck 1984. For a more recent statement, see Kitschelt 1994.

CHAPTER 3. SUPPLY-SIDE ECONOMIC STRATEGIES FROM A
COMPARATIVE PERSPECTIVE (I)

1   These figures are an average of domestic data not weighed according to GDP or population.
2   When we control for the proportion of the population that is school age, the variance remains high. Public spending on education for each 1 percent of the population younger than twenty years has ranged in all three decades from 0.3 points of GDP to 0.1 points of GDP or less.
3   A high income earner is here anyone earning five times the wage of the "average production worker," as defined by the (OECD 1990a). The effective tax rate (i.e., the proportion of the income paid in personal income tax, after all allowances are deducted and the corresponding tax rate has been applied) has been estimated for an unmarried worker.
4   Partisan control of the cabinet is measured as the share of cabinet posts controlled by socialist and communist parties every year. It runs as a continuous variable from 1 (full control of government) to 0 (no ministerial cabinets held by those parties in that given year). It has been reduced to this interval in order to facilitate its use in building several interactive variables. For the period 1960–88, my source is Lane, McKay, and Newton 1991. For 1989–90, I used my own calculations based on *Keesing's Contemporary Archives.*
5   See the definition of the organizational power of labor in Chapter 2, note 12.
6   Trade exposure is measured as the sum of exports and imports as a percentage of GDP. Financial integration is operationalized, following Cusack and Garrett 1992, as the absolute value of 1 minus the ratio of private investment to private savings.
7   Iceland and Luxembourg are thus excluded. Turkey is also excluded for lack of reliable data. Accordingly, the sample includes Australia, Austria, Belgium, Canada, Denmark, Finland, France, (West) Germany, Greece, Ireland, Italy, Japan, the Netherlands, New Zealand, Norway, Portugal, Spain, Sweden, Switzerland, the United Kingdom, and the United States of America.
8   There are continuous series for all the countries of the initial sample (listed in n. 7 except New Zealand and Switzerland).
9   In order to assess the relationship between partisan control, the organization of the domestic economy, the international economy, and gross fixed capital formation by the general government (from now on referred to as public investment), I run panel regression of time-series cross-national data for the period from 1961 to 1990 in the countries listed (except New Zealand and Switzerland, for which there are no data on public gross fixed capital formation, and Greece and Portugal, for which data on the organized power of labor are not available). The autoregressive specification for the dependent variable is chosen as the "best" using standard techniques. To compute the regression I employ the generalized least

squares (GLS) technique to correct for the violations that cross-national panel data impose on the assumptions underlying ordinary least squares (OLS) estimations. Given the potential problems that, according to Beck et al. (1993), may plague GLS estimation strategies, I have also estimated the regression using OLS with robust errors following White's general method, using the statistical procedure DPD developed by Arellano and Bond (1988, 1991). The resulting coefficients are extremely similar in both cases, and OLS robust standard errors tend to be smaller than GLS standard errors. Table 3.2 presents the results obtained through the GLS estimation technique.

10 This is true when all the terms interacting with socialist control of the government are set to 0. A more precise understanding of the impact of partisanship comes from simulations done later.

11 For the simulation, all the variables (except partisanship) have been set at their mean levels.

12 For the simulation, the rate of growth and the budget balance have been set at 0. As shown in Table 3.2, however, partisanship still has an important effect in corporatist countries through its interaction with both the rate of growth and the budget balance.

13 In all cases, I assume a country whose initial per capita income was $4,000, that grew at the OECD annual average growth rate, and where public investment was 3.5 percent of GDP in 1960. All the other variables (corporatism, trade openness, and financial integration) are set at their mean levels.

14 The assumptions made are the same described in n. 13.

15 Notice that with a growth rate of 5.2 percent after 1973, per capita income turns out to be $18,000 in 1990 (instead of $11,000).

16 Higher public investment rates do not take place merely as a result of a generalized strategy of higher spending pursued by socialist governments. When we regress government outlays (as a percentage of GDP) on public investment (as a percentage of GDP), to check the extent to which they are correlated, the $R^2 <$ .10 for all three decades. This points to the fact that socialist parties consciously target public investment to develop their most preferred economic strategy. It also accords well with current theoretical literature that has not found a clear relationship between the overall size of government and socialist parties.

17 Capital spending is excluded because it already appears in the estimates of fixed capital formation. Data are taken from UNESCO's *Statistical Yearbooks*.

18 I employ the *level* of public effort in 1970 because we lack sufficient data on the level of public effort in education in 1960 to calculate the actual evolution, or change, in spending effort during the decade.

19 This result is not reported in any table.

20 Per capita income is not used here to control for economic development because its level is in turn strongly affected by the volume of the expenditure on education. See Mankiw, Romer, and Weil 1992.

21 The organizational power of labor has no effect even when we regress partisanship, labor organization, and the interaction of both at the same time.

22 This figure refers to *public* education; private spending on education in Germany is sizable and puts total spending on education over 6 percent of GDP.

23 The data are for 1985, except those for Italy, for which 1986 is the first year reported.

24 These results get much stronger when we exclude Austria, which has the lowest level of public expenditure on manpower policies among European nations and therefore behaves as an outlier. When Austria is excluded, partisanship explains 34.2 percent of the variance (vs. 22.8 percent including Austria), and the organizational power of labor explains 40.8 percent of the variation (vs. 26.5 percent). It might be justified to exclude Austria given that it has a large nationalized sector which probably operates as a public source of worker training (see Scharpf 1984; Freeman 1989).

25 This result is not reproduced in Table 3.6.

CHAPTER 4. SUPPLY-SIDE ECONOMIC STRATEGIES FROM A COMPARATIVE PERSPECTIVE (II)

1 Although there is no doubt that public enterprises have generally served several purposes, such as channeling the redistribution of income across social strata, sectors, or regions, or smoothing the business cycle through countercyclical investment and employment decisions, their main goal has been to affect the productive conditions of the economy, promoting economic development and fostering the competitiveness of the domestic factors abroad. For a review of the theories (of either a liberal or a radical origin) justifying the existence of public enterprises, see Freeman 1989, chap. 1–2; Alt and Freeman 1994.

2 These figures are my own estimates based on national data presented in Short 1984.

3 See an analysis of the ideological evolution of the British Conservative Party in Chapter 7.

4 In some instances social democratic governments engaged in a redefinition of the specific purposes and uses of the public business sector; see n. 7 below and the discussion of the Spanish case in Chapter 5.

5 The sample is formed by all OECD nations except (a) countries with fewer than one million inhabitants, that is, Iceland and Luxembourg; (b) Switzerland and Turkey, for which complete information is unavailable; and (c) the United States, whose public business sector is insignificant and where, contrary to all other cases, political differences between Republicans and Democrats over the size of the public *business* sector are marginal. The period observed goes from 1979 to 1992 (both years included) with the following exceptions: for West Germany, it ends in October 1990, at the time of unification; in the cases in which elections held during 1993 resulted in important government changes (France, Greece, and Spain), the period examined goes beyond December 1992 through the month of 1993 in which the political situation changed; two governments have been excluded: the minority, caretaker Italian government Fanfani VI, which was formed in April 1987 and lasted less than a month, and the transitional Greek government of 1990.

6 As a matter of fact, from 1983 to 1992 the Italian authorities sold 195 public enterprises but acquired 231 companies; moreover, the enterprises acquired by the public sector were generally larger than those sold in terms of both employees and net sales (OECD 1994a).

7 For a defense of targeted privatizations as a way of rationalizing the Spanish public

business sector, see the 1989 article by Aranzadi, then president of INI. In 1985 there were 479 public enterprises in Spain; four years later, despite several privatizations, there were 553 (see IGAE, several years). Capital formation by the public business sector increased at a rate well above the rate of change of capital formation by Spanish private firms during the second half of the 1980s. For a more extended discussion, see Chapter 5. A similar case of commitment to the public business sector can be observed in Austria, where gross fixed capital formation by the public business sector represented 4.9 percent of GDP in both 1979 and 1988 (Short 1984; CEEP 1990).

8 Although this might have included a deliberate effort to redefine the goals and strategy of the state-run business sector. Again, see my discussion on the Spanish case in Chapter 5.

9 See definition in Chapter 3, n. 4.

10 The fragmentation of government is measured according to the Rae index, which equals $1 - \sum p^2$, where p is the proportion of cabinet portfolios that each party has within the government. It ranges from 0 (one-party government) to 1 (extreme fragmentation). See Taagapera and Shugart 1989 for a review and discussion of this index.

11 The index is 1 if the government commands the majority of seats; 0 if it is a minority government.

12 The following variables, which have also been regressed on the variable Strategy Toward the Public Business Sector, have been found to have no effects on the decisions adopted toward public firms: (1) the proportion of centrist (Christian Democratic) ministers in each cabinet; (2) the partisan affiliation of the minister of finance; (3) the level of public business sector investment (measured as a proportion of GDP) in 1980 and 1985, introduced to measure the preexisting levels of public ownership; (4) the organizational power of labor; (5) measures of short-term economic performance (the average GDP growth rates in each country as well as their difference in relation to the average GDP growth rates in the OECD in the five years previous to the year of formation of each government); and (6) the balance of the public budget in the first year of each government.

13 As should be evident from the discussion above, the coding of the behavior of governments into certain "strategies" conveys more accurately the actual privatization strategy pursued by each government than the pure volume of asset sales. In any case, the same results are obtained when we estimate the impact of partisanship, internal cohesion of the cabinet, and economic performance on the volume of assets sold.

14 Notice that given that the estimation in Table 4.3 is done through a nonlinear technique, the resulting parameters cannot be interpreted the way that they are in standard OLS procedures. Simulations are in this case indispensable to understand the exact size of the impact of each variable.

15 Conditions are more stringent for large privatizations to take place. For example, conservative governments, no matter how divided, are very likely to implement them if the economy has experienced low growth rates. But if real GDP per capita has grown at 3 percent, only one-party cabinets carry out privatizations (see Table 4.4B).

16 Different tax strategies are taken here to derive from different ideas about their economic consequences for the allocation of production factors. Naturally, the

choice of a tax system also involves resolving questions about the equity dimension – that is, to what extent policymakers choose to redistribute income. As a matter of fact, the efficiency and equity dimensions cannot be easily separated. For example, highly progressive systems are likely to both channel savings into the public purse and have strong redistributive effects. Still, this analysis is only secondarily concerned with taxes as instruments of income redistribution. As the specialized literature has generally stressed, the extent to which the state affects the redistribution of income depends on social transfers and public expenditure rather than on the structure of taxes.

17 Since the late 1970s, the OECD reports the income of the "average production worker" and the effective tax to be paid for a single worker and for a worker with two children. I have only estimated the case of a single worker.

18 The effective tax rate on higher incomes and the volume of revenues it generates are strongly correlated. For the late 1970s personal income taxation as a percentage of GDP and the effective tax rate on an income five times an APW's wage show a correlation coefficient of 0.79. For the late 1980s, the correlation coefficient for personal income taxation as a percentage of GDP and the effective tax rate on an income five times an APW's wage is 0.68.

19 Conversely, this does not mean that interventionist supply-side economic strategies never come jointly with more public spending across the board. A pure social democratic strategy consists of boosting capital and social spending at the same time – although the rationales for increasing each kind of expenditure are partly different. A pure conservative strategy results in a reduction of both capital and social spending. A third solution consists of cutting public investment and freeing the economy while maintaining or expanding social expenditure.

20 Even though social democratic governments resorted to countercyclical policies during the 1960s, some conservative cabinets did too – as long as the inflationary costs of propping demand up were perceived to be low. As shown in Boix 1996, Keynesianism mainly distinguished socialists from conservatives in the 1970s. It was at that time that, regardless of the institutional structure of the economy, socialist parties ran much looser fiscal policies and held interest rates lower than conservative parties.

21 As shown in Boix 1996, partisan differences over the management of demand tended to disappear in the 1980s. In corporatist countries, social democratic governments maintained the domestic real interest rate slightly below the world interest rate while balancing the budget. In noncorporatist countries, socialist cabinets sustained monetary policies that were as tight as those followed by conservative cabinets. Overall, however, monetary policy was more restrictive in the 1980s than in the 1960s.

CHAPTER 5. THE SOCIAL DEMOCRATIC PROJECT

1 The analysis of the Socialist electorate presented here refers to the 1979 General Election and relies heavily on Gunther, Sani, and Shabad 1988 and Linz and Montero 1986. Shorter studies, which incorporate a preliminary analysis of economic voting, can be found in Lancaster and Lewis-Beck 1986 and in Lewis-Beck

1988. Most data come, however, from CIS survey no. 1327, for purposes of comparison with the results of 1982 and 1993.

2 Data are fully reported in Table 6.4, in Chapter 6.

3 In spite of the PSOE's electoral manifesto explicitly calling for an "expansive policy" (PSOE 1982, 7), Minister of Economy Miguel Boyer, who had not participated in the elaboration of the manifesto, was quick to emphasize in press declarations, made after the electoral victory and before the formation of the government, that the Socialist cabinet would not pursue "either a stabilization policy or an intense expansive policy" (*El País*, 24 and 27 November, 1982).

4 By November 1981 the French minister of finance had already indicated that it was necessary "to pause before announcing further reforms." By June of 1982, that is, several months before González was elected, the French government abandoned its macroeconomic policy and implemented an austerity plan. The deflationary strategy was strengthened in the spring of 1983. See Hall 1986, 199–201.

5 For a more detailed account of this change of ideas among economists, see Serrano and Costas 1988. See also Rojo 1986. The overall consensus among Spanish economists about the causes of the crisis carried over to the economic team nominated by González in 1982 that would control the Ministry of Economy and Finance and its related ministries throughout the decade. And, even though carrying out a nonexpansionary macroeconomic strategy created strong tensions within the PSOE, the need for macroeconomic stability was eventually accepted by most sectors of the party. Thus, in the programmatic renewal movement, mainly sponsored by the center-to-the-left branch of the party in the late 1980s, that crystallized in the so-called Programa 2000, one-country demand-management policies were definitely and explicitly rejected. See Programa 2000, 1988, particularly p. 30.

6 In attempting to control the deficit, the Socialist cabinet took care to compensate for the impact of its restrictive policies with all sorts of social transfers to low-income households (Boyer 1983a, 36).

7 For the presentation of the Budget for 1986 see Solchaga in *El País*, 19 and 25 September and 3 October 1985; for 1987, see Solchaga 1986b; and for 1988, see Solchaga 1987. See also Zabalza 1987.

8 In addition, the Socialist cabinet played with the idea that, by forcing the process of European integration, it would be possible to gain enough political leverage to support a coordinated expansionary policy in the future. See, for example, the declarations of the minister of economy before the Parliament at the end of 1989 (Solchaga 1990, 33), as well as Dehesa 1988, 32–7.

9 See Zabalza 1990, 1991a, for a critique of the idea that a mere increase of private savings (achieved through tax cuts) mechanically translates into higher investment rates, and for a defense of an alternative strategy based on building up public savings and directing them to the formation of capital stock through the budget.

10 All data are for Spain excluding the Basque Country and Navarre.

11 Fiscal drag accounted for 80 percent of all new revenue through 1985 (Argimón and González-Páramo 1987; Valdés, Argimón, and Raymond 1989) and for 80 percent of the new revenue from 1986 on (Jiménez and Salas 1992).

12 See PSOE 1982, 18; Programa 2000, 1988, 163. See also Solchaga 1986a, 214ff.; Borrell 1987, 1988, 1989.

13 Although the level of taxation appears to be similar to or smaller than that in other European countries, it is probably higher when one accounts for the Spanish real per capita income. Since the latter is much smaller than that in more advanced countries and therefore its capacity to finance consumption and savings is presumably lower, the fiscal extraction suffered by the Spanish taxpayers turns out to be higher than in other countries. Thus, in 1990, real per capita income was around $5,200 at the price levels and exchange rates of 1985 and tax revenues were 35 percent of GDP. Similar proportions of tax revenues to GDP were reached only in Sweden in 1965, when per capita income was over $8,000 (again at the price levels and exchange rates of 1985); in Germany in 1972, when per capita income was $7,800; and in Italy in 1985, when per capita income came close to $7,500. All estimations are my own based on data from OECD 1991c.

14 The implementation of a value-added tax in 1986 led to a temporary upsurge in revenue from indirect taxes. For a strong statement that this situation was merely provisional and that the Socialist cabinet was committed to rely mostly on direct taxes over the long run, see the declarations of the minister of economy before Parliament in October 1986 (Solchaga 1986b, 35–37).

15 Estimations are derived from the data collected in IGAE 1991.

16 Fewer than 1 percent of all taxpayers were in that category.

17 The fact that these considerations were explicitly recognized by the government can be seen in Borrell 1990.

18 All these proportions refer to central government nonmilitary investment and they include investment by all autonomous institutes (Organismos Autónomos) and Social Security. Military investment declined over time; it represented 0.8 percent of GDP in 1987 and 0.5 percent of GDP in 1990 (IGAE 1990). Besides direct public investment, the central government financed investment by private and public enterprises through capital transfers, which fluctuated around 2 percent of GDP. Most of these enterprises will be examined in the section on public companies.

19 This figure, however, does not include major capital transfers from the central government to the two public railway companies, RENFE and FEVE, totaling Pta 535 billion (in 1990 pesetas) from 1985 to 1992. This represented 56 percent of all the investment effort made by RENFE and FEVE in the same period (Pta 947 billion in 1990 pesetas).

20 All figures on central government investment are my own estimates based on MOPTMA 1993 and MOPT, several years.

21 Around 80 percent of the new expenditure in education was directed to secondary and university education, according to data collected by Bandrés (1993) comparing 1980 with 1990.

22 All children between six and twelve years of age were already attending school in 1980.

23 These programs were also spurred by European funds, which financed 52 percent of them (Espina 1991).

24 For a history of the public enterprise sector in Spain before the 1980s, see Martín and Comín 1990 and, more generally, Comín and Martín 1991.

25 In 1986, for example, the average public enterprise had 1,600 employees, sold

Pta 15,500 million, and had assets amounting to Pta 26,000 million. The average private enterprise had 200 employees, Pta 2,900 million in sales, and Pta 3,000 million in assets (Cuervo 1989).

26 In 1985, public manufacturing enterprises exported 28.9 percent of their production, whereas all manufacturing enterprises sold 21 percent of their production abroad.

27 The PSOE, however, did not renounce the possibility of employing the public business sector in some manner as an economic and industrial policy instrument. See PSOE 1982 and also Programa 2000, 1988.

28 The Socialist cabinet nationalized only the high-tension electrical network. In 1983 it also took over RUMASA, a financial and industrial conglomerate the government judged was heading toward immediate collapse. The companies included in RUMASA were devolved to the private sector over the following years.

29 It is true, however, that the government continued to support some sectors that were sustaining heavy losses. This was, for example, the case with the coal-mining industry (Servén 1989), which was heavily concentrated in one region, Asturias, and in which employment amounted to 44 percent of all industrial employment (the data are for 1976 and can be found in Martín and Comín 1990).

30 A third of the companies that were sold were companies nationalized in the 1970s.

31 These numbers fall to 402 and 484 respectively when we exclude all commercial services as well as the Organismos Autónomos.

32 This excludes capital transfers from the state.

33 See the declarations by M. Cuenca, vice-president of INI, on 26 August 1992 El País, 27 August 1992 and by Espina (1992), secretary of state for industry since April 1991.

34 This consolidation process involved the integration of Entel and Eria in Eritel (in 1991), mainly controlled by Inisel; an accord between Inisel and Ceselsa; and a share exchange between Sainco and Inisel (see INI, several years).

35 Telefónica bought 20 percent of Entel and 43.6 percent of CTC (both of them serving the Chilean market), shares of Telefónica de Argentina and CANTV (in Venezuela), 79 percent of the Puerto Rican TLD, and part of two telephone mobile services, one in Portugal (Contactel) and one in Romania (Telefonica Romania) (see Telefónica, several years).

36 In 1992 Telefónica managed close to 14 million telephone lines in the Spanish domestic market and another 5 million through all the participating foreign companies (Telefónica 1992). Thus, the international strategy pursued by Telefónica increased its business volume by 40 percent in just three years.

37 Notice that Figure 5.2, which reports the financial balance of key public corporations, shows results in constant 1981 pesetas.

38 See n. 33 for declarations in favor of maintaining a publicly owned business sector. For recommendations in favor of partial privatizations to reduce the deficit see, for example, the statements by Solchaga, Aranzadi, and Fanjul in El País during September 1992.

39 In order to finance large investment plans, already in 1988 the government had sold shares of three electricity companies – totaling Pta 101 billion. By the following year, 24 percent of the oil company of INH, REPSOL, had also been

sold to the public. The government retained, however, the majority of shares in all these companies.

CHAPTER 6. THE POLITICAL AND ELECTORAL DIMENSIONS OF THE PSOE'S ECONOMIC STRATEGY

1 A straightforward exposition of these two alternatives and their costs and benefits by the minister of economy himself can be found in the presentation of the budget for 1989 (Solchaga 1988, 29ff.), the budget for 1990 (Solchaga 1990, 33ff.), and the budget for 1992 (Solchaga 1991b, 12ff.).

2 Moreover, given the governmental conviction that wages were the main causal component of the inflationary process, it appeared to be the most direct and less costly way to reduce inflation. See Solchaga (1988, 29). Similarly, a 1988 report prepared by the Ministry of Economy on collective bargaining since 1977 indicated that the trade unions' excessive concentration on salary increases, with little concern for productivity, had forced employers to reduce their labor force in order to control unit costs (*El País*, 9 April 1988).

   The government's attribution of inflation to wage pressure was modified, however, in the late 1980s. Instead, as the behavior of prices started to diverge between the tradable and the nontradable sectors close to EC inflation in the former but well above the EC average in the latter, the government started to focus its attention on the structure and behavior of the nontradable sectors. See Zabalza 1989, 1991a; Solchaga 1991a. See also OECD 1992, 57–76.

3 For a clear exposition of the UGT's demands, according to its general secretary, Nicolás Redondo, see Redondo 1988. See also Espina's (1991) historical analysis.

4 If the government follows a restrictive policy, both the socialist cabinet and the trade unions prefer wage moderation to wage aggressiveness. Trade unions prefer wage moderation because high wage increases only exacerbate the negative effects of tight governmental policies and lead to very high rates of unemployment.

5 See Olson 1982; and for specific applications to the labor market and the union movement, see Calmfors and Driffill 1988; Soskice 1990.

6 On neocorporatist settlements, see Goldthorpe 1984. From a slightly different perspective, which links the literature to the Olsonian model of collective action and stresses the effects of corporatism on economic performance, see Lange and Garrett 1985, 1987; Alvarez, Garrett, and Lange 1991.

7 Data taken from a CIS survey reported in *El País*, 29 May 1989.

8 Partly due to high electoral thresholds in the allocation of workers' representatives according to the results of the syndical elections, UGT and CCOO already controlled three-fourths of all syndical delegates by 1986 (*Anuario El País 1988*). Similarly, by the end of the 1980s, and despite their small membership, the two main unions, CCOO and UGT, were represented at more than 90 percent of all collective-bargaining tables (Fernández-Castro 1993).

9 It is true, however, that sector-based unions will have incentives to moderate wage claims if they internalize the output effect of wage increases – for example, if domestic demand for their goods is highly price elastic.

10 Within the framework of a tight economic policy, the government still naturally prefers union moderation to wage aggressiveness.

11 Notice that the ordering of preferences of the PSOE government is still different from the ordering of preferences of a conservative government. A conservative government *always* prefers restrictive policies over expansionary policies. As a result, the game is different: regardless of what unions do, an equilibrium takes place in the lower-left cell. See Scharpf 1987.

12 Moreover, from 1990 to 1992 real-wage increases were higher than productivity growth, which in turn led to a profit squeeze (OECD 1992, 1993a).

13 Besides the strategies of social concertation or restrictive macroeconomic policies, the government could have followed a third scenario: it could have curtailed union power and, above all, reformed the labor market to make it flexible, highly responsive to the economic cycle, and less prone to inflationary pressures. The government was either unable or unwilling to pursue that alternative. After the government legalized some forms of temporary contracts in 1984 with the acquiescence of unions, further attempts to reform a highly regulated labor market were repeatedly staved off. As a matter of fact, new legislation passed in the early 1990s enhanced union power and rigidities in the labor market. The legislation on labor procedures approved in 1990 increased the compensation to be paid to workers that had been unfairly laid off. A 1991 law on new employment contract monitoring extended the right of workers' representatives and unions to screen the legality of most new hiring contracts. Ongoing negotiations (since 1991) on the regulation of the right to strike showed the capacity of unions and the left wing of the PSOE to sustain a legal environment favorable to the former. After the cabinet had drafted a moderate proposal which excluded all the main union demands, the unions outmaneuvered the government through direct negotiations with the Socialist parliamentary group (Fernández-Castro 1993).

14 Overall, however, public investment continued to grow steadily, as shown in Chapter 5.

15 The figures represent the trade-weighted real exchange rate index of the peseta with respect to the industrial countries and based on the consumer price index. After the three devaluations in 1992–93, the peseta fell to its level of June 1989.

16 A preliminary analysis of the economic impact of an overvalued peseta can be found in Gordo and L'Hotellerie 1993, who show that, although Spanish companies did increase somewhat their export share in world markets, their participation in the domestic market diminished substantially throughout the 1980s.

17 From a constitutional point of view, this distinction corresponds respectively to those regions that were granted their autonomy through the common procedure regulated in art. 143 of the Spanish constitution (Aragón, Asturias, Baleares, Cantabria, Castille–La Mancha, Castille–León, Extremadura, Madrid, Murcia, and La Rioja), those regions that achieved limited self-rule through the special procedure of art. 151 (Andalusia, Canary Islands, Catalonia, Galicia, and Valencia), and two special *foral* regions with broader powers over the tax system (Navarre, Basque Country). This distinction is commonly used in all official and academic analysis. A recent example can be found in the last section of OECD 1993a.

18 Alone it explains 33 percent of all variation (a result not reproduced in Table 6.2).

19 The electoral results of 1982 and 1986 have been chosen to avoid the possibility that the causality operates in the reverse direction – that is, the Socialist vote driving the volume of public spending.

20 The result is likely to derive from a partial correlation between per capita income and the Socialist vote ($r = .39$). A partial F-test shows that the probability that the statistical improvement achieved by adding the variable of Socialist vote could have happened by chance is less than 5 percent.

21 The ratio of Socialist membership to population size derives from my own estimates based on data for April 1984 presented in Puhle 1986, 328. Socialist membership and the average Socialist vote in 1982–86 are partly correlated ($r = .73$).

22 Data come from "Datos de opinión" 1991, 240.

23 The most appropriate system to examine the evolution of the Socialist vote would be to analyze temporal panel surveys from 1982 to 1993 (i.e., surveys of the same individuals for that period of time). Such panel surveys have never been conducted in Spain, however.

24 Disposable family income is the sum of all wages, capital income, social income (such as pensions, etc.), and net transfers less social security contributions and direct taxes. To measure the GPP and the DFI, I use "standardized" parameters – that is, estimated relative to the national mean which is 100. For example, in 1991, Girona, enjoying the highest GPP, had a standardized GPP of 140.5, or 40.5 percent higher than the national mean, whereas Badajoz, with the lowest one, had a standardized GPP of 56.7. The difference between GPP and DFI is assumed to show the net level of transfers from the state – that is, how taxes and social expenditure affect final income and correct for strong initial inequalities. This parameter, however, fulfills its goal rather crudely. It measures neither the levels of public fixed capital formation and public employment nor the impact that the latter may have on the growth rate of each area.

25 Employment in the primary sector and public transfers are well correlated ($r = .69$). When we regress each one separately on the evolution of the Socialist vote, their impact is much bigger. In this case, each percentage point employed in the primary sector increases the Socialist vote by 0.33 points. Similarly, each point of net transfers increases the PSOE vote by 0.26 points.

CHAPTER 7. TURNING AROUND THE BRITISH
POSTWAR CONSENSUS

1 Very candid statements by top Conservative policymakers about the need to change the macroeconomic framework and then reform the supply side of the economy can be found in Thatcher 1993 (esp. pp. 41–42), Lawson 1980 (reproduced in Lawson 1992), 1984.

2 See particularly the discussion by Särlvik and Crewe (1983, chap. 5), who stress the difference between Conservative voters, whose support for the Tory Party derives from an ideological agreement with the virtues of the market economy, and Labour voters, who define their support in terms of class identity and class interests.

3 Evidence that the Conservative program was cast in terms of both economic efficiency and moral and political renewal can be directly gathered from the autobiographical works of Lawson (1992), Ridley (1991), Tebbit (1988), and Thatcher (1993).

4 First described by Butler and Stokes (1974), the process of class dealignment has been examined thoroughly by Särlvik and Crewe (1983). Although challenged by Heath, Jowell, and Curtice (1985), it has been restated by Crewe (1986), Dunleavy (1987), Scarbrough (1987), and finally broadly accepted by Heath et al. (1991).

5 A similar change, although less sharp in relative terms, took place on the issue of social services. In 1974, 38 percent of the population favored a reduction in social services; 59 percent wanted them to be either expanded or maintained. Five years later, the proportions had changed to 49 and 46 percent respectively (Särlvik and Crewe 1983, 91, table 8.4).

6 There was also some flow from the Conservative to the Liberal Party. Thus, in net terms, only one out of five 1974 Liberals cast their ballots for the Conservative Party. All the estimates are based on the data presented by Särlvik and Crewe (1983).

7 Proceeds from selling public assets are treated as a negative expenditure in the British government budget.

8 The sum of all the spending areas reported in Table 7.3 amounts to four-fifths of general government expenditure.

9 It represented close to three-fifths of all increases in that period.

10 Net general government debt declined from over 45 percent of GDP in 1983 to less than 30 percent of GDP in 1990.

11 In 1992–93, the government introduced a "lower rate" of 20 percent on the first £2,000 of income.

12 Effective tax rates are derived from applying general allowances and deductions and the corresponding nominal tax rates to an unmarried person.

13 The reform of National Insurance tax rates (NIC) increased the gains accrued by the highest incomes through the reform of personal income taxation. While the amount of income paid by average wage earners remained almost unchanged (due to the weight of NIC at those levels), the proportion of taxes paid in the upper segments dwindled drastically:

Income tax and NIC as	Married men, multiples of average earnings				
% of gross earnings	0.5	1	2	5	10
In 1978–79	21.9	27.8	31.4	50.5	66.5
In 1990–91	21.2	25.5	28.8	35.5	37.8

Source: Johnson 1993.

14 By 1983 the Conservative government had sold all of Amersham International, most of British Rail's hotels, some of the NBS's subsidiaries, part of British Aerospace, Cable and Wireless, the oil-producing side of the British National Oil Corporation, and the British Transport Docks Board.

15 The content of policy documents prepared shortly before Jenkin's proposal shows that the sale of BT was the turning point in the privatization strategy. *Public Enterprise in Crisis*, published in 1980 by John Redwood, who became actively involved in the privatization program from 1983 to 1985, made very moderate

proposals (Mitchell 1990). Similarly, the Westwell report, a Conservative Party strategy document written in the winter of 1981, scarcely mentioned privatization.

16 The Major government split British Rail into the track network and the transportation system, leasing the latter to private operators.

17 For an analysis of the efficiency gains resulting from the sale of public corporations, see Bishop and Kay 1988; Bishop and Thompson 1992.

18 Unions were weakened as well by the reduction in the proportion of the labor force in manufacturing jobs and by massive unemployment. Green (1993) attributes 30 percent of the fall in union membership to the contraction of the industrial sector.

19 These figures correspond to replacement ratios estimated under the assumption of a constant population since 1968. The average income of an unemployed worker is estimated 13 weeks (i.e., a quarter of a year) after job loss. The data come from Dilnot and Norris 1983 and are reproduced in Mayhew 1985.

20 These figures are my own estimates based on U.K. Parliament 1992.

CHAPTER 8. THE POLITICAL AND ELECTORAL DIMENSIONS OF THE
CONSERVATIVE ECONOMIC STRATEGY

1 Nigel Lawson at the Maurice Macmillan Memorial Lecture of June 1985; quoted in Lawson 1992, 206. See also Thatcher 1993, chap. 23.

2 Home ownership had constantly increased during the postwar period from a meager 26 percent in 1945. Nevertheless, the growth rates for home ownership had always been higher under Conservative governments than under Labour governments with the exception of the Heath government (my own estimates based on data in Forrest, Murie, and Williams 1990).

3 The sum of mortgage interest relief, the Housing Benefit, and current and net capital expenditure in housing reached £14.0 billion (in 1988–89 prices) in 1989–90. This was only slightly less than the sum spent in 1978–79. But the composition had varied completely. In 1978–79, 68 percent of all resources were spent in current and net capital expenditure. In 1989–90, 76 percent were directed to mortgage interest relief and Housing Benefit. Data are my own estimates from figures reported in Hills 1991.

4 See Rose and McAllister 1986, chap. 5.

5 The Labour Party only switched to favoring the privatization of council houses in 1986.

6 For a different view, see Heath et al. 1989. The data from the Heath et al. survey show, however, strong deviations from actual results in both the aggregate vote and the proportions of homeowners and council tenants.

7 The Conservative lead across the whole electorate was 8 percentage points in 1979 and 15 in 1983.

8 A logit analysis of both the vote in 1979 and that in 1992 shows clear stability in the impact of class, home ownership, and union membership on vote for the Conservative Party, with a slight strengthening of the impact of home ownership and unionization:

	Change in probability of voting Conservative	
	In 1979	In 1992
From lowest to highest class	+0.15	+0.16
From council tenant to homeowner	+0.17	+0.21
From union member to nonunionized	+0.18	+0.20

The estimation is based on 1979 and 1992 British Electoral Studies. In the analysis, class was divided into professional, managerial, routine nonmanual, skilled manual, partly skilled manual, unskilled manual. Home ownership was classified as 1 = home ownership, 0.5 = private tenancy, 0 = council tenancy. Union membership was a binary variable where 0 = unionized, 1 = nonunionized.

9 The estimate is my own based on applying the Conservative share of the vote to the 1979 proportions of housing tenure reported in Table 8.1.

10 For shares sold at a set price and allocated through a rationing scheme (the system employed in three-quarters of all sales), Vickers and Yarrow (1988) have estimated their undervaluation to be over 20 percent, or about £3 billion in forgone revenue through 1987. Veljanovski (1988) puts this figure, however, at £1.6 billion.

11 Although widely spread, share ownership was rather thin. The average holding of shares has been put at about 5 percent of wealth per household – therefore much less important than home ownership and savings on pension funds (Riddell 1989). By 1988, over half of all shareholders had invested in just one company, most of them in either British Telecom, British Gas, or Trustee Savings Bank. Fewer than a tenth held between four and nine different company shares. And a mere 300,000 had a portfolio of over ten shares. Control over the privatized companies turned out to be strongly concentrated. Over 90 percent of all shareholders were individuals in companies like BAA, British Gas, or Rolls-Royce. Yet the top 10 percent of shareholders controlled around nine-tenths of the shares (Bishop and Kay 1988).

12 See Saunders 1995 for evidence that the purchase of shares in the mid- and late 1980s raised the likelihood of voting for the Conservative Party in 1993 among 1987 Labour voters.

13 Although the effect of share ownership proves to be powerful at the individual level, its aggregate consequences are lower than home ownership, because the former is much less extended than the latter.

14 The comparison with 1979 is based on data presented in Rose 1981.

15 The data for the 1979 General Election are taken from Crewe 1981 and refer to the average for the period of the electoral campaign.

16 This is the estimate presented in the Budget for 1994/95 and is taken from the *Economist,* 4 December 1993.

17 Data from Gallup Political and Economic Index, November 1991. It is true, however, that, when asked a more structured question, over 50 percent considered it likely that a Conservative government would privatize the NHS.

18 The figures are my own estimates based on U.K. Parliament, *Social Security: The Government Expenditure Plans,* several years.

19 The average is estimated for the fiscal years 1980/81 to 1986/87, based on figures on total planned expenditure published in U.K. Parliament, *Public Expenditure Analyses*, several years.

CHAPTER 9. PARTISAN STRATEGIES AND ELECTORAL COALITIONS

1 Data are from Esping-Andersen 1985, chap. 9; Heath, Jowell, and Curtice 1985, chap. 3.

2 By contrast, the proportion was only 44 percent in France (Maravall 1995, 187).

3 For somewhat similar results among French middle classes after the socialist government of 1981–86, see Hall 1986, chap. 8.

4 Differences in the resort to public employment, however, have been only relative. Until the early 1980s public sector employment grew at average annual rate of over 4 percent in Sweden and Norway (OECD 1990b, Table 1.13). Yet, in Spain, it grew at 4.4 percent between 1979 and 1990 (OECD 1994b, Table 1.1).

5 See a preliminary analysis in Iversen 1995, chap. 6.

6 This contrasts with the greater polarization of opinions on the extent to which the state should actively intervene to secure full employment and economic growth. Similar attitudes are held among party elites. Economic interventionism is contested within conservative and liberal parties in a way that the public health system and public pensions are not.

7 The reduction is calculated by looking at the difference between 1978/79 and 1988/89, two peak years in the business cycle.

8 This competition normally takes place in the goods markets. But it equally results from the immigration of low-paid workers, who, on entering advanced countries, induce a fall in the relative price of the labor of the native unskilled workers.

9 For evidence that free trade was part of European social democratic programs already in the 1920s and 1930s, see Simmons 1994. See Katzenstein 1985 for the postwar period.

CHAPTER 10. CONCLUSIONS

1 The degree of capital mobility in fact varies depending on the type of capital and is inversely related to the latter's specificity. The less specific capital is (i.e., the more alternative uses it can be put to), the more mobile it is, and the more power or influence capital has over the state. See Alt 1987; Frieden 1991b, 19–22.

2 For an analysis of the so-called structural dependence of the state on capital, see Lindblom 1977, chap. 13; Hirschman 1981; Przeworski and Wallerstein 1988.

3 Those alternative strategies are pursued without challenging the logic of market allocation. Again, states may still implement measures that question the latter: either by nationalizing capital or by restricting its mobility.

4 It goes without saying that economic shocks may also have an immediate positive effect on the productivity of sectors and on the country's capacity to boost its social wage: the industrialization of the Western Hemisphere in the nineteenth century established the basis for the welfare state of this century; and the expan-

sion of the East Asian economies should lead to higher levels of welfare transfers in the future.

5 Low unemployment was also the result of countercyclical policies and the expansion of public employment. Notice, however, that the employment performance of the highly educated nations worsened in the early 1990s. This may derive from either a collapse of corporatist structures (Iversen 1995) or an accumulation of increasingly intense exogenous shocks (and shifts in the demand for labor), which, in spite of the existence of a well-trained labor force, cannot be easily absorbed due to the presence of excessive institutional rigidities.

6 Notice, however, that it is still unclear whether we can properly talk about similar "institutional settings" at the national level. Empirical research in this area remains at a very preliminary stage. Moreover, there is some evidence that "institutional frameworks" mostly vary across regions (see the literature on "industrial districts") and across productive sectors. The political implications of this are important. With a fully coordinated economy at the national level, governments may have little incentive to lower social wages. But, if the economy is regulated only in certain sectors, a regulated economy at the national level only works to the advantage of the coordinated sectors (which can endure regulations). In this case, reducing the social wage and "deregulating" the economy or not will depend on the strength of each sector and on the particular political alignments within the governing party.

7 German unemployment has shot upward dramatically in the mid-1990s. See n. 5 above for a possible explanation in the framework of this book's model.

8 This might explain why the Tory government's program of economic reform was much more radical than the German government's measures in the 1980s. Other factors, however, such as the strength of German unions, the greater division of power in Germany's federal system, which would have slowed down most reforms, or, more simply, the weight of Christian Democratic ideas in Germany, may account for that difference.

9 The specific policy instruments developed to secure higher rates of public investment have depended on the particular constellation of domestic institutions in each country. In highly coordinated economies, supply-side strategies, formulated jointly with trade unions, have resulted in extensive training programs. In Sweden, under the Rehn–Meidner plan, the social democratic government and the union movement agreed to combine a uniform wage policy, a tight fiscal policy, and higher indirect taxes to squeeze profits and force the least profitable companies to either shut down or become more efficient, that is, more capital-intensive. In exchange, the state spent heavily on human capital formation to retrain all workers who had been laid off in order to channel them into high-productivity jobs and established a public pool of savings and investment to compensate for a likely fall in business savings (Martin 1979; Pontusson 1991a; Swenson 1989). By contrast, in countries with a "decentralized" institutional framework, the supply-side economic strategy is developed without regard to the behavior of social partners and either involves the formation of a strong state-owned enterprise sector (the British Labour and the French and Greek Socialist strategy) or relies on direct spending on human and fixed capital formation (the Spanish experience of the 1980s).

10 It is worth emphasizing again that economic shocks include the effects of economic internationalization – a phenomenon stressed by the most recent literature on political economy (see, e.g., Keohane and Milner 1996) – but also internal structural changes. The latter are as important as or even more important than the former to understand economic change in the advanced world.

REFERENCES

Alesina, Alberto. 1987. "Macroeconomic Policy in a Two-Party System as a Repeated Game." *Quarterly Journal of Economics* 101: 651–78.

——— 1989. "Politics and Business Cycles in Industrial Democracies." *Economic Policy* 8: 57–98.

——— 1993. "Elections, Party Structure, and the Economy." Department of Government, Harvard University. Unpublished paper.

Alesina, Alberto, Gerald Cohen, and Nouriel Roubini. 1992. "Macroeconomic Policy and Elections in OECD Economies." *Economics and Politics* 4: 1–30.

Alesina, Alberto, and Roberto Perotti. 1994. "The Political Economy of Budget Deficits." NBER Working Paper Series, no. 4637. February.

Alesina, Alberto, and Dani Rodrik. 1991. "Distributive Politics and Economic Growth." NBER Working Paper Series, no. 3668.

Alesina, Alberto, and Howard Rosenthal. 1995. *Partisan Politics, Divided Governments, and the Economy.* Cambridge: Cambridge University Press.

Alesina, Alberto, and Nouriel Roubini. 1992. "Political Cycles: Evidence from OECD Economies." *Review of Economic Studies* 59: 663–88.

Alesina, Alberto, and Lawrence H. Summers. 1993. "Central Bank Independence and Macroeconomic Performance: Some Comparative Evidence." *Journal of Money, Credit, and Banking* 25: 151–62.

Alt, James E. 1984. "Dealignment and the Dynamics of Partisanship in Britain." In Dalton, Flanagan, and Beck 1984, 298–329.

——— 1985. "Political Parties, World Demand, and Unemployment: Domestic and International Sources of Economic Activity." *American Political Science Review* 79: 1016–40.

——— 1987. "Crude Politics." *British Journal of Political Science* 17(2): 149–99.

Alt, James E., and John R. Freeman. 1994. "The Politics of Public and Private Investment in Britain." In A. Hicks and T. Janoski, eds., *The Comparative*

Political Economy of the Welfare State. pp. 136–68. Cambridge: Cambridge University Press.

Alvarez, R. Michael, Geoffrey Garrett, and Peter Lange. 1991. "Government Partisanship, Labour Organization, and Macroeconomic Performance, 1967–1984." *American Political Science Review* 85: 539–56.

Anuario El País. Several years. Madrid: El País.

Arango, Joaquín, and Miguel Díez. 1993. "6-J: el sentido de una elección." *Claves de Razón Práctica* 36: 10–18.

Aranzadi, Claudio. 1989. "La política de desinversiones en el INI." *Papeles de Economía Española* 38: 258–61.

Arellano, Manuel, and Stephen Bond. 1988. "Dynamic Panel Data Estimation Using DPD: A Guide for Users." Working paper, Institute for Fiscal Studies, London.

———. 1991. "Some Tests of Specification for Panel Data: Montecarlo Evidence and an Application to Employment Equations." *Review of Economic Studies* 58: 277–97.

Argandoña, Antonio. 1990. "El conflicto entre la política monetaria y la peseta." In FEDEA, ed., *Política monetaria e inestabilidad financiera,* pp. 23–64. Madrid: FUNDES/FEDEA.

Argimón, Isabel, and José Manuel González-Páramo. 1987. "Una medición de la rémora inflacionista del IRPF, 1979–1985." *Investigaciones Económicas. Segunda Epoca* 11: 345–66.

Banco de España. 1983. *Informe Anual.* Madrid: Banco de España.

———. 1984. *Informe Anual.* Madrid: Banco de España.

———. Several years. *Informe Anual.* Apéndice estadístico. Madrid. Banco de España.

Bandrés, Eduardo. 1993. "La eficacia redistributiva de los gastos sociales. Una aplicación al caso español 1980–1990." In *I Simposio sobre Igualdad y Distribución de la Renta y la Riqueza, Fundación Argentaria,* vol. 7, pp. 123–71. Madrid: Fundación Argentaria.

Barker, Rodney. 1992. "Legitimacy in the United Kingdom: Scotland and the Poll Tax." *British Journal of Political Science* 22: 521–33.

Barro, Robert J. 1991. "Economic Growth in a Cross Section of Countries." *Quarterly Journal of Economics* 106(2): 407–43.

Bates, Robert H. 1984. *Markets and States in Tropical Africa.* Berkeley and Los Angeles: University of California Press.

Bean, Charles, and James Symmons. 1989. "Ten Years of Mrs T." *NBER Macroeconomics Annual 1989,* pp. 13–72.

Beck, Nathaniel, Jonathan N. Katz, R. Michael Alvarez, Geoffrey Garrett, and Peter Lange. 1993. "Government Partisanship, Labour Organization, and Macroeconomic Performance: A Corrigendum." *American Political Science Review* 87: 945–48.

Beer, Samuel H. 1969. *Modern British Politics.* London: Faber.

———. 1982. *Britain against Itself.* New York: Norton.

Begg, David. 1987. "Fiscal Policy." In Rudigger Dornbusch and Richard Layard, eds., *The Performance of the British Economy,* pp. 29–63. Oxford: Oxford University Press.

Behrens, Robert. 1980. *The Conservative Party from Heath to Thatcher.* London: Saxon House.

Bentolila, Samuel, and Juan José Dolado. 1993. "Fixed-Term Contracts and Wage Setting in Spanish Manufacturing Firms." *Economic Bulletin, Bank of Spain*, January, pp. 59–64.

Bertola, Giuseppe and Andrea Ichino. 1995. "Wage Inequality and Unemployment: US vs. Europe." Paper presented at the NBER Macroeconomics Annual Conference.

Bishop, Matthew, and John A. Kay. 1988. "Does Privatisation Work? Lessons from the UK." Centre for Business Strategy, London Business School. Unpublished paper.

Bishop, Matthew, and David Thompson. 1992. "Privatisation in the UK: Internal Organization and Productive Efficiency." *Annals of Public and Cooperative Economy* 63: 171–88.

Blanchard, Olivier J. 1991. "Wage Bargaining and Unemployment Persistence." *Journal of Money, Credit, and Banking* 23:277–92.

Blanchard, Olivier J., and Lawrence H. Summers. 1987. "Hysteresis in Unemployment." *European Economic Review* 31: 288–95.

Blank, Rebecca M., ed. 1994. *Social Protection versus Economic Flexibility: Is There a Trade-off?* Chicago: University of Chicago Press.

Blank, Rebecca M., and Richard B. Freeman. 1994. "Evaluating the Connection between Social Protection and Economic Flexibility." In Blank 1994, 21–41.

Boix, Carles. 1996. "Partisan Governments and Macroeconomic Policies in OECD Countries, 1961–1993." Paper presented at the 1996 Annual Meeting of the American Political Science Association, San Francisco.

Borrell, José. 1987. "Balance del sistema tributario." *Papeles de Economía Española* 30–31: 56–63.

1988. "Evolución y tendencias del gasto público." *Papeles de Economía Española* 37: 174–93.

1989. "Economía y fiscalidad en Europa." *Papeles de Economía Española* 41: 91–101.

1990. "De la Constitución a Europa: una década de política fiscal." *Información Comercial Española* 680: 9–37.

Boussard, Isabel. 1992. "Maastricht: Le refus des agriculteurs et des ruraux." *Revue Politique et Parlementaire* 94(961): 25–28.

Boyer, Miguel. 1983a. "Discursos parlamentarios." *Hacienda Pública Española* 82: 19–50.

1983b. "Opiniones." *Papeles de Economía Española*, 16: 366–68.

1984. "Características de los presupuestos generales del Estado para 1984." *Hacienda Pública Española* 85: 145–51.

Bruno, Michael, and Jeffrey Sachs. 1985. *Economics of Worldwide Stagflation*. Cambridge: Harvard University Press.

Budge, Ian, David Robertson, and Derek Hearl, eds. 1987. *Ideology, Strategy, and Party Change: Spatial Analyses of Post-war Election Programmes in 19 Democracies*. New York: Cambridge University Press.

Butler, David E., and Donald Stokes. 1974. *Political Change in Britain: The Evolution of Electoral Choice*. London: Macmillan.

Calmfors, Lars, and John Driffill. 1988. "Bargaining Structure, Corporatism and Macroeconomic Performance." *Economic Policy* 6: 14–61.

Cameron, David. 1984. "Social Democracy, Corporatism, Labour Quiescence, and the Representation of Economic Interest in Advanced Capitalist Society." In Goldthorpe 1984, 143–178.

CEEP. 1990. *L'enterprise publique dans la Communauté Economique Européenne.* Brussels: Centre Européen de l'Enterprise Publique.

CIDE. 1992. *El sistema educativo español, 1991.* Madrid: Ministerio de Educación y Ciencia, Centro de Investigación, Documentación, y Evaluación.

Comín, Francisco, and Pablo Martín, eds. 1991. *Historia de la empresa pública en España.* Madrid: Espasa-Calpe.

Corugedo, I., et al. 1991. *Un análisis coste-beneficio de la Enseñanza Media en España.* Madrid: Ministerio de Educación y Ciencia, Centro de Investigación, Documentación y Evaluación.

Cox, Gary W. 1997. *Making Votes Count: Strategic Coordination in the World's Electoral Systems.* New York: Cambridge University Press.

Crewe, Ivor. 1981. "Why the Conservatives Won." In Howard R. Penniman, ed., *Britain at the Polls, 1979: A Study of the General Election,* pp. 263–305. Washington, D.C.: American Enterprise Institute for Public Policy Research.

———. 1986. "On the Death and Resurrection of Class Voting." *Political Studies* 34: 620–38.

———. 1991. "Labour Force Changes, Working Decline, and the Labour Vote: Social and Electoral Issues in Postwar Britain." In Frances Fox Priven, ed., *Labour Parties in Post-Industrial Societies,* pp.20–46. Oxford: Oxford University Press.

Crewe, Ivor, Neil Day, and Anthony Fox. 1991. *The British Electorate, 1963–1987: A Compendium of Data from the British Election Studies.* Cambridge: Cambridge University Press.

Crewe, Ivor, Anthony Fox, and Neil Day. 1995. *The British Electorate, 1963–1992: A Compendium of Data from the British Election Studies.* Cambridge: Cambridge University Press.

Cuervo García, Alvaro. 1989. "La empresa pública: estructura financiera, rentabilidad y costes financieros." *Papeles de Economía Española* 38: 177–98.

Cusack, Thomas R., and Geoffrey Garrett. 1992. "Economic Decline, Interdependence, and the Public Economy: The Politics of Government Spending, 1962–1988." Wissenschaftszentrum Berlin. Unpublished paper.

Dalton, Russell J., Scott C. Flanagan, and Paul A. Beck, eds. 1984. *Electoral Change in Advanced Industrial Democracies.* Princeton: Princeton University Press.

"Datos de opinión: los españoles ante el pago de los impuestos." 1991. *Revistas Española de Investigaciones Socioloógicas* 55 (July–September).

Dehesa, Guillermo de la. 1988. "Los límites de la política económica española." *Leviatán* 32: 27–37.

De la Cruz, Rafael. 1986. "Editorial." *Hacienda Pública Española* 102–3: 3–15.

Dilnot, A. W., and C. N. Norris. 1983. "Private Costs and Benefits of Unemployment: Measuring Replacement Rates." In C. Greenhalgh, P. R. G. Layard, and A. J. Oswald, eds., *The Causes of Unemployment,* pp. 321–340. Oxford: Oxford University Press.

Dorey, Peter. 1993. "One Step at a Time: The Conservative Government's Approach to the Reform of Industrial Relations since 1979." *Political Quarterly* 64: 24–36.

Douglas, James. 1989. "Review Article: The Changing Tide – Some Recent Studies of Thatcherism." *British Journal of Political Science* 19: 399–424.

Dunleavy, Patrick J. 1987. "Class Dealignment in Britain Revisited." *West European Politics* 10: 400–419.

EIU. 1994. *Country Report: United Kingdom*. London: Economist Intelligence Unit.

Espina, Alvaro. 1991. *Empleo, democracia y relaciones industriales*. Madrid: Ministerio de Trabajo y Seguridad Social.

____. 1992. *Recursos humanos y política industrial: España ante la Unión Europea*. Madrid: Fundesco.

Esping-Andersen, Gösta. 1985. *Politics against Markets: The Social Democratic Road to Power*. Princeton: Princeton University Press.

____. 1990. *The Three Worlds of Welfare Capitalism*. Cambridge: Polity.

Fariñas, José Carlos, Jordi Jaumandreu, and Gonzalo Mato. 1989. "La empresa pública industrial española: 1981–1986." *Papeles de Economía Española* 38: 199–216.

Fernández-Castro, Joaquín. 1993. "The Creation of a New Industrial Relations System and Political Change: The Case of Spain." Massachusetts Institute of Technology. Unpublished paper. September.

Finegold, David, and David Soskice. 1988. "The Failure of Training in Britain: Analysis and Prescription." *Oxford Review of Economic Policy* 4: 21–53.

Fischer, Stanley. 1991. "Growth, Macroeconomics, and Development." *NBER Macroeconomics Annual 1991*, pp. 329–79.

Flora, Peter, and Jans Alber. 1981. "Modernization, Democratization, and the Development of Welfare States in Western Europe." In Peter Flora and Arnold J. Heidenheimer, eds., *The Development of Welfare States in Europe and America*, pp. 37–80. New Brunswick, N.J.: Transaction Books.

Forrest, Ray, Alan Murie, and Peter Williams. 1990. *Home Ownership: Differentiation and Fragmentation*. London: Unwyn Hyman.

Franklin, Mark. 1985. *The Decline of Class Voting in Britain*. Oxford: Oxford University Press.

Freeman, John R. 1989. *Democracy and Markets: The Politics of Mixed Economies*. Ithaca: Cornell University Press.

Freeman, Richard B., and Lawrence F. Katz. 1994. "Rising Wage Inequality: The United States vs. Other Advanced Countries." In Richard B. Freeman, ed., *Working under Different Rules*, pp. 29–63. New York: Russell Sage Foundation.

Freeman, Richard B., and J. Pelletier. 1990. "The Impact of Industrial Relations Legislation on British Union Density." *British Journal of Industrial Relations* 28: 141–64.

Frieden, Jeffry A. 1991a. "Invested Interests: The Politics of National Economic Policies in a World of Global Finance." *International Organization* 45: 425–51.

____. 1991b. *Debt, Development, and Democracy: Modern Political Economy and Latin America, 1965–1985*. Princeton: Princeton University Press.

Frieden, Jeffry A., and Ronald Rogowski. 1996. "The Impact of the International Economy on National Policies: An Analytical Overview." In Robert O.

Keohane and Helen Milner, eds., *Internationalization and Domestic Politics*, pp. 25–47. New York: Cambridge University Press.

Friedman, Milton. 1968. "The Role of Monetary Policy." *American Economic Review* 58: 1–17.

Fuentes Quintana, Enrique. 1979. "La crisis económica española." *Papeles de Economía Española* 1: 84–136.

García-Blanch, José, et al. 1990. "Política de infraestructuras de transporte." *Presupuesto y Gasto Público* 28: 139–53.

García Hermoso, José Manuel. 1989. "El INI como grupo de negocios: Presente y futuro." *Papeles de Economía Española* 38: 262–76.

García Perea, Pilar, and Ramón Gómez. 1993. "Aspectos institucionales del mercado de trabajo español, en comparación con otros países comunitarios." *Banco de España, Boletín Económico*, September, pp. 29–47.

Garrett, Geoffrey. 1994. "Internationalization and Economic Policy in the Industrial Democracies, 1962–1988." Paper presented at the Third Workshop on European Political Economy and Institutional Analysis, Cambridge, Mass., 18–19 February.

Garrett, Geoffrey, and Peter Lange. 1991. "Political Responses to Interdependence: What's 'Left' for the Left?" *International Organization* 45: 539–64.

Gillespie, Richard. 1989. *The Spanish Socialist Party: A History of Factionalism*. Oxford: Clarendon Press.

Gimeno, Andrés. 1993. "Incidencia del gasto público por niveles de renta (España 1990 vs. 1980)." In *I Simposio sobre Igualdad y Distribución de la Renta y la Riqueza, Fundación Argentaria*, vol. 7, pp. 63–121. Madrid: Fundación Argentaria.

Godé Sánchez, José Antonio. 1990. "Los gastos sociales en el Presupuesto de 1990." *Presupuesto y Gasto Público* 2: 131–44.

Golden, Miriam, and Michael Wallerstein. 1994. "Trade Union Organization and Industrial Relations in the Postwar Era in 16 Nations." Paper presented at the 1994 Annual Meeting of the American Political Science Association, New York.

Goldthorpe, John H., ed. 1984. *Order and Conflict in Contemporary Capitalism*. Oxford: Clarendon Press.

González-Páramo, José Manuel, and J. M. Roldán. 1992. "La orientación de la política presupuestaria en España: evolución reciente y perspectivas de convergencia." *Papeles de Economía Española* 52–53: 167–79.

Goodman, John B., and Louwis W. Pauly. 1993. "The Obsolescence of Capital Controls? Economic Management in an Age of Global Markets." *World Politics* 46: 50–82.

Gordo, Esther, and Pilar L'Hotellerie. 1993. "La competitividad de la industria española en una perspectiva macroeconómica." *Banco de España, Boletín Económico*, October, pp. 43–52.

Green, Francis. 1993. "Recent Trends in British Trade Union Density: How Much of a Compositional Effect?" *British Journal of Industrial Relations* 30: 445–58.

Grilli, Vittorio, Donato Mascianidaro, and Guido Tabellini. 1991. "Political and Monetary Institutions and Public Financial Policies in the Industrial Countries." *Economic Policy* 13: 341–92.

Grunberg, Gérard. 1994. "Les français et l'Europe." *Revue Politique et Parliamentaire* 96(970): 20–25.

Gunther, Richard. 1986. "El realineamiento del sistema de partidos de 1982." In Linz and Montero 1986, pp. 27–69.

Gunther, Richard, Giacomo Sani, and Goldie Shabad. 1988. *Spain after Franco: The Making of a Competitive Party System*. Berkeley and Los Angeles: University of California Press.

Guyomarch, A. 1993. "The 1993 Parliamentary Election in France." *Parliamentary Affairs* 46: 605–26.

Haggard, Stephan. 1990. *Pathways from the Periphery. The Politics of Growth in the Newly Industrializing Countries*. Ithaca: Cornell University Press.

Hall, Peter A. 1986. *Governing the Economy. The Politics of State Intervention in Britain and France*. Oxford: Oxford University Press.

———. 1992. "The Movement from Keynesianism to Monetarism: Institutional Analysis and British Economic Policy in the 1970s." In Sven Steinmo, Kathleen Thelen, and Frank Longstreth, eds., *Structuring Politics: Historical Institutionalism in Comparative Analysis*, pp. 90–113. New York: Cambridge University Press.

———. 1993. "Policy Paradigms, Social Learning, and the State: The Case of Economic Policymaking in Britain." *Comparative Politics* 25: 275–96.

———. 1995. "The Political Economy of Europe in an Era of Interdependence." Center for European Studies, Harvard University. Unpublished paper.

———. ed. 1989. *The Political Power of Economic Ideas: Keynesianism across Nations*. Princeton: Princeton University Press.

Heath, Anthony, Roger Jowell, and John Curtice. 1985. *How Britain Votes*. Oxford: Pergamon Press.

Heath, Anthony, Roger Jowell, John Curtice, and Geoff Evans. 1989. "The Extension of Popular Capitalism." Strathclyde Papers on Government and Politics, no. 60. Department of Politics, University of Strathclyde.

Heath, Anthony, et al. 1991. *Understanding Political Change: The British Voter, 1964–1987*. Oxford: Pergamon Press.

Helm, Dieter, Colin Mayer, and Ken Mayhew. 1991. "The Assessment: Microeconomic Policy in the 1980s." *Oxford Review of Economic Policy* 7(3): 1–12.

Hibbs, Douglas A., Jr. 1977. "Political Parties and Macroeconomic Policy." *American Political Science Review* 71: 1467–87.

———. 1987. *The American Political Economy: Macroeconomics and Electoral Politics*. Cambridge: Harvard University Press.

———. 1992. "Partisan Theory after Fifteen Years." *European Journal of Political Economy* 8: 361–73.

Hills, John. 1991. *Unravelling Housing Finance: Subsidies, Benefits, and Taxation*. Oxford: Clarendon Press.

Hirschman, Albert O. 1981. "Exit, Voice, and the State." In Albert O. Hirschman, *Essays in Trespassing: Economics to Politics and Beyond*, pp. 246–65. Cambridge: Cambridge University Press.

HM Central Statistical Office. 1993. "The Effects of Taxes and Benefits on Household Income." *Economic Trends*, January, pp. 147–87.

IGAE. 1990. *Actuación económica y financiera de las Administraciones Públicas*. Madrid: Intervención General de la Administración del Estado.

1991. *Actuación económica y financiera de las Administraciones Públicas.* Madrid: Intervención General de la Administración del Estado.

1993. *Boletín de información estadística del sector público, 1991.* Madrid: Intervención General de la Administración del Estado.

Several years. *El sector público empresarial.* Madrid: Intervención General de la Administración del Estado.

Inglehart, Ronald. 1984. "The Changing Structure of Political Cleavages in Western Society." In Dalton, Flanagan, and Beck, 1984, pp. 25–69.

INI. Several years. *Informe Anual.* Madrid: Instituto Nacional de Industria.

Iversen, Torben. 1995. "Contested Economic Institutions: The Politics of Macroeconomics and Wage Bargaining in Organized Capitalism." Ph.D. diss., Duke University.

Jiménez, Miguel, and Rafael Salas. 1992. "Causas del incremento en la recaudación del IRPF, 1982–1987." In Instituto de Estudios Fiscales, *La reforma del IRPF. Número monográfico de "Hacienda Pública Española,"* pp. 145–57. Madrid: Instituto de Estudios Fiscales.

Jiménez Fernández, Adolfo. 1990. "La Seguridad Social en 1990: el presupuesto del consenso social." *Presupuesto y Gasto Público* 2: 75–96.

1991. "La política de prestaciones que informa el contenido del presupuesto de la Seguridad Social para 1991 y breve descripción de este último." *Presupuesto y Gasto Público* 4: 97–126.

Johnson, Christopher. 1993. *The Grand Experiment. Mrs. Thatcher's Economy and How It Spread.* Boulder: Westview.

Jowell, Roger, Lindsay Brook, and Bridget Taylor, eds. 1991. *British Social Attitudes: The 8th Report.* London: Darmouth.

Juliá Díaz, Santos, ed. 1988. *La desavenencia: partido, sindicato, y huelga general.* Madrid: El País/Aguilar.

Katz, Lawrence F. 1986. "Efficiency Wage Theories: A Partial Evaluation." *NBER Macroeconomics Annual* 1: 235–76.

Katzenstein, Peter. 1985. *Small States in World Markets: Industrial Policy in Europe.* Ithaca: Cornell University Press.

Keegan, William. 1984. *Mrs. Thatcher's Economic Experiment.* London: Allen Lane.

Keohane, Robert O., and Helen V. Milner, eds. 1996. *Internationalization and Domestic Politics.* New York: Cambridge University Press.

King, Anthony. 1975. "The Election That Everyone Lost." In Howard R. Penniman, ed., *Britain at the Polls: The Parliamentary Elections of 1974,* pp. 3–31. Washington, D.C.: American Enterprise Institute for Public Policy Research.

1993. "The Implication of One-Party Government." In Anthony King et al., *Britain at the Polls. 1992,* pp. 223–48. Chatham, N.J.: Chatham House Publishers.

King, Desmond S. 1993. "The Conservatives and Training Policy, 1979–1992: From a Tripartite to a Neoliberal Regime." *Political Studies* 41: 214–35.

King, Gary, Robert O. Keohane, and Sidney Verba. 1994. *Designing Social Inquiry: Scientific Inference in Qualitative Research.* Princeton: Princeton University Press.

Kitschelt, Herbert. 1994. *The Transformation of European Social Democracy.* New York: Cambridge University Press.

Lagares, Manuel J. 1992. "Comportamiento del sector público: perspectiva de una década y planteamientos de futuro." *Papeles de Economía Española* 52/53: 132–66.

Lancaster, Thomas, and Michael S. Lewis-Beck. 1986. "The Spanish Voter: Tradition, Economics, Ideology." *Journal of Politics* 48: 648–74.

Lane, Jan-Erik, David McKay, and Kenneth Newton. 1991. *Political Data Handbook: OECD Countries*. New York: Oxford University Press.

Lange, Peter, and Geoffrey Garrett. 1985. "The Politics of Growth: Strategic Interaction and Economic Performance in the Advanced Industrial Democracies, 1974–1980." *Journal of Politics* 47: 792–827.

1987. "The Politics of Growth Reconsidered." *Journal of Politics* 49: 257–74.

Lange, Peter, Michael Wallerstein, and Miriam Golden. 1995. "The End of Corporatism? Wage Setting in the Nordic and Germanic Countries." In Sanford M. Jacoby, ed., *The Workers of Nations. Industrial Relations in a Global Economy*, pp. 76–100. Oxford: Oxford University Press.

Lasheras, Miguel Angel, Isabel Rabadán, and Rafael Salas. 1993. "Política redistributiva en el IRPF entre 1982 y 1990." *Cuadernos de Actualidad de Hacienda Pública Española* 7: 165–72.

Laver, Michael J., and W. Bent Hunt. 1992. *Policy and Party Competition*. New York: Routledge.

Lawson, Nigel. 1980. *The New Conservatism*. London: Conservative Political Centre.

1984. *The British Experiment*. The Fifth Mais Lecture. London: City University Business School.

1992. *The View from No. 11: Memoirs of a Tory Radical*. London: Bantam Press.

Layard, Richard, Stephen Nickell, and Richard Jackman. 1994. *The Unemployment Crisis*. Oxford: Oxford University Press.

Leape, Jonathan I. 1993. "Tax Policies in the 1980s and 1990s: The Case of the United Kingdom." In Anthonie Knoester, ed., *Taxation in the United States and Europe. Theory and Practice*, pp. 276–311. New York: St. Martin's Press.

Lee, Bradford A. 1989. "The Miscarriage of Necessity and Invention: Proto-Keynesianism and Democratic States in the 1930s." In Hall 1989, 129–170.

Lewis-Beck, Michael S. 1988. *Economics and Elections: The Major Western Democracies*. Ann Arbor: University of Michigan Press.

Lindbeck, Assar, and Dennis J. Snower. 1985. "Explanations of Unemployment." *Oxford Review of Economic Policy* 1(2): 34–59.

Lindblom, Charles E. 1977. *Politics and Markets*. New York: Basic Books.

Linz, Juan J., and J. R. Montero, eds. 1986. *Crisis y cambio: electores y partidos en la España de los años ochenta*. Madrid: Centro de Estudios Constitucionales.

Lipset, Seymour. 1983. *Political Man*. Reprint, Garden City, N.Y.: Anchor.

Lucas, Robert E., Jr. 1972. "Expectations and the Neutrality of Money." *Journal of Economic Theory* 4: 103–24.

1988. "On the Mechanisms of Economic Development." *Journal of Monetary Economics* 22: 3–42.

1990. "Why Doesn't Capital Flow from Rich to Poor Countries?" *American Economic Review* 82: 1–13.

Machin, Howard, and Vincent Wright. 1982. "The French Presidential Elections of April–May 1981." *West European Politics* 5(1): 5–35.

Mankiw, N. Gregory, David Romer, and David Weil. 1992. "A Contribution to the Empirics of Economic Growth." *Quarterly Journal of Economics* 107: 407–37.

Maravall, José María. 1981. *La política de la transición, 1975–1980.* Madrid: Taurus.

——— 1992. "From Opposition to Government: The Politics and Policies of the PSOE." In J. M. Maravall et al., *Socialist Parties in Europe*, pp. 7–34 Barcelona: Institut de Ciències Polítiques i Socials.

——— 1995. *Los resultados de la democracia.* Madrid: Alianza Editorial.

Martin, Andrew. 1979. "The Dynamics of Change in a Keynesian Political Economy." In Colin Crouch, ed., *State and Economy in Contemporary Capitalism*, pp. 88–121. London: Croom Helm.

Martín, Pablo, and Francisco Comín. 1990. "La acción regional del Instituto Nacional de Industria, 1941–1976." In Jordi Nadal and Albert Carreras, eds., *Pautas regionales de la industrialización española (siglos XIX y XX)*, pp. 379–419. Barcelona: Ariel.

Mayhew, Ken. 1985. "Reforming the Labour Market." *Oxford Review of Economic Policy* 1(2): 60–79.

Meltzer, A. H. and S. F. Richards. 1981. "A Rational Theory of the Size of Government." *Journal of Political Economy* 89: 914–27.

Metcalf, D. 1991. "British Unions: Dissolution or Resurgence?" *Oxford Review of Economic Policy* 7: 18–32.

Miller, Marcus. 1985. "Measuring the Stance of Fiscal Policy." *Oxford Review of Economic Policy* 1(1): 44–57.

Miller, W. L., H. D. Clarke, M. L. Harrop, L. Ledul, and P. Whiteley. 1990. *How Voters Change.* Oxford: Clarendon Press.

Minford, Patrick. 1988. "Monetary Policy in the U.K. under Mrs. Thatcher." *Finanzmarket und Portfolio Management* 4: 43–46, and *IEA Inquiry* 5. Reproduced in Patrick Minford, 1991. *The Supply Side Revolution in Britain*, pp. 56–73. Aldershot: Institute of Economic Affairs, 1991.

Ministerio de Economía y Hacienda. 1989. *Informe sobre el Impuesto de la Renta de las Personas Físicas y sobre el Patrimonio.* Madrid: Instituto de Estudios Fiscales.

Mitchell, James. 1990. "U.K.: Privatisation as Myth?" In J. J. Richardson, ed., *Privatisation and Deregulation in Canada and Britain*, pp. 14–37. Aldershot: Darmouth.

MOPT. Several years. *Los transportes y las comunicaciones.* Madrid: Instituto de Estudios del Transporte y las Comunicaciones.

MOPTMA. 1993. *Anuario Estadístico 1992.* Madrid: Ministerio de Obras Públicas, Transporte y Medio Ambiente, Dirección General de Programación Económica y Presupuestaria.

Newton, Kenneth. 1993. "Caring and Competence: The Long, Long Campaign." In Anthony King et al., *Britain at the Polls, 1992*, pp. 129–70. Chatham, N.J.: Chatham House Publishers.

Nickell, Stephen. 1990. "Inflation and the U.K. Labour Market." *Oxford Review of Economic Policy* 6(4): 26–35.

Nordhaus, William. 1975. "The Political Business Cycle." *Review of Economic Studies* 42: 169–90.

——— 1989. "Alternative Models to Political Business Cycles." *Brookings Papers on Economic Activity* 2: 1–56.

Norton, Philip. 1993. "The Conservative Party from Thatcher to Major." In Anthony King et al., *Britain at the Polls, 1992*, pp. 29–69. Chatham, N.J.: Chatham House Publishers.

OECD. 1981. *OECD Economic Surveys. United Kingdom*. Paris: OECD.

1988. *OECD Economic Surveys of 1987–88. Spain*. Paris: OECD.

1989. *Economies in Transition: Structural Adjustment in OECD Countries*. Paris: OECD.

1990a. *The Personal Income Tax Base: A Comparative Survey*. Paris: OECD.

1990b. *OECD Historical Statistics, 1960–1990*. Paris: OECD.

1991a. *OECD Economic Surveys of 1990–1991: United Kingdom*. Paris: OECD.

1991b. *Revenue Statistics for OECD Member Countries, 1965–1990*. Paris: OECD.

1991c. *OECD National Accounts. Main Aggregates, 1960–89*. Vol. 1. Paris: OECD.

1992. *OECD Economic Surveys of 1991–92: Spain*. Paris: OECD.

1993a. *OECD Economic Surveys of 1992–93: Spain*. Paris: OECD.

1993b. *OECD Economic Surveys of 1992–1993: United Kingdom*. Paris: OECD.

1993c. *OECD Economic Outlook, December*. Paris: OECD.

1993d. *OECD Employment Perspectives, 1993*. Paris: OECD.

1994a. *OECD Economic Surveys of 1993–94: Italy*. Paris: OECD.

1994b. *The Jobs Study*. Paris: OECD.

Olson, Mancur. 1982. *The Rise and Decline of Nations*. New Haven: Yale University Press.

Oxley, Howard, and John P. Martin. 1991. "Controlling Government Spending and Deficits: Trends in the 1980s and Prospects for the 1990s." *OECD Economic Studies* 17: 145–189.

PEMP. 1985. *Plan Económico a Medio y Largo Plazo*. 4 vols. Madrid: Ministerio de Economía y Hacienda.

Pérez, Pedro and José Juan Ruiz. 1989. "La economía española ante la década de los noventa: expectativas de futuro y lecciones del pasado." *Información Comercial Española* 676–77: 71–97.

Plasser, Fritz and Peter A. Ulram. 1995. "Konstanz und Wandel im österreichischen Wählerverhalten." In Wolfgang C. Müller, Fritz Plasser, and Peter A. Ulram, eds., *Wählerverhalten und Parteienwettbewerb: Analysen zur Nationalratswahl 1994*, pp. 341–406. Vienna: Schriftenreihe des Zentrums für Angewandte Politikforschung.

Pontusson, Jonas. 1988. "Swedish Social Democracy and British Labour: Essays on the Nature and Condition of Social Democratic Hegemony." Western Societies Program Occasional Paper no. 19, Center for International Studies, Cornell University.

1991a. "The Crisis of Swedish Social Democracy." Cornell University, Unpublished paper. March.

1991b. *The Limits of Social Democracy: Investment Politics in Sweden*. Ithaca: Cornell University Press.

Poveda, Ramón. 1986. "Política monetaria y financiera." In Luis Gámir, ed., *Política económica española*, pp. 29–48. Madrid: Alianza.

Programa 2000. 1988. *La economía española a debate*. Madrid: Siglo XXI.

Przeworski, Adam, and John Sprague. 1986. *Paper Stones: A History of Electoral Socialism*. Chicago: University of Chicago Press.

Przeworski, Adam, and Michael Wallerstein. 1986. "Democratic Capitalism at the

Crossroads." In A. Przeworski, *Capitalism and Social Democracy*, pp. 205–221. Cambridge: Cambridge University Press.

1988. "Structural Dependence of the State on Capital." *American Political Science Review* 82: 11–30.

PSOE. 1982. *Programa electoral*. Madrid: Partido Socialista Obrero Español.

Puerto, Mariano. 1991. "La reforma de la enseñanza no universitaria: aspectos económicos y presupuestarios, *Presupuesto y Gasto Público* 4: 153–70.

Puhle, Hans-Jürgen. 1986. "El PSOE: un partido dominante y heterogéneo." In Linz and Montero 1986, pp. 289–344.

Purcell, John. 1993. "The End of Institutional Industrial Relations." *Political Quarterly* 64: 6–23.

Quinn, Dennis P., and Robert P. Shapiro. 1991. "Economic Growth Strategies: The Effects of Ideological Partisanship on Interest Rates and Business Taxation in the United States." *American Journal of Political Science* 35:656–85.

Reason Foundation. 1986–92. *Privatization*. Santa Monica, Calif.: Reason Foundation.

Redondo, Nicolás. 1988. "Los objetivos del sindicalismo." In *Anuario El País 1988*, p. 357. Madrid: PRISA.

Riddell, Peter. 1989. *The Thatcher Decade*. Oxford: Basil Blackwell.

Ridley, Nicholas. 1991. *"My Style of Government": The Thatcher Years*. London: Hutchinson.

Riviere, Angel, and Fernando Rueda. 1993. "Igualdad social y política educativa." In *I Simposio sobre Igualdad y Distribución de la Renta y la Riqueza. Fundación Argentaria*. vol. 8, pp. 8–34. Madrid: Fundación Argentaria.

Rodríguez López, Julio. 1989. "Crédito oficial: la transición." *Papeles de Economía Española* 38: 340–48.

Rogowski, Ronald. 1989. *Commerce and Coalitions: How Trade Affects Domestic Political Alignments*. Princeton: Princeton University Press.

Rojo, Luis Angel. 1981. "Desempleo y factores reales." *Papeles de Economía Española* 8: 124–36.

1986. *Discurso pronunciado en el acto de recepción del Premio Rey Juan Carlos de Economía instituido por la Fundación Celma Prieto*. Madrid: Banco de España.

Romer, Paul M. 1986. "Increasing Returns and Long-Run Growth." *Journal of Political Economy* 94: 1002–37.

Rose, Richard. 1981. "Toward Normality: Public Opinion Polls in the 1979 Election." In Howard R. Penniman, ed., *Britain at the Polls, 1979: A Study of the General Election*, pp. 177–209. Washington, D.C.: American Enterprise Institute for Public Policy Research.

Rose, Richard, and Ian McAllister. 1986. *Voters Begin to Choose: From Closed-Class to Open Election in Britain*. Beverly Hills, Calif.: Sage.

Rothstein, Bo. 1993. "The Crisis of the Swedish Social Democrats and the Future of the Universal Welfare State." *Governance* 6: 492–517.

Ruggie, John. 1982. "International Regimes, Transactions, and Change: Embedded Liberalism in the Postwar Economic Order." *International Organization* 36: 379–415.

Ruiz Álvarez, José Luis. 1992. "Un análisis económico de las recientes políticas presupuestarias del mercado de trabajo." *Presupuesto y Gasto Público* 7: 7–17.

Rus, Ginés de. 1989. "Las empresas públicas del transporte en España." *Papeles de Economía Española* 38: 349–82.

Sachs, Jeffrey, and Charles Wyplosz. 1986. "The Economic Consequences of President Mitterrand." *Economic Policy* 2: 257–313.

Sánchez Revenga, Jaime. 1990. "La inversión en infraestructuras públicas en el Presupuesto para 1990." *Presupuesto y Gasto Público* 2: 97–130.

Sanders, David. 1991. "Government Popularity and the Next General Election." *Political Quarterly* 62: 235–61.

———. 1993. "Why the Conservative Party Won – Again." In Anthony King et al., *Britain at the Polls, 1992*, pp. 171–222. Chatham, N.J.: Chatham House Publishers.

Sargent, T., and N. Wallace. 1975. "Rational Expectations: The Optimal Monetary Instrument and the Optimal Money Supply Rule." *Journal of Political Economy* 83: 241–54.

Särlvik, Bo, and Ivor Crewe. 1983. *Decade of Dealignment: The Conservative Victory of 1979 and the Electoral Trends of the 1970s*. Cambridge: Cambridge University Press.

Saunders, Peter. 1995. "Privatization, Share Ownership, and Voting." *British Journal of Political Science* 25: 131–37.

Scarbrough, Elinor. 1987. "Review Article: The British Electorate Twenty Years On – Electoral Change and Election Surveys." *British Journal of Political Science* 17: 219–46.

Scharpf, Fritz W. 1984. "Economic and Institutional Constraints of Full-Employment Strategies: Sweden, Austria, and Western Germany, 1973–1982." In Goldthorpe 1984, 227–57.

———. 1987. "A Game-Theoretical Interpretation of Inflation and Unemployment in Western Europe." *Journal of Public Policy* 7: 227–57.

———. 1991. *Crisis and Choice in European Social Democracy*. Ithaca: Cornell University Press.

Serrano Sanz, José María, and Antón Costas Comesaña. 1988. "Ideas y políticas en la economía española de la crisis." University of Zaragoza: Unpublished paper.

Servén, Luis. 1989. "La empresa pública en un sector estratégico: HUNOSA." *Papeles de Economía Española* 38: 383–89.

Shepsle, Kenneth. 1991. *Models of Multiparty Electoral Competition*. Chur, Switzerland: Harwood Academic Publishers.

Short, R. P. 1984. "The Role of Public Enterprises: An International Comparison." In Robert H. Floyd, Clive S. Gray, and R. P. Short, *Public Enterprises in Mixed Economies: Some Macroeconomic Aspects*, pp. 110–196. Washington, D.C.: International Monetary Fund.

Simmons, Beth. 1994. *Who Adjusts? Domestic Sources of Foreign Economic Policy during the Interwar Years*. Princeton: Princeton University Press.

Skidelsky, Robert. 1979. "The Decline of Keynesian Politics." In Colin Crouch, ed., *State and Economy in Contemporary Capitalism*, pp. 55–87. London: Croom Helm.

Solchaga, Carlos. 1986a. "Discurso parlamentario sobre la reforma del IRPF." *Hacienda Pública Española* 99: 205–20.

———. 1986b. "Discurso en la presentación de la Ley de Presupuestos Generales del Estado para 1987 ante el Congreso de Diputados." *Hacienda Pública Española* 102–3: 17–46.

1987. "Presentación del proyecto de Ley de Presupuestos Generales del Estado para 1988." *Hacienda Pública Española* 105–106: 23–61.

1988. "Presentación del proyecto de Ley de Presupuestos Generales del Estado para 1989." *Hacienda Pública Española* 112: 15–44.

1990. "Presentación del proyecto de Ley de Presupuestos Generales del Estado para 1990." *Presupuesto y Gasto Público* 2: 15–54.

1991a. "Presentación del proyecto de Ley de Presupuestos Generales del Estado para 1991." *Presupuesto y Gasto Público* 4: 13–28.

1991b. "Presentación del proyecto de Ley de Presupuestos Generales del Estado para 1992." *Presupuesto y Gasto Público* 6: 7–24.

Soskice, David. 1990. "Wage Determination: The Changing Role of Institutions in Advanced Industrial Countries." *Oxford Review of Economic Policy* 6: 36–61.

1991. "The Institutional Infrastructure for International Competitiveness: A Comparative Analysis of the U.K. and Germany." In Anthony B. Atkinson and Renato Brunetta, eds., *Economics of the New Europe*, pp. 45–66. London: Macmillan.

1995. "Finer Varieties of Advanced Capitalism: Industry- versus Group-Based Coordination in Germany and Japan." Wissenschaftszentrum Berlin. Unpublished paper.

Stevens, Barrie. 1992. "Prospects for Privatisation in OECD Countries." *National Westminster Bank Quarterly Review*, August, pp. 2–10.

Streeck, Wolfgang. 1991. "On the Institutional Conditions of Diversified Quality Production." In Egon Matzner and Wolfgang Streeck, eds., *Beyond Keynesianism. The Socio-economics of Production and Full Employment*, pp. 21–61. London: Edward Elgar

Strom, Kaare. 1990. "A Behavioral Theory of Competitive Political Parties." *American Journal of Political Science* 34: 565–98.

Swank, Duane. 1992. "Politics and the Structural Dependence of the State in Democratic Capitalist Nations." *American Political Science Review* 86: 38–54.

1993. "Social Democracy, Equity, and Efficiency in an Interdependent World." Paper prepared for delivery at the 1993 Annual Meeting of the American Political Science Association, Washington, 2–5 September.

Swenson, Peter. 1989. *Fair Shares: Unions, Pay, and Politics in Sweden and Germany.* Ithaca: Cornell University Press.

1991. "Bringing Capital Back In, or Social Democracy Reconsidered: Employer Power, Cross-Class Alliances, and Centralization of Industrial Relations in Denmark and Sweden." *World Politics* 43: 513–45.

Taagapera, Rein, and Matthew S. Shugart. 1989. *Seats and Votes: The Effects and Determinants of Electoral Systems.* New Haven: Yale University Press.

Tebbit, Norman. 1988. *Upwardly Mobile.* London: Weidenfeld and Nicolson.

Telefónica. Several years. *Informe Anual.* Madrid: Telefónica.

Téneo. 1992. *Informe Anual.* Madrid: Téneo.

Thatcher, Margaret. 1993. *The Downing Street Years.* London: HarperCollins.

Traxler, Franz. 1994. *The Level and Coverage of Collective Bargaining: A Cross-National Study of Patterns and Trends.* Paris: OECD.

U.K. Parliament. Several years. *The Government's Expenditure Plans.* Command papers. London: HMSO.

Several years. *Public Expenditure Analyses.* London: HMSO.

1992. *Public Expenditure Analyses to 1994–95*. Statistical Supplement to the 1991 Autumn Statement. Presented to Parliament by the Chancellor of the Exchequer by Command of Her Majesty. January. Command paper no. 1920. London: HMSO.

UNESCO. Several years. *Statistical Yearbook*. Paris: UNESCO.

Valdés, T., Isabel Argimón, and José Luis Raymond. 1989. "Evolución de la recaudación del IRPF: determinación de las causas y estimación de los efectos." *Investigaciones Económicas* 13: 14–44.

Veljanovski, Cento. 1988. *Selling the State: Privatisation in Britain*. London: Weidenfeld and Nicolson.

Vernon, Raymond, ed. 1988. *The Promise of Privatization: A Challenge for U.S. Policy*. New York: Council on Foreign Relations.

Vickers, John, and Vincent Wright, eds. 1989. *The Politics of Privatization in Western Europe*. London: Frank Cass.

Vickers, John, and George Yarrow. 1988. *Privatization: An Economic Analysis*. Cambridge: MIT Press.

Walters, Alan. 1986. *Britain's Economic Renaissance: Margaret Thatcher's Reforms, 1979– 1984*. Oxford: Oxford University Press.

Weir, Margaret. 1989."Ideas and Politics: The Acceptance of Keynesianism in Britain and the United States." In Hall, 1989, 53–86.

Wilensky, Harold L. 1981. "Leftism, Catholicism, and Democratic Corporatism: The Role of Political Parties in Recent Welfare State Development." In Peter Flora and Arnold J. Heidenheimer, eds., *The Development of Welfare States in Europe and America*, pp.345–82. New Brunswick, N.J.: Transaction Books.

Wilks, Stephen. 1985. "Conservative Industrial Policy, 1979–83." In Peter Jackson, ed., *Implementing Government Policy Initiatives: The Thatcher Administration, 1979–83*, pp. 123–43. London: Royal Institute of Public Administration.

Wood, Adrian. 1994. *North–South Trade, Employment, and Inequality*. Oxford: Oxford University Press.

Zabalza, Antonio. 1987. "El contexto macroeconómico del presupuesto de 1988." *Hacienda Pública Española* 105–6: 87–98.

1988a. "La inversión pública: evolución y perspectivas." *Papeles de Economía Española* 37: 332–54.

1988b. "El impacto macroeconómico del presupuesto de 1989." *Hacienda Pública Española* 112: 45–52.

1988c. "Perspectivas de inversión pública en infraestructuras." *Economistas* 35: 268–72.

1989. "Crecimiento, empleo, y política fiscal en la CEE y en España." *Papeles de Economía Española* 41: 29–36.

1990. "El Presupuesto y su contexto económico." *Presupuesto y Gasto Público* 2: 57–62.

1991a. "El sector público español ante el mercado único." *Papeles de Economía Española* 48: 37–49.

1991b. "La política fiscal y las demandas sociales en el presupuesto de 1991." *Presupuesto y Gasto Público* 4: 31–42.

1991c. "La reforma de l'IRPF i la política fiscal." *Revista Econòmica de Catalunya* 15: 51–57.

Zaragoza Rameau, José. 1989. "Los desequilibrios regionales en España: su correc-
    ción." *Economía Industrial* 269: 63–73.
Zufiaur, José María. 1985. "El sindicalismo español en la transición y la crisis." *Papeles
    de Economía Española* 22: 202–34.

INDEX